The road to Brexit

MANCHESTER
1824

Manchester University Press

The road to Brexit

A cultural perspective on British attitudes to Europe

Edited by

Ina Habermann

Manchester University Press

Published by Manchester University Press
Oxford Road, Manchester M13 9PL
www.manchesteruniversitypress.co.uk

British Library Cataloguing-in-Publication Data
A catalogue record for this book is available from the British Library

ISBN   978 1 5261 4508 6   hardback
ISBN   978 1 5261 6380 6   paperback

First published 2020
Paperback published 2022

Typeset by Newgen Publishing UK

For M.

Contents

List of figures and table   *page* ix
List of contributors   x
Preface   xiv
Acknowledgements   xvi

Introduction: Understanding the past, facing the future   1
    Ina Habermann

Part I Britain and Europe: political entanglements   15

1 Not with a bang but a whimper: Brexit in historical
    perspective   17
    Robert Holland

2 'This is something which we know, in our bones, we cannot
    do': hopes and fears for a united Europe in Britain after
    the Second World War   44
    Lara Feigel and Alisa Miller

3 EU enlargement and the freedom of movement: imagined
    communities in the Conservative Party's discourse on
    Europe (1997–2016)   69
    Marlene Herrschaft-Iden

4 The discursive role of Europe in a disunited kingdom   87
    Klaus Stolz

Part II British discourses of Europe in literature and film   105

5 'Extr'ord'nary people, the Germans': Germans as aliens in
   post-war British popular culture   107
   Judith Vonberg

6 'I don't want to be a European': the European Other in British
   cultural discourse   126
   Menno Spiering

7 The dystopian nightmare of a European superstate: British
   fiction and the EU   143
   Lisa Bischoff

8 A case for a Green Brexit? Paul Kingsnorth, John Berger and
   the pros and cons of a sense of place   162
   Christian Schmitt-Kilb

9 Brexit and the Tudor turn: Philippa Gregory's narratives
   of national grievance   179
   Siobhan O'Connor

**Part III Negotiating borders in British travel writing
and memoir**   197

10 Guards of Brexit? Revisiting the cultural significance of the
    white cliffs of Dover   199
    Melanie Küng

11 From Iron Curtains to Iron Cliffs: British travel writing
    between East and West   215
    Blanka Blagojevic

12 Fifty years of Unbelonging: a Gibraltarian writer's personal
    testimonial on the road to Brexit   234
    M.G. Sanchez

Index   245

Figures and table

Figures

5.1 *Sink the Bismarck!* (1960), dir. Lewis Gilbert; prod.
    Twentieth Century Fox; dist. Twentieth Century Fox.
    DVD (screenshot by author)   *page* 111
5.2 *Sink the Bismarck!* (1960), dir. Lewis Gilbert; prod.
    Twentieth Century Fox; dist. Twentieth Century
    Fox. DVD (screenshot by author)   113
5.3 *The One That Got Away* (1957), dir. Roy Ward Baker;
    prod. Julian Wintle; dist. Rank. DVD (screenshot by author)   117
5.4 *The One That Got Away* (1957), dir. Roy Ward Baker;
    prod. Julian Wintle; dist. Rank. DVD (screenshot by author)   121
5.5 *The One That Got Away* (1957), dir. Roy Ward Baker;
    prod. Julian Wintle; dist. Rank. DVD (screenshot by author)   122
5.6 *The One That Got Away* (1957), dir. Roy Ward Baker;
    prod. Julian Wintle; dist. Rank. DVD (screenshot by author)   122
5.7 *The One That Got Away* (1957), dir. Roy Ward Baker;
    prod. Julian Wintle; dist. Rank. DVD (screenshot by author)   123

Table

3.1 List of analysed Conservative leaders' speeches on enlargement   71

Contributors

Lisa Bischoff took her PhD in British Cultural Studies at Ruhr University Bochum, Germany, with a thesis entitled *DysEUtopia: British Novels and the European Union*. Prior to starting her PhD, she obtained a Master's degree in European Culture and Economy. Her research interests include British–EU relations, national identity and dystopian fiction. In summer 2017, she was a visiting scholar at the Department of Politics and International Relations at the University of Oxford.

Blanka Blagojevic studied English Language and Literature in Belgrade and Bern, Switzerland, where she obtained her MA. She was a member of the 'British Discourses of Europe' research project at the University of Basel with a grant from the Swiss National Science Foundation and is currently completing her PhD on British literary and cultural representations of Eastern Europe from the interwar period until today. Her research interests include Anglophone travel writing and poetry. In spring 2017, she was a visiting scholar at the University of Exeter on the invitation of Vesna Goldsworthy.

Lara Feigel is a Reader in Modern Literature and Culture at King's College, London, where she co-directs the Centre for Modern Literature and Culture. She studied English Literature at Oxford University and UCL and obtained a PhD from the University of Sussex. Since 2013, she has been working on a project about culture in post-war Germany entitled 'Beyond Enemy Lines', supported by a European Research Council Starting Grant. Her publications include *Literature, Cinema and Politics 1930–1945: Reading Between the Frames* (Edinburgh University Press 2010), *The Love Charm of Bombs: Restless Lives in the Second World War* (Bloomsbury 2013) and *The Bitter Taste of Victory: In the Ruins of the*

Reich (Bloomsbury 2016). She reviews regularly for publications such as the *Guardian* and the *Observer*.

Ina Habermann is Professor of English Literature at the University of Basel and acted as Director of the Centre of Competence Cultural Topographies from 2009 to 2017. Her publications include *Myth, Memory and the Middlebrow: Priestley, du Maurier and the Symbolic Form of Englishness* (Palgrave Macmillan 2010) and, as editor with Daniela Keller, *English Topographies in Literature and Culture. Space, Place, Identity* (Brill Rodopi 2016). She ran the Swiss National Science Foundation project 'British Literary and Cultural Discourses of Europe' (2014–17), and her research interests include middlebrow writing, Britishness and Englishness, and literary otherworlds.

Marlene Herrschaft-Iden is a research assistant at the University of Passau, Germany, where she teaches Cultural Studies. She obtained her PhD in 2018 with a thesis entitled *To Be, or Not to Be European? The Liberal Democrats Imagining Britain and Europe in Parliamentary Discourse, 1997–2010*. Her research interests include British–European relations, nations and identity as well as cultural diplomacy, and she is a member of the Association for the Study of British Cultures and the 'Arbeitskreis Deutsche England-Forschung'.

Robert Holland has specialised in British overseas history, with a focus on the Mediterranean during the nineteenth and twentieth centuries. He spent the bulk of his academic career at the Institute of Commonwealth Studies in London University's School of Advanced Studies. Currently he is a Senior Research Fellow at that institution and a Visiting Professor at the Centre for Hellenic Studies at King's College London. Amongst his book publications are *The Pursuit of Greatness: Britain and the World Role, 1900–1970* (Fontana 1991), *Blue-Water Empire: The British in the Mediterranean since 1800* (Penguin 2013) and *The Warm South: How the Mediterranean Shaped the British Imagination* (Yale University Press 2018).

Melanie Küng obtained her PhD as a member of the project 'British Literary and Cultural Discourses of Europe' at the Department of English, University of Basel. Her thesis is entitled *Bordering Europe: The Cultural and Literary Production of the English Channel in the 20th and 21st Centuries*. Her research interests include twentieth- and twenty-first-century British and Irish literature, the relationship between memory, space and identity, and border studies. In spring 2016, she was a visiting scholar at the School of Critical Studies at the University of Glasgow.

Alisa Miller holds degrees from the University of Michigan and the London School of Economics, and completed her DPhil at the University of Oxford. She has published widely on the comparative development of war cultures in twentieth-century Europe and the United States, examining how evolving literary networks – utilising different forms of media and technology – influence political discourses and perceptions of violence. She joined King's College London as a post-doctoral Research Associate in 2016 on the European Research Council funded projects Beyond Enemy Lines and Ego-media. She is the author of *Rupert Brooke in the First World War* (Clemson University Press and Liverpool University Press 2018).

Siobhan O'Connor took her PhD at Manchester Metropolitan University. Her thesis, entitled *The Tudor Turn: The Politics and Poetics of Englishness*, examines the relationship between historical fiction and national identity. It centres specifically on the proliferating literary re-imaginings of Henry VIII's court and what these illuminate about contemporary Englishness. Siobhan O'Connor is the author of 'History, Nation and Self: *Wolf Hall* and the Machinery of Memory', in Eileen Pollard and Ginette Carpenter (eds), *Contemporary Critical Perspectives: Hilary Mantel* (Bloomsbury 2018).

M.G. Sanchez is a Gibraltarian writer based in the UK. He studied at the University of Leeds, where he obtained BA, MA and PhD degrees in English Literature. He has written various fiction and non-fiction books about Gibraltar, including three novels, *The Escape Artist* (2013), *Solitude House* (2015) and *Jonathan Gallardo* (2015), as well as several collections of short stories. His writing focuses on Gibraltarian identity politics and on the geopolitical challenges facing the Rock and its inhabitants. He is also interested in borders, national stereotypes and colonial/postcolonial discourses of 'otherness'. More information can be found at www.mgsanchez.net/.

Christian Schmitt-Kilb is Professor of British Literature at the University of Rostock, Germany. His current research interests are in the fields of ecocriticism and environmental literary studies. His publications include *'Never was the Albion Nation without Poetrie': Poetik, Rhetorik und Nation im England der Frühen Neuzeit* (2004) and, as editor, *Britain at War*, a special issue of the *Journal for the Study of British Cultures*, vol. 14:2 (2007).

Menno Spiering is a Lecturer of European Studies at the University of Amsterdam. He has lectured for extended periods at the Universities of Minnesota and Hull (UK), and published widely on European and national identity as well as the relationship between 'Britain and Europe'. He is the author of *A Cultural History of British Euroscepticism* (Palgrave Macmillan 2015).

Klaus Stolz is a political scientist and Professor of British and American Social and Cultural Studies at the Technische Universität Chemnitz, Germany. He has taught at the universities of Freiburg, Mannheim, Göttingen and Chemnitz and published widely on British politics, regions and regionalism in Europe, political professionalisation and political careers. His research interests include British territorial politics and Scottish politics, and he is the author of *Towards a Regional Political Class? Professional Politicians and Regional Institutions in Catalonia and Scotland* (Manchester University Press 2010).

Judith Vonberg obtained her PhD from the University of East Anglia, and her research interests include Anglo-German cultural relations, national identity and popular culture. Her publications include 'The *Denken/ Handeln* Topos: Hamlet in Post-1945 Germany', in *Angermion: Yearbook for Anglo-German Literary Criticism, Intellectual History and Cultural Transfers* (2014). As a journalist, she has contributed to the *New Statesman*, the *Guardian*, *New Humanist* and *CNN International*.

Preface

As I revisit the introduction to this collection, I wish I could say that some of the problems outlined here had been addressed in the meantime. Unfortunately, however, while Britain has left the EU, these problems remain. They concern the legal and practical implementation of Brexit, the economic and political consequences, the cultural and political fault-lines within the British Isles, and Britain's relationship to Continental Europe. In British politics, narratives of British exceptionalism continue to be foregrounded. While lorries are queueing up in the Dover region, Gibraltar has entered the Schengen area and hostilities are breaking out over customs checks in Northern Ireland, the negative economic impact of Brexit has not yet been balanced out by the other profitable alliances envisioned by the Leave Campaign. If anything, the devastating Covid pandemic has served to camouflage the effects of Brexit, though there is no doubt that they will eventually emerge most starkly. We argue in this collection that a thorough understanding of the British-European relationship past and present must be the basis of a realistic vision for a future, mutually beneficial collaboration. This argument remains as relevant, if not more relevant, than when the book first went to press.

Without attempting a comprehensive review of the many books about Brexit that appeared in the last two years, this preface offers a brief update on the academic debates in literary and cultural studies. Responding to the proliferation of borders and border conflicts in recent years, Brexit is increasingly discussed in the context of Border Studies. This is a highly dynamic field, acknowledged for example in the launch of MUP's 'Rethinking Borders' series, with titles such as *Border images, border narratives: The political aesthetics of boundaries and crossings* (2021), edited by Johan Schimanski and Jopi Nyman, which speaks to the issue of British discourses of national identity as regards the 'island myth', Britain's domestic national boundaries (cf. also Naomi Lloyd-Jones and Margaret M. Scull ed., *Four Nations Approaches to Modern 'British' History. A (Dis) United Kingdom?* Palgrave Macmillan 2018) and the English Channel as a border zone. Borders, conceived as performative demarcations of space, are studied in terms of border poetics and aesthetics, entangled with matters of materiality and violence. Melanie Küng, a contributor to our collection, is finalizing a book about the Channel as a borderscape both real and imagined, and the collection *Bordertextures. A Complexity Approach to Cultural Border Studies*, edited by Christian Wille, Astrid M. Fellner and Eva Nossem (Transcript, autumn 2022), promises new theoretical departures.

Now widely available in paperback and accessible in style, our collection contributes to these negotiations of borders as well as to the debates about British attitudes to Europe and about BrexLit, which have recently received new momentum with the publication of Kristian Shaw's extensive study *BrexLit. British Literature and the European Project* (Bloomsbury 2021). It is to be hoped that the vibrant interdisciplinary research in our fields will increasingly inform wider debates about the British-European relationship after Brexit.

Ina Habermann, Basel, February 2022

Acknowledgements

This collection emerged from my research project 'British Literary and Cultural Discourses of Europe' at the University of Basel, funded by the Swiss Science Foundation, 2014–17. During these years and beyond, I am very grateful for innumerable conversations and valuable input about the riddled relationship between Britain and Europe with experts in history, politics and literature as well as cultural and media studies, and with guest speakers, colleagues and students at our workshops, conferences and other events. While it is impossible to list everyone, I would like to mention Christine Berberich, Wendy Bracewell, Gabriele Clemens, Gerard Delanty, Jacob Dittmar, Alex Drace-Francis, Robert Eaglestone, Ann-Marie Einhaus, Rainer Emig, Maurice Fitzpatrick, Michael Gardiner, Janine Hauthal, Sabina Horber, Stefan Howald, Daniela Keller, Annette Kern-Stähler, Barbara Korte, Gill Plain, Petra Rau, Joanna Rostek, Elmar Schenkel, Georg Sedlmayr, Kristian Shaw, Richard Stinshoff, Adam Thorpe, Alex Van Lierde and Anne Julia Zwierlein. Particularly, I would like to thank the contributors to this volume for their patience, co-operation and excellent work. Personal thanks go to friends in Britain who are affected in one way or another by the Brexit decision: Anke Bernau, Bernhard Klein, David Matthews and Gordon McMullan. It is reassuring to feel that our friendship will endure regardless of what happens on the political stage.

Thanks also go to Michelle Witen for her help with the typescript, to Alexandra Grasso, as ever, for her excellent editing and formatting work, to Matthew Frost, Tom Dark and particularly Paul Clarke of Manchester University Press for their support and the excellent collaboration throughout this project, to the publisher's copy editors, and to the anonymous reviewers for their encouragement and helpful comments. When I started work on this project in 2011 as an extension of my previous work on Englishness, I was of course aware that British discourses of Europe was a crucially important and understudied field, but I had no idea how topical it would soon become. I would be glad if we could contribute a little to a better understanding of the Brexit decision and the cultural frames of the debate about a possible future for Britain in Europe.

Introduction: Understanding the past, facing the future

Ina Habermann

Brexit means Brexit

Brexit brings out the worst in people. The interminable fight over what Brexit actually means, beyond (former) Prime Minister May's mesmerising tautology, has produced, and revealed, multiple faultlines in an increasingly dis-United Kingdom, on the level of nations, regions, political parties and social classes, down to the most intimate levels of families, friends and relationships. To a certain extent, this was caused by the stark binarism of the choice that the British people were given – yes or no, in or out. Woefully inadequate to the complexity of the situation, such binarisms erase all subtlety and are thus guaranteed to make people act more narrow-mindedly than they would under normal circumstances, to become partisan, even to risk re-awakening the ghosts of violent Irish sectarianism. While Brexit was sold to the British people as a way out of an impasse, several years into the process, it has become glaringly obvious that this move in itself will solve neither economic and social problems, nor those related to an English identity crisis. This collection of essays seeks to contribute to the Brexit debate, not being concerned, however, with the day-to-day political process and the technical difficulties of 'getting Brexit done', as Boris Johnson liked to put it. Rather, we are interested in the origins, the logic behind and the longer-term consequences of the developments that culminated on 23 June 2016, when a majority of British people voted to leave the European Union. In other words, we seek to help trace the road to Brexit.

We argue that in order to address the Brexit situation adequately, we need to understand British attitudes to Europe more deeply. As has often been pointed out, the Brexit vote represents a kind of category error – ordinary people wishing to punish the political class for their callousness and inability to develop policies that will allow people to deal with the consequences of austerity politics and the global challenges of the twenty-first century (see McGarvey, 2017). While this is most probably true, we suggest that it is not accidental that it was possible to re-direct people's anger, which should, according to this line of argument, have focused on the class system and rampant neo-liberal global capitalism. Even though the immediate critical target was the EU as a supranational political and economic organisation, many people's anger was in fact re-directed to Europe as a cultural, political and historical entity. The question is how this particular type of scapegoating could be so successful. The main reason is, we claim, that many people in Britain are in denial about the strength of the country's ties to continental Europe – ties that are in fact geographic, ethnic, historical, cultural, political, economic and often personal. This denial may take the form of open hostility, as it has in debates about immigration and political sovereignty, but even more fre-quently, it surfaces as a lack of interest in Europe or things European, fostered perhaps by the increasingly monolingual culture and dwindling grasp on history caused in Britain by 'stripped-down' curricula in schools and universities. There may come a time when people will not know any more that Queen Victoria's mother tongue was German. At its worst, this historical and cultural amnesia leads to a parochialism Britain can ill afford, especially if it wishes to 'stand alone' again in the winds of global change. It does make a difference after all whether or not the navel at which one gazes also happens to be the navel of the world, as in the days of the British Empire to which many look back with nostalgia – times up to the early twentieth century where, in Jan Morris's words, 'the British travelled all the world like the children of rich parents. Not for a moment did I think of myself as European. I was a privileged transient from another kind of country, an oceanic country whose frontiers extended from Tasmania to Newfoundland' (Morris, 2006: 4).

If we are to understand British attitudes to Europe, we need to pay close attention to cultural memory and the cultural imaginary. Many attempts at explaining the Leave victory and current British (and particu-larly English) 'Euroscepticism' (Spiering, 2015) focus quite narrowly on economic, legal and political factors, underestimating more 'fuzzy' phe-nomena such as cultural myths, narratives and images which circulate in literature, travel writing, films and other media, influencing people on a visceral level, sometimes even against their better judgement. There is now a growing public awareness of this, but it took about two years after the referendum to emerge. As Robert Eaglestone stated in a collection published in late 2018, 'Brexit is not only political, economic and admin-istrative: perhaps most significantly it is an event in culture, too. Brexit grew from cultural beliefs, real or imaginary, about Europe and the UK; the arguments before, during and after the referendum were – and are – arguments about culture; its impact on the cultural life of these islands may last for generations' (Eaglestone, 2018: 1). Looking at the build-up to the referendum, it is striking that Leave campaigners were very good at exploiting myths and stereotypes for their own ends, tapping into the reservoirs of cultural memory in search of narratives and images that would have an impact, while Remainers did not manage, or did not care, to offer powerful narratives in favour of European integration. For example, the UKIP poster that shows three huge escalators cutting into the white cliffs of Dover, prime symbol of British Exceptionalism and the 'island myth' (see chapter 10), says more than a thousand words; its impact cannot be countered with a considered and bland argument about change, cultural hybridity and the ultimately beneficial effects of immigration. In recent years, the British 'island story' (see Christinidis, 2015) has been foregrounded again, and if international ties are acknowledged, the emphasis is on the Commonwealth and the United States, downplaying the ways in which Britain is historically, culturally and economically entangled with Europe. John Robert Seeley famously suggested in 1883 that the British had acquired their empire in a 'fit of absence of mind', and it sometimes appears as if they had also embarked on their exit from Europe in this half-conscious state. If anything, the need for a candid debate about British and English identity and the nature of the country's relations to Europe is even more obvious now, three years into the Brexit negotiations. As this book goes to press, three projected exit dates, 29 March, 12 April and 31 October 2019, have come and gone, and there is still a conspicuous lack of values and visions that could guide the political negotiations. If Britannia once ruled the waves, she is now adrift, and we argue that Britain will have to face Europe, *really* to engage with it and to take an interest, if it is to make informed decisions about the future.

More kin than kind

For many centuries, England/Britain has had a close, difficult and often violent relationship with continental Europe. In order to understand this particular entanglement and its role in the Brexit decision in 2016, one has to take a close look at the historical situation in conjunction with the debates about Britishness and Englishness that emerged in the last twenty years. After the demise of the British Empire and during decolonisation, Britain had to come to terms, in the context of post-war austerity and Cold War politics, with the loss of its imperial status. As Jodi

Burkett shows in *Constructing Post-Imperial Britain* (Burkett, 2013), attempts were made by organisations such as the Campaign for Nuclear Disarmament to replace Britain's geopolitical and economic dominance with a moral claim to leadership. In parallel, as Dominic Sandbrook argues in *The Great British Dream Factory* (2016), Britain transformed itself into a 'cultural superpower', exporting lifestyles, fashion, literature, films and music. Despite these developments, the British public had to accept Britain's diminished role in the world and to suffer the effects of their country's weak economy, at the same time facing a (Western) continental Europe that was recovering fast and building supra-national organisations. As Benjamin Grob-Fitzgibbon observes in *Continental Drift* (2016), Britons thus developed a Euroscepticism that became inseparable from post-imperial nostalgia (see Paul Gilroy on postcolonial melancholia, 2004), not least in view of the excruciating structural changes of the Thatcherite 1980s. While 'Cool Britannia' seemed the way forward for a while in the relatively prosperous 1990s under New Labour, the end of the Cold War and the devolution process put the interrogation of Englishness on the agenda with increasing urgency, and in the years leading up to the referendum, the volume was turned up on arguments against un-English influences. The notion of the 'Norman Yoke' was resurrected (Kingsnorth, 2014; see chapter 8), and with the dismissal of 'Hanoverian thinking' (Gardiner, 2018: 106) and postcolonial multiculturalism (UKIP and the Conservative government's 'hostile environment', see chapters 10 and 12), Englishness has time and again emerged as an antler-shaking, folksy version of Anglo-Saxonism (see, for example, the production of D.C. Moore's *Common* at the National Theatre in London in 2017). Ironically, of course, the Anglo-Saxons were migrants from what is today Denmark and northern Germany. Such is the nature of national identity that peeling away the layers of perceived foreignness, one is ultimately left with nothing. The ubiquitous metaphor of 'roots' has tended to mislead people here, since movement rather than stasis has always been the default condition. This is a truism which the powers that be choose to deny, thus attempting to cement the status quo.

Even though Britain did join the European Economic Community in 1973 in a time of economic crisis, it failed to acknowledge the strength of its relations to continental Europe, considering itself separate and aloof to such an extent that when Article 50 of the Treaty on European Union was triggered in March 2017, the British government forgot to make adequate provisions for its continental European territory, Gibraltar (see Habermann, 2018), as well as for Ireland. Europe is 'the Other', both for Conservatives and those on the left (see MacShane, 2015, 2016, 2017), often cast in the role of a tedious relative who will persistently pop up at family parties, displaying irritatingly familiar personality traits and getting in the way of the much more interesting American and Commonwealth crowds. While Britain had a 'multicultural moment' in the 1990s and into the very early years of the new millennium, after the financial crisis in 2008–9 there was a marked return to English heritage and nostalgia, country houses, the royal family, snobbish TV productions such as *Downton Abbey* (2010–15), and of course to that 'finest hour' when the 'island nation' purportedly stood alone. As regards recent popular culture and the media, films such as Jonathan Teplitzky's *Churchill* (2017), Joe Wright's *Darkest Hour* (2017) and Christopher Nolan's *Dunkirk* (2017) cannot but be interpreted now in the light of Brexit, invested as they are in the heroic success story that re-signifies a chaotic retreat from mainland Europe into a moral victory. Taking a relational perspective, this collection explores the British-European entanglement in the face of British Exceptionalism, the 'island myth' shadowed by the invasion scare narrative, and dys-EUtopia.

British-European entanglements

No attempt will of course be made here to revisit the long history of British–European relations from the time of the Roman occupation, and through the various waves of migration to the present day, trying to cover aspects of commerce, warfare, exile, custom, language and dynastic relation (see Simms, 2017). Rather, I will touch upon a selection of issues that had, or have, a particular impact on the British cultural memory and imagination. Countering the notion of the 'island fortress', in his book *Blue Water Empire* Robert Holland gives a detailed account of the important place of the Mediterranean in British history and the British imagination. In a large-scale historical survey, he shows how strongly the Mediterranean was shaped by British influence. Inquiring into the 'British experience of the Mediterranean, and the Mediterranean experience of the British' (Holland, 2013: 6) since 1800, he argues that if 'there has in modern times been a predominant instrument for integrating the Mediterranean as a single theatre it was the British … It was the British presence in the Mediterranean, and the stability it provided, which made the region what an eminent historian writing in 1904 incapsulated as the "keyboard of Europe": if that was shaken, everything else would shake too' (Holland, 2013: 6).[1]

While, given the cultural and political importance of the Mediterranean, Britain has thus crucially shaped Europe, the same holds true the other way round, as Holland shows in his study *The Warm South: How the*

Mediterranean Shaped the British Imagination. Offering an extended discussion of the Romantic infatuation with the Mediterranean, Holland moves on to the twentieth century, where he singles out Peter Mayle's best-selling memoir *A Year in Provence* (1989), turned into a TV mini-series in 1993, as an important landmark. This was 'the story of a fifty-something couple moving to the south of France and their travails with dodgy builders and other eccentric locals while converting a derelict farmhouse into their idealized escape' (Holland, 2018: 259). Before long, 'a whole flood of British retirees were on the move southwards, creating de facto communities, transforming corners of Tuscany into Chiantishire, the somewhat less affluent making do with cramped apartments on Spanish coasts' (Holland, 2018: 259). He concludes: 'Nothing could replicate the warm South as a benchmark and inspiration, because of the relentless pull exerted from the Graeco-Roman past, and the range and power of its more modern manifestations' (Holland, 2018: 259). This continues to be reflected in a sizable amount of more or less middlebrow works for light holiday reading as well as in mainstream literature by British authors based abroad, such as Tim Parks or Adam Thorpe, whose memoir *Notes from the Cévennes: Half a Lifetime in Provincial France* was published in 2018, or the Francophile Julian Barnes, whose collection of stories *Cross Channel* (1996) offers a literary exploration of the English Channel as a contact zone. Identity is always relational: as any historical inquiry will show, Europe would not be what it is without Britain, and Britain as we know it would not exist without Europe.

The road to Brexit

Our analysis of the road to Brexit is subdivided into three parts: the chapters in part I, 'Britain and Europe: political entanglements', take stock of the political status quo and its historical causes, addressing the process of European integration and British party politics, and paying attention to Britain's internal faultlines. Robert Holland opens the collection with a wide-ranging chapter on Britain's oblique relation to Europe, exploring the 'tendency for British influence to drape itself around Europe's outer rims' and reviewing the chequered history of negotiations with the EU and its predecessors. Ironically, Holland emphasises, those in Britain who do not like to negotiate with the EU will have to face the fact that the need for negotiation will increase after Brexit. In chapter 2, Lara Feigel and Alisa Miller focus on the twentieth century, and particularly the period after the Second World War. The chapter addresses visions for a unified Europe in the aftermath of war, debates about British leadership and the contributions of writers such as Stephen Spender and T.S. Eliot. Feigel and Miller argue that the European project needs to be kept alive as a cultural vision. Chapter 3 by Marlene Herrschaft-Iden offers an in-depth analysis of the Conservative Party's discourse on Europe between 1997 and 2015. It emerges that when in opposition, the Conservatives did nothing to criticise Labour's policy of free movement after the 2004 EU enlargement, and that the hostile rhetoric signalling the rise of immigration to the top of the political agenda only crept in after 2011 as part of an argumentative U-turn. It is therefore demonstrably disingenuous to blame Labour exclusively for the consequences of Britain's open policy in the early 2000s. Chapter 4 by Klaus Stolz discusses Britain's internal divisions, tracing the ways in which Europe was used in domestic constitutional debates and showing that European discourses always first and foremost served domestic purposes.

Studying the discourses of national identity in Britain, one cannot help but notice the crucial role that literature plays in them, from early modern authors such as Spenser, Shakespeare, Bunyan and Milton via the eighteenth-century novel and the Gothic novel, the Romanticism of Scott, Wordsworth, Byron, Shelley and Blake, the condition-of-England novel, the fin-de-siècle spy and invasion scare fiction as well as the projections of a dangerous Europe evoked by E.M. Forster and Henry James, to twentieth-century counterfactual and dystopian literature and travel writing. This may be so, as Michael Gardiner argues, because 'in the absence of a codified constitution … English Literature continued to act as an informal or anti-formal constitution' (Gardiner, 2013: 1; see also Gardiner, 2004 and Westhall and Gardiner, 2013). Over centuries, literature effected a flexible and dialogic debate about identity, structurally able to negotiate otherness as it defined Englishness and Britishness, rhetorically beating the bounds, and shaping the contours of the nation in a geographical and social imaginary epitomised in John of Gaunt's (aka Jean de Gant) vision of the 'sceptre'd isle' as dramatised in Shakespeare's *Richard II* (see chapter 10). According to Gardiner, this system has come under pressure in the new millennium in a post-colonial paradigm: 'If the informal constitution was indeed cultural, could English Literature really retain the civilizing and universalizing shape it had had during imperial and consensual times?' (2013: 5). Gardiner concludes that the 'long-accepted universalism that ties together British state and English Literature … can and should be historicized' (2013: 9), especially now that English Literature is increasingly turned into expensive heritage through exorbitant study fees. Possibly, 'BrexLit' projects such as Ali Smith's writing to the moment in her Seasonal Quartet (*Autumn*, 2016; *Winter*, 2017; *Spring*, 2019) or the Poet Laureate Carol Ann Duffy's communal drama *My Country: A*

Work in Progress (2017) seek to recapture literature's role as a space for constitutional debate.[2] This reading would seem to be endorsed by the fact that each of Smith's novels abounds with literary echoes and is linked to a Shakespeare play. In *Spring*, in line with its refugee theme, this is *Pericles*, a play that charts its characters' wanderings across the Eastern Mediterranean, effecting miraculous reunions.

Given this crucial importance of literature in the context of British discourses of identity, the second and third parts of the collection will deal mainly with literature. While our approach is necessarily selective, we emphasise some particularly resonant themes such as the role of Germany (chapters 2, 5 and 7) and British Exceptionalism and isolationism underpinned by the topographical narrative of the island nation (chapters 1, 4, 6, 10, 11 and 12). This narrative is related in turn to the tropes of immigration scare stories, which have been used to great advantage by Leave campaigners and the Europhobe press, to stereotypes of Eastern Europe and fears of mass immigration from the East (chapters 6 and 11).

In detail, part II, 'British discourses of Europe in film and literature', is devoted to exemplary case studies in film, dystopian and historical fiction. Understandably, after the Second World War, the British found it particularly difficult to come to terms with Germany (see Rau, 2013). As Judith Vonberg shows in chapter 5, the 1960 film *Sink the Bismarck!* establishes images of Britishness and Germanness congruent with the dominant wartime stereotypes. Vonberg proceeds to contrast this with the 1957 box office hit *The One That Got Away*, whose likeable protagonist, played by the dashing German actor Hardy Krüger, elicited ambivalent responses in Britain. Was it really acceptable to side with an escaped German prisoner? Menno Spiering, in chapter 6, revisits the concept of British Exceptionalism, intrinsically connected to the conspicuous negative projections of the European in anti-Catholic and anti-European novels. Chapter 7 by Lisa Bischoff continues the discussion of Eurosceptic novels with an in-depth analysis of Andrew Roberts' influential novel *The Aachen Memorandum*, originally published in 1995 and re-issued in 2012 by Biteback Publishing. The subsequent two chapters address historical fiction: In chapter 8, Christian Schmitt-Kilb reads Paul Kingsnorth's *The Wake* (2014) as a Brexit novel. Set at the time of the Norman invasion and focused on resistance to the 'Norman yoke', the novel constructs an authentic Anglo-Saxon Englishness obliterated through invasion. Schmitt-Kilb links this to Fintan O'Toole's argument about the structures of feeling that led to Brexit: in *Heroic Failure: Brexit and the Politics of Pain*, O'Toole diagnoses an English 'desire to *have actually been invaded* so that one could – gloriously – resist' (O'Toole, 2018: 44; emphasis in original). A similar dynamic is at work in the popular, best-selling fictions set in the Tudor period. In chapter 9, Siobhan O'Connor analyses Philippa Gregory's *The King's Curse* (2014) and *The Taming of the Queen* (2015) in terms of expressions of 'postcolonial melancholia' (Gilroy, 2004). In these novels, 'native' Plantagenet culture is seen as threatened by Tudor tyranny – a foreign usurpation that also brings contagion through the sweating sickness, the 'Tudor disease'. Schmitt-Kilb's and O'Connor's case studies throw into relief the arbitrary nature of prelapsarian visions of England. Ironically, in the Tudor novels, the invaders of earlier times are cast as people with a native birth right, proponents of a class-inflected, indigenous culture. Despite their dominant political message, these novels thus undermine their own claims of origin with their failure to imagine a Britain, or England, prior to, and 'untainted' by, European migration.

Part III, 'Negotiating borders in British travel writing and memoir', deals with constructions of identity in non-fictional literature. In chapter 10, Melanie Küng focuses on the English Channel as a liminal space, analysing the significance of the white cliffs of Dover as a prime symbol of British Exceptionalism. The symbol, creating white cliffs of the mind as ostensible geographical proof of insular separatism, becomes so strong as to obliterate the reality of constant exchange. If this is considered properly, it becomes less surprising, if still deplorable, that the Conservative politician Dominic Raab admitted publicly, a few days before he stepped down as Brexit minister in November 2018, that he had had no idea of the cross-Channel volume of trade. Chapter 11 by Blanka Blagojevic continues the discussion of borders and boundaries, analysing the trope of the 'Iron Curtain' in British travel writing pre- and post-1989. In readings of David Shears' *The Ugly Frontier* (1970), Anthony Bailey's *Along the Edge of the Forest: An Iron Curtain Journey* (1983) and Tim Moore's *The Cyclist Who Went Out in the Cold: Adventures along the Iron Curtain Trail* (2016), she traces the trajectory of British conceptions of Eastern Europe. Again, it emerges that seemingly natural boundaries are surprisingly mobile. Finally, one of the crucial British–European entanglements that was forgotten when Britain triggered Article 50 to begin the Brexit process, along with the issue of Ireland,[3] was British Gibraltar. Unsurprisingly, although pre-Brexit Gibraltar was almost invisible to large parts of the British population, the post-Brexit status of Gibraltar has become a bone of contention. Acknowledging this, the collection finishes with a brief memoir by the British-Gibraltarian writer M.G. Sanchez, who says that, given his experiences in Britain over the years, and the nature of his encounters, in Gibraltar and elsewhere, with people from 'mainland Britain', he was surprised to see Leave win only by such a narrow margin.

The Aftermath

To conclude this brief introduction, I want to focus on one example that puts in a nutshell what I mean when I speak about British, and especially English, denial, rejection and oblivion with regard to Europe. In 2013, Rhidian Brook published *The Aftermath*, a novel set in the ruins of Hamburg after the Second World War and based on his own family history. His grandfather, Colonel Walter Brook, was 'governor of the Kreis (county) district of Pinneberg, immediately to the west of Hamburg, and responsible for its reconstruction and the feeding, rehousing and de-Nazification of thousands of displaced people' (Brook, 2014). When Colonel Brook requisitioned a villa to live in, he took the unusual decision to allow the previous owners to stay, so that Rhidian Brook's father grew up between 1946 and 1951 in close contact with the Ladige family, ignoring the injunction not to 'fraternize' with the defeated enemy, and a friendship developed between the Brook and Ladige children. When Rhidian Brook heard about this history, as late as 2001, he decided to go on a trip down memory lane and to learn about his grandfather, bonding with his own father in the process. As they travelled to Hamburg together, met Theo and Heike Ladige and rekindled memories, it turned out that Brook's father can actually still speak German.

> Flying home, my father expressed relief. Theo and Heike remembered that time with gratitude and fondness. How curious that my grandfather's simple act of kindness had led to his son and grandson making this trip together 60 years later.
>
> I asked what influence Walter's action had had on Dad's own life. He liked to think he'd inherited his father's tendency to question 'the expected patterns of behaviour' and that he'd continued his 'always open door' policy in his own home. But the most telling legacy for him was to be found in Theo's and Heike's responses. He'd always had an idea of what his father was like but their memories made him more real.
>
> The distance between Hamburg and London is surprisingly small.
> (Brook, 2014)

Brook also recounts that the Germans were punning on Walter Brook's name, praising him as a builder of bridges, given that the name Brook sounds similar to the German *Brücke* (bridge). So this is a story of reconciliation after a cataclysmic historical event, where Colonel Walter Brook displayed the (British) decency and graciousness that won over so many people on the Continent after the war. I consider it unfortunate, but also quite typical, that this contact was not sustained and the episode fell into oblivion. It is equally unfortunate and typical that, to a certain extent, Rhidian Brook betrays the story by romanticising it, adding sexual interest and focusing on an adulterous affair between the wife of the British Army officer and the German occupant of the house. There seems to be a need, almost a compulsion, to re-imagine the British–European encounter in terms of an illicit love affair. Thus distorted into cliché, the potentially uplifting episode is overwhelmed by the dynamics of British Europhobia: since the narrative takes its frisson and interest from transgressive sexual desire, it casts all contact with the European 'Other' as dangerous. (A blueprint for this can be found in Henry James' novels.) This almost automatic plot device is in fact both acknowledged and questioned in E.M. Forster's novel *A Passage to India* (1924), where the young Englishwoman Adela Quested misreads the disturbing impact that India's otherness has on her as sexual assault. This leads initially to a charge against the Indian Doctor Aziz which Adela then has the courage to withdraw when she realises that she has made a mistake, thus alienating the British colonial community. Significantly, the problem is noticed with regard to India rather than Europe. Postcolonial literary studies have done much for a critique of the British Empire, showing that there is no British identity outside an imperial paradigm, which is of crucial importance, given the quasi-constitutional role of literature. We need a Euro-British literary studies to do the same for the relationship between Britain and continental Europe, recapturing and highlighting all that disavowed Europeanness. What does it mean that Will Ladislaw in George Eliot's *Middlemarch* has Polish ancestry? How to interpret all those European settings in British fiction and the immense bulk of travel writing?[4]

The film *The Aftermath*, based on Brook's novel and released in late 2018, amplifies the novel's romantic frisson, reducing bombed Hamburg to a picturesque backdrop for rather bland English period drama.[5] So far, the film has mainly been discussed, and dismissed, in terms of old-school romance and soapy period drama, as reviews and social media commentary focused on the choice of actors, Keira Knightley's period appeal, her dresses, the morals of a film that asks spectators to countenance 'cheating' on one's husband. Moreover, producers apparently could not find it in their hearts to cast an actual German as the male love interest, who is played by Alexander Skarsgård. Unfortunately, then, in terms of the relationship between Britain and the Continent, in this case the particularly riddled one with Germany, *The Aftermath* is not even a 'brief encounter', to recall the title of the famous Second World War film melodrama; it is more like two ships passing in the night. In the case of the Brook family, in contrast, contact was made through the children who were thrown together by destiny, doing what comes naturally to children – talking, playing, making a new beginning.[6] But in order for this healing power to emerge, there must be contact and dialogue, there must be curiosity, respect, openness and goodwill. These qualities, amply displayed by Colonel Walter Brook, are severely under pressure in our age of renewed borders and walls.

Speaking about borders and walls – I promised myself that I would leave my personal stake in the matter out of this academic inquiry, but in questions such as these it seems there is no neutral ground. I grew up during the Cold War as an anglophile in the Western part of a divided (and occupied) Germany fostered by American help, but also crucially shaped by the cultural 'projection of Britain', for many years promoted institutionally by the British Council. Having studied Englishness, English literature, history and culture, and British–European relations over years and in some depth, I am convinced that, in its own best interest as for the benefit of the Continent, Britain must acknowledge its inextricable entanglement with Europe, and continue to play its part, as it has always done in the past, so that together we can face the challenges of the future. If Brexit brought that home to a significant number of people in Britain, and if it forced both Britain and the EU to face some home truths about Europe's increasingly marginal role in the world, that would not be entirely a bad thing.

Notes

1   The 'eminent historian' in question was Julian Corbett (in Corbett, 1904: 314).
2   The term 'BrexLit' was coined by Kristian Shaw, whose book *BrexLit* will be published by Bloomsbury in 2020. For the emerging BrexLit phenomenon see also Shaw (2018).
3   For an excellent discussion of Brexit and Ireland, see Connelly (2018).
4   For an important discussion of the European dimension in British interwar travel and travel writing see Fussell (1980).
5   *The Aftermath* (UK, Germany, USA, dir. James Kent, prod. Ridley Scott *et al.*, Fox Searchlight Pictures).
6   For detailed historical accounts of the situation in post-war Germany and Europe see Judt (2005), Hitchcock (2008) and Buruma (2013).

References

Brook, Rhidian (2013), *The Aftermath* (New York: Knopf).
    (2014), 'Hamburg after the war: how my dad made friends with the Germans', *Guardian*, 1 November. www.theguardian.com/lifeandstyle/2014/nov/01/hamburg-after-the-war-how-my-dad-made-friends-with-the-germans (last accessed 12 April 2019).

Burkett, Jodi (2013), *Constructing Post-Imperial Britain: Britishness, 'Race' and the Radical Left in the 1960s* (Basingstoke: Palgrave Macmillan).

Buruma, Ian (2013), *Year Zero: A History of 1945* (London: Atlantic Books).

Christinidis, Georgia (2015), 'Our island story: renegotiating national history', *Journal for the Study of British Cultures* 22:2, pp. 209–25.

Connelly, Tony (2018), *Brexit & Ireland: The Dangers, the Opportunities, and the Inside Story of the Irish Response* (London: Penguin).

Corbett, Julian (1904), *England in the Mediterranean: A Study of the Rise and Influence of British Power within the Straits 1603–1713*, 2 vols (London: Longmans Green).

Eaglestone, Robert (ed.) (2018), *Brexit and Literature: Critical and Cultural Responses* (London: Routledge).

Fussell, Paul (1980), *Abroad: British Literary Traveling Between the Wars* (Oxford: Oxford University Press).

Gardiner, Michael (2004), *The Cultural Roots of British Devolution* (Edinburgh: Edinburgh University Press).

—— (2013), *The Constitution of English Literature: The State, the Nation and the Canon* (London: Bloomsbury Academic).

—— (2018), 'Brexit and the Aesthetics of Anachronism' in Robert Eaglestone (ed.), *Brexit and Literature: Critical and Cultural Responses* (London: Routledge), pp. 105–17.

Gilroy, Paul (2004), *Postcolonial Melancholia* (New York: Columbia University Press).

Grob-Fitzgibbon, Benjamin (2016), *Continental Drift: Britain and Europe from the End of Empire to the Rise of Euroscepticism* (Cambridge: Cambridge University Press).

Habermann, Ina (2018), 'European topologies: M.G. Sanchez' *The Escape Artist* and the case of Gibraltar', in Janine Hauthal, Christophe Collard and Lesley Penné (eds), special issue *Spaces of Entanglement: Negotiating European Crossroads, Journal for Literary and Intermedial Crossings*. www.jlic.be/doku.php?id=spaces_of_entanglement.

Hitchcock, William I. (2008), *The Bitter Road to Freedom: The Human Cost of Allied Victory in World War II Europe* (New York: Free Press).

Holland, Robert (2013), *Blue-Water Empire: The British in the Mediterranean Since 1800* (London: Penguin).

—— (2018), *The Warm South: How the Mediterranean Shaped the British Imagination* (New Haven and London: Yale University Press).

Judt, Tony (2005), *Postwar: A History of Europe Since 1945* (London: Penguin).

Kingsnorth, Paul (2014), *The Wake* (London: Unbound).

McGarvey, Darren (2017), *Poverty Safari: Understanding the Anger of Britain's Underclass* (Edinburgh: Luath Press Limited).

MacShane, Denis (2015), *Brexit: How Britain Will Leave Europe* (London: I.B. Tauris).

—— (2016), *How Britain Left Europe* (London: I.B. Tauris).

—— (2017), *Brexit, No Exit: Why (in the End) Britain Won't Leave Europe* (London: I.B. Tauris).

Morris, Jan (2006), *Europe: An Intimate Journey* (London: Faber & Faber).

O'Toole, Fintan (2018), *Heroic Failure: Brexit and the Politics of Pain* (London: Head of Zeus).

Rau, Petra (2013), *Our Nazis: Representations of Fascism in Contemporary Literature and Film* (Edinburgh: Edinburgh University Press).

Sandbrook, Dominic (2016), *The Great British Dream Factory: The Strange History of Our National Imagination* (London: Penguin).

Shaw, Kristian (2018), 'BrexLit' in Robert Eaglestone (ed.), *Brexit and Literature: Critical and Cultural Responses* (London: Routledge), pp. 15–30.

Simms, Brendan (2017), *Britain's Europe: A Thousand Years of Conflict and Cooperation* (London: Allen Lane).

Spiering, Menno (2015), *A Cultural History of British Euroscepticism* (Basingstoke: Palgrave Macmillan).

Westhall, Claire and Michael Gardiner (eds) (2013), *Literature of an Independent England: Revisions of England, Englishness, and English Literature* (Basingstoke: Palgrave Macmillan).

Part I

Britain and Europe: political entanglements

1

Not with a bang but a whimper: Brexit in historical perspective

Robert Holland

Exploring the nature of Brexit in historical perspective is inevitably like pinning down the proverbial butterfly. 'Brexit means Brexit', Theresa May famously declared early in her premiership, and although at the time this seemed to critics merely frustratingly elusive, much later it is surely rather reflective of an inherently ungraspable proposition, impossible to effect in any truly satisfactory fashion. Looking again at innumerable press clippings gathered during the three years that followed the June 2016 referendum, what above all strikes this commentator is how little the debate has shifted. There has not effectively been a substantive 'debate' at all, as there was, for example, in the years leading up to the United Kingdom's original adhesion to the Treaty of Rome in 1973. This failure to resolve the underlying dilemmas lay at the heart of the paralysis gripping the country as the originally scheduled day of departure from the European Union – 29 March 2019 – came and went.

Amidst the hubbub of the impending referendum a desire quickly surfaced to find meaningful *historical* pointers in a process that otherwise the Electoral Reform Society found to have 'glaring deficiencies' as an exercise of democratic will. A pro-Brexit 'Historians for Britain' emerged, with its epicentre in Cambridge University whose case for abandoning the EU rested on an exceptionalism defined, as one declaratory statement had it, by 'the distinctive character of the United Kingdom, rooted in its largely uninterrupted history since the Middle Ages'. Without such a sense that the United Kingdom, by nature and historical experience, is wholly separate from Europe, and that Europe itself constitutes the 'Other', Brexit could never have displayed the staying power and ideological mobilisation over the next few years in the face of a host of practical objections. It did not take long, however, for an entirely opposite group to articulate the view that far from being exceptional and uninterrupted, British history has in fact experienced numerous ruptures, most of them connected to similar phenomena on the Continent, with which the UK's relationship has always been organic and ultimately compelling.

One telling irony was that leading 'Historians for Britain' often appeared to be specialists in something other than the history of the United Kingdom itself. A chief spokesperson was the chronicler of the Mediterranean, David Abulafia, who perhaps found in an idealised vision of a seamless British history some soothing counter-point to the bewildering disruptions of the region with which his own work was concerned (Abulafia, 2011). Another example of this tendency was the pro-Brexit historian of France, Robert Tombs, who published a volume entitled *The English and Their History* (2015), including the judgment that after the Napoleonic wars Great Britain had 'captured the future' and secured hegemonic control of the Western world. This was the same Britain which in 1823 could not stop restored Bourbon France from invading Spain, so reversing the effects of Wellington's triumphs in the recent Peninsular campaigns, or in 1830 from seizing Algiers. A sense of British power hugely out of proportion to any nineteenth-century or, as we shall see, early twentieth-century reality – a long era when Paris far outshone London as the world's cultural metropole – was a recurring feature of Brexit's historical underpinning.

Some advocates of Brexit latched onto the English Reformation and the split from Rome as providing a notable sixteenth-century historical analogue, though specialists on the subject were quick to point out that this ignored the fact that the Reformation in England was only part of an international, essentially German-led movement (MacCulloch, 2016). There was also the slight awkwardness, as the writer Peter Frankopan observed, that Henry VIII might have 'taken back control', but his actions also sowed the seeds of a later civil war (Frankopan, 2017). As for the reformed English Church and state, the emerging Elizabethan 'Anglican' settlement by the 1580s and 1590s had anyway been hedged about with all sorts of compromises and contradictions. Querying how Protestant that settlement was, one expert has recently observed that the outcome was not at all what true or advanced Reformers had really wanted in the first place (Younger, 2018). Theresa May's 'deal' for Brexit as it emerged in late 2018 was surely 'Anglican' in exactly this late Tudor sense of desperately balancing antithetical elements in the hope of discovering a workable *via media* reflecting English particularities. The fact that these latter-day ideals were so intensely *English*, however, was also a significant weakness when translated into the setting of a wider British Union.

Another reflection of a historicist instinct immediately before and after June 2016 was a temptation to claim the mantle of Winston Churchill.

One of the leading Brexiteers, Boris Johnson, sought to literally take on a Churchillian persona, including gruffly-voiced classical allusions and talk of roaring lions. Churchill seemed to be everywhere you looked in Brexit-inclined Britain. There were three blockbuster films in 2017 alone. One leading London bookshop, Hatchards in Piccadilly, devoted a whole corner of their shelves to the great man – more than for the seventeenth century or the French Revolution or China. In history-writing this fixation climaxed during October 2018 with a massive new biography by the right-wing historian Andrew Roberts, and although one reviewer complains unkindly about 'one thousand pages of literary purgatory',[1] there was no doubt that such accounts of the great man testify to an insatiable appetite for the subject among the mass British public, even when the narrative has been endlessly repeated.

The trouble with Churchill as an inspiration for Brexit was that his long career pointed in so many different directions before trailing off into complete enigma in the last few years of his life. The prominent historian of contemporary times, Vernon Bogdanor, remarked on the eve of the referendum that Churchill's ambivalence towards European unification, far from signifying any firm conclusions on his own part, merely tracked the uncertainties of British people over a long period, with many ebbs and flows along the way (Bogdanor, 2016). Bogdanor's instinct was that, had Churchill possessed a vote in 2016, he would have thought hard, and reluctantly voted Remain on the grounds that Europe was inherent in the United Kingdom's physical security. But to this might be added something more. It was a key belief of Churchill that there was no greater error than to pretend to a position, and degree of leverage, that you did not actually have, since you would surely be found out. Such a deep fragility was to show up painfully as Theresa May's negotiation with the EU evolved.

A Churchillian streak embedded in the British public mind was surely not unconnected with a somewhat older stereotype of a distinctively English 'apartness': that of John Bull. This fitted a long-standing pattern when periods of growing involvement with, or vulnerability to, the adjoining Continent have been interlaced with phases of sharp nativist reaction. Such a phenomenon might be traced back to the struggles to fend off marauding Vikings – the last true English army had been destroyed by King Cnut at the battle of Assandun on an Essex hillside on 18 October 1016 – and the stories of Robin Hood and his Merry Saxons hitting back at arrogant Norman-French overlords after the conquest of 1066. The anti-foreigner figure of John Bull arose from the much more modern context in which a new Dutch king after 1688, William III, involved his freshly-acquired English kingdom in European wars, culminating in the War of Spanish Succession after 1700. John Bull, with his fierce predilection for warm beer, quietness and Protestantism at home, and all entanglements beyond the sea to 'go hang', was the cutting edge of a new political satire. Boris Johnson's call for the EU in mid-2017 to 'go hang' in insisting that Britain pay for all outstanding liabilities as a departing member was in this edgy mould.

It must also be said that, however confected the figure of John Bull might have been, his prejudices were not without a good deal of historical validity. When John Major became prime minister in November 1990 following the dramatic fall of Margaret Thatcher, he said that Britain must thereafter be 'at the heart of Europe' and not just sulk on the sidelines. Yet on a long view the brutal truth has been that Britain's attempts to be an effective power-player at the heart of Europe have rarely, if ever, turned out well. The Anglo-Normans fought to keep their territories in France but even Calais was lost in the end under Queen Mary; her heart, she said, would on death be found to bear the imprint of the town's name. Later attempted interventions on the Continent invariably ended badly, as with the disastrous campaign in 1791 on the island of Walcheren and the attempt in 1793 to sustain the French Royalist hold on Toulon against the republican forces including a very youthful Captain Napoleon Bonaparte. The field of Waterloo in 1815 offered some kind of compensation, though even then only with last-minute help from the Prussians. In the mid-nineteenth century, when British ascendency was expanding elsewhere, key issues on the European mainland, such as the Schleswig-Holstein Question, were resolved with minimal reference to British views as the power of a unifying Germany took shape. The British got on fine so long as they kept to their ships, but once they got on land – at least on European land – strategically speaking their swagger seemed to disappear, as fighting in the Crimea during the 1850s cruelly exemplified.

The twentieth century only confirmed this skewed reality, but at greater cost in blood and cash. After August 1914 the British Expeditionary Force was soon on the ropes, and the reason why it was placed *away* from the French coast in the panic of the retreat towards Paris during those early months of the conflict was that it was rumoured that the British army under Sir John French might be preparing to make a dash back home (Cassar, 1977: 286). Afterwards Lord Kitchener's conscripted New Armies represented a massive attempt to prove that the British *could* be a truly continental force when they put their minds to it. But by the spring of 1918 it was the British army that was closest to cracking, which was why General Ludendorff's ultimately failed offensive was aimed primarily at their lines (Holland, 1991: 82–3). Only the arrival of large-scale reinforcements from the 'associated' power of the United States saved the day. Even then it was a French Supreme Commander, Marshal Foch, who presided over the Allied forces on the Western Front in the final phases of the war. In its last weeks, French power flooded into eastern Europe whilst the British Army of Salonica under General Milne diverted to Constantinople and remote parts of what was now increasingly termed 'the Middle East'. This is what best suited British capacities and instincts. Suggestively, the biggest British legend of the 1914–18 war was the distantly exotic one of Lawrence of Arabia – there was nothing comparable on the Western Front.

1939–45 simply reconfirmed the same underlying lesson. From the start there was little possibility of the British making the same attempt to 'continentalise' themselves as they had unavailingly tried after 1915–16. The British expeditionary force in 1939/40 was ramshackle, and its swift eviction from Dunkirk was decisive and lasting in its effects. Yet the image of all those little ships and the national camaraderie involved made it feel curiously familiar, indeed *right*, something that the Blitz over London and other British cities only accentuated. Prime Minister Churchill might assure the French leadership at the height of the crisis in May–June 1940 that Britain, after withdrawing behind the Channel draw-bridge, would one day return and 'win it all back' for them – that is, restore a truly free France – but few really believed that at the time (Ismay, 1960: 139–40).[2]

Churchill's war strategy after 1940 hinged on winning successes at the margins, above all in the Mediterranean. This provided the *sort* of war that the British people might be prepared to sustain for some time, one without the sacrifices of the previous great conflict. From such a vantage-point maintaining a British stake in Greece took on a special significance for Churchill (Holland, 2013: 172–3, 248–50, 269–70, 272–5). Although this commitment went wrong quite quickly in 1941 with the British army's evacuation from the mainland Peloponnese, and then from Crete, in 1943–44 a re-entry into Greece was one of the British leader's key priorities; his visit with Anthony Eden to Athens at the outset of the civil war in that country during December 1944 was one of the great episodes of his life. To Churchill's far more powerful American ally, this seemed just a canny way to avoid what was really needed to end the war that really mattered, the re-invasion of continental Europe. In June 1944 President Roosevelt and Supreme Allied Commander Eisenhower eventually dragged a still reluctant Churchill into the D-Day landings (Colville, 2004: 462; Holland, 1991: 87–8). This reluctance nonetheless sprang from an authentic belief that whoever might prove the beneficiary of a definitive outcome at the heart of Europe, it could not any longer be Britain. In this Churchill was surely right, and from this stems a great deal of the complexity and dissimulation that was afterwards to surround British policy towards recovery and consolidation on the Continent.

It is in such repeated recoils from a failure to be a successful protagonist on the continent of Europe that we can detect a persisting obliqueness in British geopolitics. Critics of latter-day Brexit have lambasted it as a retreat into isolationism. There are of course elements of that. But it would be truer to say that it represents something subtly different: a reversion to a long-standing oblique or *peripheral* tendency that comes naturally to British psychology and that is rooted in a good deal of hard experience in war and diplomacy, and which earlier lay at the heart of Churchillian war strategy.

A peripheral bias in British thinking has not only been a product of two great modern conflicts. It had previously been reinforced by imperial expansion going back to the eighteenth century. Yet the importance of this aspect can be overdone. Empire was always a subsidiary element in the British make-up. The old Victorian joke was that the quickest way to empty the House of Commons was to inaugurate a debate on the Colonies. During the Second World War data collected by the Ministry of Information indicated that most Britons at home had very little interest in anything that happened outside Europe (McLaine, 1979: 274), which was why the British army that fought in Burma gained the tag 'Forgotten'. When the British Raj ceased to exist in August 1947, the British public did not register any strong interest. This was hardly surprising, given that their aspirations for the future hinged on a 'New Jerusalem' at home, not one abroad. Britain had undoubtedly possessed a great empire, but it was an 'imperial nation' only in limited and sporadic ways, and which under stress evaporated altogether. An indigenous nativism always went much deeper.

Legacies of empire have nonetheless featured significantly in Brexit. Leaving the EU has been occasionally scoffed at as 'Empire 2.0' precisely because its advocates sought to press a powerful button in drumming up a renewed vision of a globalist, all-conquering Britain back on the ocean waves at last. But as the commentator Janan Ganesh pointed out, this was to get the contemporary, post-post-imperial mood of British people very wrong (Ganesh, 2017). 'The terminal point of empire is introspection', he remarks 'not a restless desire to do it all again'. Strikingly, Professor Philip Murphy, the Director of the Institute of Commonwealth Studies in London University, and as such somebody with the credentials to make a judgement on the matter, published a book in April 2018 entitled *The Empire's New Clothes: The Myth of the Commonwealth* (Murphy, 2018), exploring in detail just how far from reality were those elements in the Brexit rationale exploiting the United Kingdom's old transoceanic links as a template for future strategy. The modern Commonwealth was in truth an immensely more concocted, diffuse association with few purposes that had much to do with any constructive action. But such attempts at informed correctives – like many 'expert' blasts at the constitutive elements of Brexit – had little effect. Before long the defence secretary in Theresa May's government, Gavin Williamson, was still robustly asserting that the abandonment of 'east of Suez' introduced in the 1960s was to be reversed, and new military bases set up in as yet unspecified places in the Far East and the Caribbean, all buttressed by allegedly still operative links from an imperial past. Where the money was to come from was a moot point.

The obliqueness most relevant in the Brexit context, however, had a more specifically geographical, rather than imperial, relationship to the old continental heartland. This has been the tendency for British influence to drape itself around Europe's outer rims. In the south such a habit was defined by the Mediterranean as a default-zone for British overseas power (Rachman, 2016). The successive acquisitions of vantage-points in that region – Gibraltar (1704), Malta (1815), Cyprus (1878), Alexandria (1882) – had been central to the operation of British power in the world, and not only, or even principally, because they lay on the route to India. This distinctively European variant of British peripheralism also had a northern-cum-Scandinavian expression, and tokens of this in modern history include Admiral Nelson's naval triumph at Copenhagen (1801), and the fact that a disastrous military intervention in Norway provided the backdrop to Churchill's elevation to war leadership in May 1940. During the later 1950s, Britain was driven to establish the Anglo-Scandinavian European Free Trade Association (EFTA). No surprise then that a 'Norway model' eventually became one of the competing scenarios at the climax of the road to Brexit. So it is that the United Kingdom's relations with Europe have habitually been defined by liminal prepositions – 'by', or 'around', but crucially not 'of', except in very qualified ways.

The problem was that the effectiveness of such a strategy towards Europe – essentially tangential, indirect, sideways – hinged on weakness and division at the heart of Europe, so that bringing power to bear from the margins might be sufficient for Britain's needs. This was often in essence a matter of playing off one continental power-centre against another, a tactic that went back to at least the fifteenth century. Never entirely successful, once Europe tentatively began to integrate after circa 1950, the scope for such an approach got progressively eliminated. The Suez crisis of 1956 had effects that went far beyond merely colonial policy (Egypt, after all, was not a colony in the first place). French anger at the botched expedition along the Nile led their Fourth Republic to abandon a policy of co-operating with Britain in diplomatic and extra-European matters, and teamed up instead with the West Germans in a goal of continental unification.

One underestimated factor here was the strong dislike of the then chancellor of the Bundesrepublik, Konrad Adenauer, for the innate tendencies perceived in British policymaking; according to one British 'insider' of that period, Adenauer regarded the British as 'some kind of maritime pirates, jolly good at swiping chunks of Africa and looking after their own interests, but not very reliable in a European context' (Charlton, 1983: 2017).[3] With these sentiments gaining ground in some continental quarters as the 1950s proceeded, a 'Paris-Bonn motor' came tentatively into being, and there was no easy way for the British to push it aside. The long-run outcome, as the historian Harold James has expressed it in one of the most insightful *resumés* after June 2016, was that the British had become 'bewildered and alienated by the Franco-German psychodrama that is at the real heart of modern Europe' (James, 2016). Rooted to the margins as this bewilderment took shape at the end of the 1950s, the fear now arose of Britain being *marginalised*, which was not at all what was meant to happen.

The suspicion crystallising on the Continent as to British good faith on pan-European issues requires more explanation, because, on both sides, it goes to the heart of why the United Kingdom's original entry to the European Community was so long delayed. This has to be seen in proportion. One reason why rationing continued in Britain through the later 1940s was to divert supplies to ensure that the British-occupied sector in defeated Germany did not actually starve. It was always a vital British interest that Europe should be *stable*. But over and above having sufficient basic food, the real issue concerning Europe after the Second World War was: should it be rebuilt and, if so, how quickly? The Americans had no hesitation on this. They needed to guarantee a market for their huge export capacity that had expanded during the war. The British were very differently placed. Their economy, so disproportionately geared to war after 1940, needed time to convert back to peacetime conditions. Putting mainland European industries back on their feet was anything but a priority; even perhaps the reverse. 'It is not pleasant', the Federation of British Industries, the predecessor of today's Confederation of British Industry, summed up the feeling in 1946 at a time of a darkening outlook, 'for us [in Britain] to face the need to encourage the revival of past competitors' (German Reparations Committee, 1946).[4]

Against that background, the British subsequently had to be encouraged by the Americans into the operations of the Marshall Plan to reconstruct Europe after 1947, just as Roosevelt had earlier dragged Churchill into the full liberation of Europe from Hitler. This was a passing phase, and there could be little doubt that ultimately a prosperous Europe was a British as well as a continental interest. Nevertheless, a degree of British reserve about the reconstruction of Europe was something that other Europeans could not help noticing, and suspicions on both sides came to the surface once the issues passed beyond merely consolidating recovery and after circa 1953–54 crystallised around longer-term issues of integration and development. Those issues were the crux of the Treaty of Rome signed by the six continental signatories during January 1957 and which established a Common Market.

The narrative of how the Treaty of Rome proceeded to operate on a Brexit basis – that is, with the United Kingdom standing rigidly but nervously aloof – is well known. It was inherent in the dilemmas of successive British governments that they should seek to limit, and even stymie, any integrationist process from which they had excluded themselves. From a European perspective this could seem wantonly destructive, a self-serving attempt to sabotage a process of pacification critical for a better future for a whole continent. Not only was the formation of EFTA interpreted as a gambit to shatter the nascent experiment, but the unavailing attempts at the end of the 1950s led by Reginald Maudling, Chancellor of the Exchequer in Harold Macmillan's post-Suez Conservative government, to negotiate a place for Britain in relation to the new organism with all sorts of privileges – a case of 'have your cake and eat it' – were viewed in the same light.[5] George Ball, a highly experienced and Anglophile American official closely involved in tracking these efforts, looked back from the vantage-point of 1983 and noted that the EFTA move in particular had been a major tactical error by the British precisely because it played into ambivalent feelings in leading European countries about the real character of British aims (Charlton, 1983: 215).

Frustrated at the attempt to secure a deal in which the United Kingdom might be half-in and half-out of the new European grouping, the government of Harold Macmillan in 1961 *did* first lodge an application to become a full signatory of the Treaty of Rome, and in 1973 the British finally succeeded in joining (taking the Irish Republic and Denmark with them). One of the striking aspects of the 2016 referendum is how little recall or discussion there was as to the reasons, right or wrong, which led Britain so reluctantly to go down that route. After all, if you are later thinking of leaving a club or organisation, it might be thought sensible to factor into the calculations what had led you to join in the first place.

Harold Macmillan had won the general election in 1959 on the slogan of 'You've never had it so good'. But this failed to conceal that many continental Europeans were starting to have it better. 1960 was the year that West German living-standards overtook the average in the United Kingdom. This was remarkable coming when memories of devastated, war-wracked German towns were still so fresh. But even more important was the dead-end that the Macmillan government felt the country was entering as an independent power. For the prime minister himself, the crucial moment of insight had come when at an international summit in Paris during May 1960 he failed to play the role of indispensable broker between the two superpowers; their leaders had simply flicked his presumptuous efforts aside. Macmillan's official biographer, Alistair Horne, has written that 'this was the moment that he [Macmillan] suddenly realized that Britain counted for nothing … [it] represented a real watershed in his life' (Horne, 1989: 224). 'Nothing', of course, should hardly be taken literally. The United Kingdom was still immensely more influential in the world at large in 1960–61 than it was to be, say, in 2016. But what Macmillan had begun to recognise was that it could not now be truly 'global' in its reach, and had to situate its interests and leverage in the appropriate regional setting.

The first British attempt to join the Common Market, however, crashed to earth on 14 January 1963 when President Charles de Gaulle called an impromptu televised press conference at the Elysée Palace in which he categorically rebuffed any such possibility. 'England is insular' de Gaulle stated and referred to Macmillan with what Horne describes as 'insulting condescension'. The prime minister complained to President Kennedy that the French president, who in 1960 had been invited to London in what was the most fêted state visit to the United Kingdom during the century, was 'simply inventing any means whatever to knock us out', and he privately admitted that 'all our policies are in ruins at home and abroad' (Horne, 1989: 447). For British public opinion, the nature of the United Kingdom's snubbing at French hands was a painful intimation of national decline. In the following years that *reduction* was most potently expressed through downward pressures on sterling. It was no accident that within days during November 1967 a renewed British application to join the Common Market was halted by de Gaulle in another publicly orchestrated veto whilst the pound was finally devalued after a long and humiliating struggle.

These sequences were to enter deeply into British consciousness, though it is arguably only in the light of latter-day Brexit that they can be fully appreciated. It was *because* the British 'turn to Europe' crystallising in the 1960s was rooted in a sense of weakness and vulnerability, both financial and political, that the very notion of 'belonging' to Europe became suffused with ineradicable negative feelings. This was a uniquely British phenomenon compared to other member states, all of which had entered

into this new association with a positive as opposed to grimly defensive
agenda. It brought about in British circumstances a psychological resentment of 'Europe' that came naturally to a certain sort of Tory mind in
particular.

The impulsion behind Britain's erratic European course at that earlier
phase needs closer inspection. As de Gaulle's patronising declarations of
'non' in 1963 and 1967 did not fail to emphasise, the difficulties besetting
the United Kingdom – and which in his view made it incompatible with a
fully European identity – included both an internal economic dimension
as well as an Anglo-Saxon, pro-American imperative in its foreign policy.
The American George Ball again reflected retrospectively: 'I had a very
strong belief during the whole of this period that Britain was going to
have a very bad time resolving the problem of [internal] industrialization
if they were left within a strictly national context, but that in a broader
context many things would have been possible' (Charlton, 1983: 273).
This logic was vital to what happened. The British – once de Gaulle had
been replaced in the French presidency by the more sympathetic Georges
Pompidou – successfully 'joined Europe' not because it held out specific
solutions to contemporary problems, and even less because it offered cash
benefits (quite the opposite). It did so because membership of a Common
Market provided a screen, a framework, some safety-valve when at last
confronting obstacles to social and economic reform at home. This certainly did not mean that the latter transformations passed off quietly.
Tensions rooted in labour unions, the 'three-day week' and the 'winter of
discontent' in the 1970s as well as the bitter miners' strike in the mid-1980s,
offered proof of that. But the United Kingdom did recast its economy and
society – as it happened, according to the radical Tory vision of Margaret
Thatcher – in a way that would almost certainly not have been possible if
the country had not been a member of the European Union. The reason
is that in a purely insular Britain – the one de Gaulle had scorned – these
pressures would have been bottled up even more within the constraints of
an exclusively national setting. Classes and groups would have been pitted
even more directly against each other, and potentially set up serious civil
conflict. Such an impasse was avoided, however narrowly, just as, indeed,
EU grants were to play a vital part in regenerating those British regions
hit hardest by a de-industrialisation part and parcel of the Thatcherite
doctrine. The paradoxes of this in the later emergence of Brexit were to be
exquisitely ironical.

There were two concrete topics in 1960s debates about Britain's puta-
tive adhesion to the Common Market that echo loudly in Brexit. The first
is agriculture. In the 1950s British farmers did not see the European idea
as having any attraction for themselves. The British countryside had long

been consolidated ('modernised') into large private holdings. Rural producers enjoyed their own system of purely national subsidies introduced in the 1930s, and which had been further developed under war conditions after 1939. British farmers looked down on continental smallholders as 'peasants'. The stereotype that got carried over into British mass culture was the French onion-grower, beret-hatted and with an extremely wobbly bicycle.

Such imagery became so embedded that it has never been entirely displaced, but in strictly practical terms views in the British countryside as to what Europe might have to offer started gradually to shift in 1960–61. Lord Soames, Macmillan's minister of agriculture (and Churchill's son-in-law) explained later that this key Conservative interest group started to grasp that there was no more cash for subsidies to be squeezed from the hard-pressed Exchequer in Whitehall; as the situation was summarised, 'the agricultural policy would have to be changed anyway because the level of support ... necessary [for farmers] was beyond the ability of the country to carry' (Charlton, 1983: 242). As events evolved, British farmers, in their conversion to the merits of Europe's Common Agricultural Policy (CAP), showed little sentimentality in casting loose their New Zealand and Australian counterparts long dependent on preferential access to the British market. The latter were amongst the most visible sacrificial lambs of Britain's signature of the Treaty of Rome by Edward Heath as Conservative Prime Minister on 22 January 1972. Even then, however, in the light of later events it is highly important that Heath had relied on the support of several dozen Labour MPs to get the necessary legislation through Parliament.

Afterwards British farmers did very well out of EU membership. They did not even have to mobilise to get much of what they wanted. French rural producers, anyway so used to being 'bolshy', did the grunt work by blocking their own auto-routes and hectoring French deputies in remote provinces. Similar tactics never worked in Britain because in the more urbanised political culture of the United Kingdom they were not effective. But through the roundabout mechanisms of Brussels what worked in France in terms of gaining enhanced support for farms got recycled into Britain, and rural interests entered a golden age of prosperity. Yet any memory of how this came about grew dim with time. By 2016 British farmers associated the EU with 'red tape'. Not having to have done much to secure the benefits of the current support system, many supposed they could easily replace what they had through purely national means and so obtain a system of subsidy shaped *entirely* by their own concerns, and not any longer have to bother with taking into account the needs of French, Spanish or Italian farmers.

It was only slowly after the referendum that British farming interests saw possible pitfalls ahead. The government of Theresa May was quick to guarantee equivalent support to that of the EU during any transitional period for Brexit, but there was an ominous silence about what might come after that. The Agriculture and Horticulture Development Board eventually published research showing that British rural incomes could be halved without an immediate free trade agreement with the EU on exit.[6] But of course there was no possibility of such an immediate settlement on the intractable matters involved. Even worse, in a 'no deal' scenario, which May and her ministers touted as a genuine prospect if only to gain leverage in negotiations with the European Commission, whole sectors of the British countryside, such as hill-farmers in Wales, might be commercially wiped out because so much of their product depended on European markets and associated income-supplements. By late 2018 the National Farmers Union, up until now studiously coy on the issues, started to utter anguished warnings. All this was just one aspect of acute contradictions in British political economy as the implications of Brexit clarified. Fishing provided another glaring example. It dawned on certain producer groups that who got what post-Brexit would depend on trade-offs, and in urban and consumer-dominated Britain farmers and fishermen usually came low in the pecking order. Again, quite paradoxically, the UK's membership in the EU had provided a foil to that long-standing tendency. Slowly but surely the possibility dawned that doing without the foil might prove dangerous.

The second aspect of British debates about Europe in the 1960s requiring more attention here is the Commonwealth in its specifically economic dimension. The vision of more integrated economic ties between Britain and an empire of overseas settlement had resonated over decades. They usually came to the fore during times of difficulty. The Conservative Unionist politician in the early 1900s, Joseph Chamberlain – a politician whose essentially provincial ideas were said to have a strong influence on Theresa May on becoming prime minister herself[7] – had been a champion of this idea under the banner headline of 'Tariff Reform'. The theme had resurfaced in the Great Depression. In 1932 a great Imperial Economic Conference was convened in Ottawa to thrash out a new system of mutual trading. Yet such ideas never got anywhere because the imperial interests were so divergent. They all hinged on raising prices to satisfy empire-wide producer groups, and the fall-guy expected to pay for this was the long-suffering British metropolitan consumer – above all, the working class, since the extra taxes mostly fell on basic foodstuffs – at the heart of the system. In the end no government in London was prepared to present its own electorate with the bill. At Ottawa in 1932 certain agreements were made to great fanfare, but when a Canadian economic historian in the 1970s crunched the numbers he found that the economic effects had been vestigial (Drummond, 1974). Still, quoting Australia and New Zealand as key examples of countries outside Europe eager to enter into a more intensive commercial exchange with the UK remained central to Brexit rhetoric on trade; though strikingly little such use could be made in regard to the old dependency of India because for historical reasons that country – so much larger than Britain's Antipodean connections – had never shown any strong desire to revivify their connection with the ex-imperial ruler. Indeed, it is notable here that even the pre-1947 British-run 'Government of India', fearing to be at odds with local opinion, had held itself severely aloof from schemes to boost empire trade with the distant United Kingdom.

What then, against all this background, were the fundamental drivers of Brexit? It is probably true that the most powerful levers of the Leave campaign in the referendum related to immigration; and though some may regard this as having been xenophobic in character, even many Remainers would concede that it gelled with genuine concerns in many communities that had seen their identity altered in recent times. Arguably, however, even the immigration factor was only a sub-set of something that went deeper in British mentalities. 'I won't have Britain barged about', Ernest Bevin, Foreign Secretary in the Labour government had declared when arriving in Berlin immediately after the general election in 1945 to attend the Potsdam Conference (Holland, 1991: 201). One consistent thread thereafter has been an instant reaction in British opinion at any hint of the country being barged about by 'Johnny Foreigner', and as usual the most sensitive barging is perceived to come from those living just over the hill, or in the case of an island just across the sea. Continental nations were hardly immune to the same sort of sensations but they had been so exposed to war, mass destruction and starvation in the first half of the twentieth century that the sort of 'barging', or mutual haggling, that went on within the institutions of an integrating Europe during the century's second half was a small price to pay for the benefits secured.

British experience had been different, and, as the Cambridge historian David Reynolds has argued, a 'purist' form of sovereignty remained lodged in most British minds (Reynolds, 2017). The full measure of the extent of this phenomenon was summed up in the core Brexit belief – one very widely held in the general public – that through membership of the EU the country's true independence had been forfeited and now needed to be regained. The contrast with the cast of mind in other EU states was often glaring. 'Words like "patriotism", "control" and "sovereignty" mean very different things in a country less than two hundred years old, which was created as a post-national state', as a Belgian contributor to a selection of continental appreciations on the issue commented: 'Those words, which are battered about *ad nauseam* in Brexit debates, come pre-packed inside inverted commas in Belgium' (McGuinness, 2019: 5). In Britain any use at all of inverted commas in these contexts would simply be confusing and even suspect. There was in this a very basic intellectual, even moral, difference.

The result in British political culture is that any challenge to sovereignty as a fundamental, undifferentiated entity is liable to trigger visceral reactions, usually validated by being mixed up with memories of an island kingdom's survival in existential struggles. At different times key foreign leaders had long provided touchstones, Napoleon and Hitler being key examples. What made the fate of Suez so emotive was that Gamal Abdel Nasser – so often compared in British media to Hitler after coming to power in Cairo during 1952 – was elevated briefly into this category. Subsequently there was something in the very status of the presidency of the European Commission that conjured up not dissimilar effects, at least in the surreal world of British tabloid newspapers. The most famous header in the latter genre is surely that of 1 November 1990 in the *Sun*, following a stirring call by the then president, Jacques Delors, for an acceleration in the integration process, especially in the monetary sphere. 'UP YOURS DELORS' ran the thick print, and underneath the additional advice: 'At midday tomorrow *Sun* readers are urged to tell the French fool where to stuff the ECU.'[8] Half the page was taken up by the pictorial rendition of a fingered V-sign. As Reynolds argues, a British failure to engage in realistic terms with what sovereignty consists of under contemporary circumstances was part of a wider problem: the absence of a convincing meta-narrative to understand how the United Kingdom might best conduct itself. In the resulting vacuum a crude tabloid culture took hold in a swathe of British political discourse.

In the Brexit era Jean-Claude Juncker has had a very similar effect in Britain to that of the unfortunate Delors before him. Behind all this was something fundamental: the 'trade-offs' that were part and parcel of the institutional and regulatory nature of EU mechanisms could not be accommodated into British political culture quite as they were into that of other EU members (Giles, 2018). Preconceptions of 'Victory' and 'Defeat' remained too primordial in Britain, and above all in England, to fit into messy sequences of give here and take there on a pan-continental basis. Yet – and here the ironies start to kick in most awkwardly – if an innate instinct to reject bargaining involving any infringements of national sovereignty as innately illegitimate underlay the final emergence of Brexit, the self-same phenomenon made Brexit itself potentially even worse than 'remaining'. Trade-offs were necessarily the essence of how an exit from the EU could be managed without exposing the British economy to a heart-attack. Theresa May's 'deal' at the end of 2018 sought to min-imise this by casting a decent veil over the bargaining, with the inescap-able losers and scapegoats, that would have to follow any passage through the British Parliament in terms of a future UK–EU trade treaty – 'kicking the can down the road'. But it was clear that in the sphere of trade-offs this would soon be a case of 'you ain't seen nothing yet'.

Nevertheless, though an idealised notion of sovereign nationality, frozen in aspic, marked Britain out in European context, it did not make Brexit itself inevitable. That phenomenon could still continue to have been finessed within existing EU membership. Rather it was the internal warfare over Europe inside British Toryism that tipped the balance. There was something curiously appropriate that the very day of the appearance of the *Sun* tabloid master-quote, 'Up Yours Delors', in November 1990 was also the day that Geoffrey Howe, having resigned as Chancellor of the Exchequer in Margaret Thatcher's government, delivered a speech in the House of Commons triggering the dramatic crisis that brought her down. 'Here', the journalist Andrew Marr commented as 2018 ended with the road to Brexit careering towards a series of forbidding cliff-edges, 'is where the real lessons and parallels for today begin' (Marr, 2018).

Geoffrey Howe – above all in his radical budget of 1981 – had been the architect of the Thatcherite revolution of slashed government expenditure and deregulation. In the early and mid-1980s, in intra-Tory terms, the battle over that formula had been fought out between a moderate, 'one nation', often rather patrician Conservative faction originally labelled by their enemies 'the wets', and a far more ideological, draconian and sub-aristocratic group known as 'the dries'. Thatcher manoeuvred between them, but victory in the war with Argentina over the Falklands in 1982, and a big majority gained in the 1983 general election, allowed her to move her revolution forward in a very dry direction. Tokens of this were the ending of subsidies that led to the great strike in the coalmines, the 'big bang' of deregulation in the finance sector and, also deeply ironic given later events, her championship of the Single European Market seeking to eliminate all those national imperfections that had continued to mark the reality of the existing format of the Common Market.

By the late 1980s, however, it was Europe itself that, in Marr's words, 'represented a fundamental and widening division in the Tory family'. The gut issue was whether the new equilibrium created by successive Thatcher governments should continue within the existing milieu of the EU – one defined by continental social democracy – or seek a head-on confron-tation with the values for which Jacques Delors had made himself the personification. On this matter Howe and Thatcher were now on opposite sides. Once the latter had been deposed in effectively a palace coup within her party, her successor, John Major, sought to smooth a path towards a different stance on Europe, speaking on entering office of a country now 'at ease with itself' and of a need, as we remarked earlier, for Britain to assume a leadership role at the heart of the EU, not merely throwing brickbats from the sidelines. This was anathema to a new Tory cohort who deeply resented the defenestration of a leader identified with so many of their deepest feelings, who had become opposed to the basic principles of the EU and for whom being 'at ease' therefore was anything but desirable. At the time these people seemed maverick and marginal, even distinctly odd-ball, but in fact they were the first wave, directed with fierce if unavailing antagonism against the UK's ratification of the Maastricht Treaty, of a fresh Tory *ultra* activism.

The vision of a Britain in the image of Tony Blair's successive governments after 1997 – multicultural, big city-oriented, social-leftish, a bit hip, essentially Europhile barring the critical exception of the single currency – only further stirred up antagonistic drives amongst Tories for whom the new dispensation was at odds with almost all their beliefs. In these circles the memory of Thatcher took on a folk dimension, cut loose from any connection with her erstwhile push for the European Single Market. What was remembered was her 'handbagging' of the EU during her successful campaign to secure a British rebate on its fiscal contributions. None of her successors in the party leadership seemed able to contain these forces. It was a characteristic attempt to 'solve' this problem with a brave – some thought foolhardy – throw of the dice that David Cameron, having gambled and won on a referendum on Scottish independence, finally sought to do the same on the matter of British membership of the EU in June 2016. You might say the rest is history.

Yet it is no such thing. The issues involved are so structural that all the majority vote to leave the EU did was to reframe long-standing questions in more intense and insoluble ways. This went beyond the mere imponderable of *how* to leave the EU, since within that 'how' was secreted immensely complicated matters of what sort of principles should govern post-Brexit Britain in relation to the outside world. Theresa May's strategy after becoming prime minister following Cameron's swift resignation was to anaesthetise such matters under the nebulous mantra of 'Brexit means Brexit'. This worked so long as vagueness could prevail, though even then it did not prevent her losing a clear parliamentary majority at the ill-advised election of June 2017.

The dangerous moment was bound to come when May had to put on the table a 'deal' negotiated with the EU since, however vague this might be in the longer term, it could hardly avoid giving some basic sense of the direction of travel. When that moment came in December 2018, civil war among the different wings of her own party swiftly broke surface. For the authentic Brexiteer, the prime minister's awkward construct of opposing elements was even worse than remaining in the EU itself. 'They have invested too much in the struggle' a political scientist remarked 'to be content with an outcome that gives them a half-baked version of their own heart's desire. A compromised Brexit ... does more to devalue the price they have paid to get here than an outright rebuff' (Runciman, 2019).

'If you think Britain needs a further bout of Thatcherite radicalism', Andrew Marr's astute summary of the underlying impasse traces this dynamic a stage further, 'then Brexit is the necessary – but, of course, not sufficient – first step. People [in the party] don't talk much about this in case it frightens the horses. But their real aim is a different kind of Britain' (Marr, 2018). The same old Britain, including one tied into the EU's regulatory universe, and only nominally outside the EU proper, was to true Brexiteers absolutely at odds with their real goals not only in regard to the EU but the governance and social balance of the country.

By this route we arrive at what are the most critical stress-fractures at the heart of Brexit. After the 2016 referendum there was a great deal of discussion about the sociological implications of the vote. Amidst the many competing explanations, the basic consensus was that those who wanted to leave the EU were for the most part people who felt left behind in the Britain that had come into being during the early twenty-first century. They had nostalgia for what had been lost, and wanted to regain wherever possible what had been, as they saw it, thoughtlessly discarded. This often took the form of a wave of aspirational 'bring-backery', of restoring lost certainties, so that in one analysis the really telling question distinguishing Brexit fundamentalism was said to be whether a death penalty should be reinstituted in the judicial system (Burton, 2016). Certainly, reduced immigration was a basic prerequisite in this worldview, and one Theresa May recognised as the principal base-line in post-Brexit Britain, embodied in her fierce commitment to its limitation to 'tens of thousands' rather than 'hundreds of thousands', regardless of the fact that the effects could only be very damaging to a range of industries – not least in the health and care sector – and weigh down the UK's already very poor productivity on which its long-term prosperity hinged. This was something that Carolyn Fairbairn, the director-general of the Confederation of British Industries, pointed out on numerous occasions, though without getting any answer on the substance of the issues (Hilton, 2019).

Yet in truth nostalgia and the restoration of a now old-fashioned, really irrecoverable world, was not what true Brexit *ultras* – as opposed to the simplified provincialism of Theresa May – were really after. They suspected, surely rightly, that such an attempt could never last for long. A new millennial generation was in the making, and there had to be a fast-growing, globalist, pulsating, re-Thatcherised form of Brexit if it were to stand any chance of taking root by holding out some prospect of material betterment. Faster economic growth was essential, and that growth could only be fed by *continuing* inward migration at a high level. Indeed, one way that the Leave campaign attracted votes in June 2016 from ethnic minorities – so that Remain did not win substantially in Birmingham as it did in London – had been to promise South Asian voters that after Brexit there would be *more* scope for entry into Britain from Pakistan and India. This had been in referendum parlance the 'curry house factor', referring specifically to the shortage of immigrant (and low-paid) cooks in Britain's restaurants when *chicken tikka masala*, not cod and chips, had long since emerged as the UK's most popular national dish.

The imponderable here, however, was that mostly unskilled, working-class, often northern *white* leavers were widely considered to have voted to keep migrants out pure and simple, and they had no desire simply for Poles, Hungarians and Bulgarians to be replaced by yet more people from Karachi, Bangalore and Afghanistan. Behind this was an even more delicate matter – one that could not easily be expressed in public – of how many white Brexit voters might feel once it became clear that a non-EU Britain, far from becoming more like them, would inevitably end up more culturally and racially diverse as European migrants stopped coming and were replaced by others from much further afield. But as the writer John Lanchester predicted in the immediate wake of the referendum, the most likely outcome of Brexit was always the betrayal of the white working class by those who had hijacked its grievances for their own purposes, though he had searingly added 'They should be used to that by now' (Lanchester, 2016).

One other sting in the tail of Brexit provides an unerring indication of how deeply the issues resonate in the history of our society. This is the matter of Ireland. At all the great moments of British history – 1640, 1688, 1798, 1846–48, 1914–16, 1967–68 – tensions surrounding Anglo-Irish relations have complicated events on the larger mainland. Brexit is no different. This time it has taken the form of the controversy surrounding the 'backstop' during a transitional period (it is precisely because everybody knows that any such transition will last for many years that the stakes are so high). The fact that the parliamentary votes of the Democratic Unionist Party (DUP) in Ulster were indispensable to May's government after June 2017 made this dimension even more volatile. Still, even those who find the DUP's politics hard to stomach on many grounds, including social libertarianism, might admit that on the Brexit 'backstop', Arlene Foster and her colleagues are from their own point of view entirely right and consistent. Any checks on goods and transit that take place anywhere other than along the existing lines of the border will sooner or later mean that the latter demarcations cease to have any meaning at all, and will herald the unification of Ireland, mediated through a border poll already allowed for in the Good Friday Agreement.

For our purposes most immediately relevant here are the psychological currents consequently flowing into British politics. A BBC *Newsnight* journalist reported on 11 December 2018 that a leading Tory had sidled up to him to say 'We simply cannot allow the Irish to treat us like this' (Watt, 2018). In fact, if there was one country that British negotiators had expected to be able to chip apart from an opposing EU front in talks on Brexit – by sheer dint of economic necessity – it was the Irish Republic. This was just part of the inbred belief, one articulated quite openly, amongst Brexit supporters that the EU was a decrepit body that only needed a few nudges to fall apart completely.[9] Not only did this not happen, but the EU27 had proved absolutely resolute in sticking to the 'red lines' established by the Fine Gael government in Dublin. The British misreading of this situation had partly come about because it had never digested the extent to which the EU was committed to smoothing out disparities between large and small nations within the EU itself (that France had been able, mentally, to do this, despite the Gaullist legacy, in a way that the United Kingdom had not, was itself remarkable).

Perhaps even more important, however, was that the Irish Republic's red lines were bound up with the integrity of the regulated Single Market that was the ultimate modus operandi of the European Union itself. The practical meaning in the realm of Anglo-Irish relations was that in the long list of earlier crises, for the first time it was now Dublin that held the whip hand over London. The resentment this created was acute. Not even hints of blackmail by some leading Tories that they might be prepared to see a hard border in Ireland even if it meant a recrudescence of the violence that the Good Friday Agreement had ended seemed able to grab back the initiative. On the eve of the 'meaningful vote' on Theresa May's much-bedraggled deal on 15 January 2019, one of her loyal supporters in Cabinet, the prisons minister Rory Stewart, even sought to load the whole blame for any defeat on the Irish Republic by saying it was up to Dublin to save the day and avert the 'no-deal' threat by nodding through critical concession to the Tory right-wing on the 'back-stop'.[10] Just how far such tactics might eventually go when push came to shove remained unresolved, but the Irish poison running in the Tory bloodstream was palpable.[11] Yet, perhaps most crucially of all, by this stage in the process, the generality of Ulster opinion now veered to the view that, if there had to be frictions at a customs frontier, that frontier should be set in the Irish Sea, not on the island of Ireland itself (Carroll, 2019). One of the most acute ironies of Brexit is that what in the end seemed likely to foreshadow the final disintegration of Protestant Ulster as a political force DUP-style was the unintended effects of its alter ego, an unbridled English nationalism. Boris Johnson's abrupt betrayal of the DUP when he came as May's successor in Downing Street to negotiate his own 'deal' with the EU, effectively tracing a distinct demarcation between Ulster and the British mainland, was in line with this.

'We're heading for the greatest humiliation since Suez' wrote the independently inclined Conservative commentator, Matthew Parris, in the *Times* on 15 October 2016, and certainly as the climax of departure from the EU under the Article 50 process unfolded the word 'humiliation' multiplied. But it is doubtful if this really resonated with the UK's Brexit generation. For the great majority Suez was ancient history, assuming that people had any cognisance of it at all. The effects of that experience had at the time anyway been relatively contained. The distinguished US foreign policy maker, Dean Acheson, famously remarked in 1962 that the British had 'lost an empire but not yet found a role'. Although American sympathy with this predicament was limited, not least when the British failed to commit troops to the war in Vietnam, they had afterwards assisted a soft landing in such ways as allowing the gentle myth of a 'special relationship' to continue, and by co-operating in the sleight of hand of the UK's so-called 'national' nuclear deterrent (it was nothing of the kind, since the indispensable Polaris launch technology was American).[12] This did not solve the real underlying problem of Britain's future orientation and status, one, we have seen, which was central to ensuing debates over Europe during the 1960s. The essential dilemma was embedded in a remark by Richard Mayne, once a personal assistant of Jean Monnet, the symbolic architect of European unity, during a debate on BBC television during 1967: 'I think that whatever we do', he stated, 'we're going to go closer to somebody – we are going to be sucked towards a power centre … this is the drama of the thing' (Moncrieff, 1967: 121).[13]

This remains the drama of the thing. But in the event after 1973 membership of the European Union provided just such a power centre for the UK, a framework within which its voice was clearly heard through a raft of institutions, and whereby the UK has conserved its essentially national identity anchored in a larger setting. As a result, for the ensuing decades from the mid-1970s the British have been broadly comfortable with their place in the world. That sense of being *adrift*, of vulnerability in a world full of hostilities and challenges, so palpable as the 1960s wore on and which during the tense days of May 1968 even led to rumours that a *coup* might take place against the Labour government in London,[14] disappeared and indeed has been wholly forgotten. Crudely inflated expectations of a reinvigorated Anglo-American special relationship on the part of leading Brexiteers have nonetheless been a tacit admission that after withdrawal from the EU the UK would in the twenty-first century have to attach itself to some larger entity, though what form 'special' might take in relation to President Donald Trump worried many people. As yet attention had not turned to a rather different scenario posed by the looming 2020 presidential election in the United States: the possibility of a new Democratic administration reverting to a previous assumption in US foreign policy that the utility of any special connection with the UK hinged on the latter's full participation in European affairs, since beyond that the British had in reality very little to offer contemporary American necessities.

It has been the recrystallisation of old uncertainties, as well as the appearance of new ones, that have been the most ominous aspect as British departure from the EU loomed as a real-time event, embodied in a deadlocked, irretrievably divided and paralysed polity, a once-great but now creaking Union whose component elements – perhaps between regions as well as nations – were in danger of shearing apart from each other (Stevens, 2019). The degree to which discussion about successive Brexit withdrawal deals with the EU hinged on the matter of an Irish 'backstop' obscured the reality that the crucial battle for the Union was being fought out in Scotland. Whilst almost all other leading British politicians seemed to fumble as the Brexit issue proceeded there was one who seemed to be playing a brilliant game in pursuit of their own objectives. This was Nicola Sturgeon, the leader of the Scottish National Party (SNP). An apparently reasoned and co-operative approach alongside other anti-Brexit protagonists overlay an unapologetic intention to collapse the British state itself. In the 2014 referendum the proposition of independence had been fended off in part because of a revival of Scottish Toryism under the leadership of Ruth Davidson. The latter's resignation now suggested this process had gone into reverse. Whether Sturgeon's SNP could reduce Tory Unionists north of the border to a mere rump again at the 2019 general election remained to be seen. Meanwhile the insistence by Prime Minister Johnson – who had been booed by crowds during a visit to Scotland almost immediately after assuming office – that there could be no re-run of a referendum on independence regardless of new election results for Westminster or indeed for the Scottish Parliament in 2021, testified to the real nervousness as to what was afoot (Brooks, 2019). Ramming home an essentially English Brexit had inevitably breached a core principle of the Union of 1707: that Scottish views should be considered with a seriousness not necessarily proportionate with a relatively small population. That the traditional party of Union – the Conservatives – had pressed on with little regard for this basic pre-conception in the British constitutional order was a measure of the degree to which they had become prisoners of a particular form of zealotry.

Boris Johnson had become leader of his party, and in the circumstances therefore prime minister, because Theresa May had been destroyed by the very insolubility of Brexit itself as revealed by the repeated failures of her own legislation on EU withdrawal in the House of Commons. Such insolubility was dictated by the baffling conundrum as to how to translate a binary yes-or-no referendum on an issue of huge complexity into a form consonant with a historically defined representative democracy. The latter required detailed scrutiny, analysis of costs and benefits, and hard-fought compromises all round. By its nature, Brexit would grind to a halt amidst such investigation. Johnson's decision in late October 2019 not to press on with his own deal with the EU despite the fact that it had just passed an initial test in the House of Commons with a clear majority, but instead to unleash all the obfuscations and generalised partisanship consequent on a general election, showed his awareness that really nothing had changed. Yet in this vein Brexit – by sucking the life out of British politics in a much broader sense – posed questions about the country and society as a whole, and as such went beyond the mistakes or failings of any individual political party. Had the nation lost the capacity to discuss issues on which its future welfare truly depended – economic, social, environmental, cli-matic – and merely sought refuge in the displacement activity offered by Brexit? Certainly the debacle during Theresa May's leadership during the 2017 general election over social care had underlined for many politicians that to try and talk about anything other than Brexit held huge dangers in offending interest groups opposed to any meaningful reform of the status quo. *Plus ça change, plus c'est la même chose* was, superficially at least, both Brexit's weakness and its essential appeal. This, too, was why in some quarters the faux late Victorian poses of a figure such as Jacob Rees-Mogg, ostentatiously splayed out almost horizontal on the ministerial benches as Leader of the House of Commons, reminiscent (and one suspects consciously so) of the superior aristocratic ease of Arthur Balfour in the same role in the 1890s, could somehow catch something about the elusive dreams of a generation struggling to seriously engage with the structural challenges of much later times.

With the 2019 general election in full flood, optimism about the future in relation to Brexit could therefore take two main, if very opposed, forms, both of them with a marked historic backdrop. For those committed to leaving the EU, there was the hope – epitomised by Johnson himself – that a new domestic political reality was in the making, one that enshrined a return to a sturdy 'John Bull-type' independence free from all external constraints and capable of regenerating fresh expansive energies. For Remainers, there was yet the possibility that after all the noise and braggadocio of Brexit could be pushed aside, a fuller and this time decisive understanding would dawn of Britain's true position in the world, including an appreciation that an effective role for itself could only be found by unalloyed membership of the neighbourhood in which it was actually situated. For liberal pessimists, however, there appeared a grimmer prospect: that the process of a degraded public discourse – part of a wider Anglo-Saxon phenomenon – had now gone too far for any 'educational moment' to arrive and restore the balance, soberness and civic decency that had been the real virtues behind the 'greatness' in Great Britain. Where in all this the pendulum might finally come to lie nobody could say with any confidence at all.

Notes

1   See the review of Robert's *Churchill: Walking with Destiny* – the title says it all – by Richard Toye, *Times Literary Supplement*, 31 October 2018.

2   For an account of this episode that helps to explain later French attitudes to the United Kingdom see Gates (1981).

3   It was said one incident in particular during Adenauer's life contributed to his feelings about Britain. Although having an impeccable anti-Nazi record, he had been imprisoned for a short while when British troops arrived in his home area during liberation. The British officer responsible went on to become Chief of the Imperial General Staff as Field-Marshal Lord Harding. See Prittie (1972).

4   Quoted in Robert Holland, 'The Federation of British Industries: war, reconstruction and devaluation, 1939–49' (unpublished paper). The records of the Federation, the precursor of today's CBI, including the German Reparations Committee, are held by the Modern Records Centre in Warwick University Library.

5   The indispensable account of the United Kingdom's interaction with the European 'core' at this time is Camps (1964).

6   'Farmers warned income will halve in absence of Brussels trade deal', 'Brexit Briefing', *Financial Times*, 10 October 2017.

7   Nick Timothy was one of May's key political advisors that she took with her when she moved from the Home Office to 10 Downing Street. Timothy was a staunch admirer, and biographer, of Joseph Chamberlain, convinced that the values he stood for provided a blueprint for Brexit. See Montgomerie (2016). A partial knowledge of history can sometimes be misleading.

8   The ECU was the basket of currencies of EU member states foreshadowing the euro before the latter's introduction in January 1999.

9   An example of this genre is Martin (2017).

10   'May's Brexit Crisis', *Evening Standard*, 10 January 2019.

11   Anything to do with Ireland has an uncanny knack of bringing out what amounts to a 'blood' feud embedded in English culture, primarily, but by no means exclusively, in a Tory milieu. After two British Army corporals were murdered at a funeral in west Belfast during March 1988, British parliamentarians, according to an official report in Whitehall at the time, expressed the view that the Army should leave the island of Ireland and let the Irish 'go on butchering each other'. See McCárthaig (2018). A cavalier attitude during Brexit to restoring a hard border in Ireland – which Sir Hugh Orde, ex-Chief Constable in Ulster, said would inevitably play into the hands of men of violence – amounted to the same flippant disregard for what happened across the Irish Sea.

12   The classic study is Pierre (1972). By contrast the French nuclear deterrent was from the first an authentically national construct. See Scheinman (1965).

13   These transcripts of the discussions on BBC provide a telling overview of the arguments on all sides, conducted with a breadth and sophistication patently lacking in the public realm – and not least on the BBC itself – during and after the referendum of June 2016.

14   These rumours originated with the press baron Cecil King, with some attempt to make use of the name of the Queen's cousin, Lord Mountbatten. See Holland (1991: 336) and King (1972: 192–3). What mattered here was not the feeble reality of any 'plot', but how it reflected the brittle mood of the day.

References

Abulafia, David (2011), *The Great Sea: A Human History of the Mediterranean* (Oxford: Oxford University Press).

Bogdanor, Vernon (2016), 'Churchill would think hard and vote remain', *The Times*, 30 May.

Brooks, Libby (2019), 'Johnson makes "cast iron" pledge to Scotland: no new referendum', *Guardian*, 8 November.

Burton, Alex (2016), 'The link between Brexit and the death penalty', *BBC Magazine*, 17 July.

Camps, Miriam (1964), *Britain and the European Community 1955–1963* (Princeton: Princeton University Press).

Carroll, Rory (2019), 'In need of a wizard, Northern Ireland gets blundering Bradley', *Guardian*, 11 March.

Cassar, George H. (1977), *Kitchener: Architect of Victory* (London: W. Kimber).

Charlton, Michael (1983), *The Price of Victory* (London: British Broadcasting Corporation).

Colville, John (2004), *The Fringes of Power: Downing Street Diaries, 1939–1955* (London: Weidenfeld & Nicolson).

Drummond, I.D. (1974), *Imperial Economic Policy, 1917–39* (London: Allen & Unwin).

Frankopan, Peter (2017), 'Henry VIII "took back control" but it eventually led to civil war', *London Evening Standard*, 15 September.

Ganesh, Janan (2017), 'Forget empire: Britain wants less no more', *Financial Times*, 11 April.

Gates, Eleanor M. (1981), *The End of an Affair: The Collapse of the Anglo-French Alliance, 1939–40* (London: Allen & Unwin).

Giles, Chris (2018), 'Trade-offs are the answer if Britain is to move forward', *Financial Times*, 6 December.

Hilton, Anthony (2019), 'We will soon see the true cost of cutting EU migration', *Evening Standard*, 10 January.

Holland, Robert (1991), *The Pursuit of Greatness: Britain and the World Role, 1900–1970* (London: Fontana Press).

Holland, Robert (2013), *Blue-Water Empire: The British in the Mediterranean since 1800* (London: Penguin Books).

Horne, Alistair (1989), *Macmillan, 1957–1986: Vol. II of the Official Biography* (London: Macmillan).

Ismay, Hastings Lionel (1960), *The Memoirs of General Lord Ismay* (London: Heinemann).

James, Harold (2016), 'The tragic legacy of Britain's indecision over its identity', *Financial Times*, 27 October.

King, Cecil (1972), *The Cecil King Diary 1965–70* (London: Jonathan Cape).

Lanchester, John (2016), 'Brexit blues', *London Review of Books* 38:15, pp. 3–6.

McCárthaig, Seán (2018), 'United Ireland would cause worst civil war, Thatcher says', *The Times*, 28 December.

MacCulloch, Diarmaid (2016), 'Not first Brexit, but a glorious revolution', *New European*, 29 July.

McGuinness, Patrick (2019), 'What Europeans talk about when they discuss Brexit', *London Review of Books*, 41:1, pp. 5–10.

McLaine, Ian M. (1979), *Ministry of Morale: Home Front Morale and the Ministry of Information in World War II* (London: Allen & Unwin).

Marr, Andrew (2018), 'This contest isn't about Theresa, but Margaret', *Sunday Times*, 15 December.

Martin, Iain (2017), 'Look at the rickety EU and be glad we're out', *The Times*, 2 March.

Moncrieff, Anthony (1967), *Britain and the Common Market, 1967: Seven B.B.C. Broadcasts* (London: British Broadcasting Corporation).

Montgomerie, Tim (2016), 'Political tsar with a hankering for old Conservatism', *The Times*, 16 July.

Murphy, Philip (2018), *The Empire's New Clothes: The Myth of the Commonwealth* (London: C. Hurst & Co Publishers).

Pierre, Andrew J. (1972), *Nuclear Politics: The British Experience with an Independent Strategic Force, 1939–1970* (London: Oxford University Press).

Prittie, Terence (1972), *Konrad Adenauer, 1872–1967* (London: Tom Stacey).

Rachman, Gideon (2016), 'Rival historians trade blows over Brexit', *Financial Times*, 13 May.

Reynolds, David (2017), 'Britain, the two world wars, and the problem of narrative', *Historical Journal*, 60:1, pp. 195–231.

Runciman, David (2019), 'Which way to the exit?', *London Review of Books*, 41:1, p. 4.

Scheinman, Lawrence (1965), *Atomic Energy Policy in France under the Fourth Republic* (Princeton: Princeton University Press).

Stevens, Phillip (2019), 'Brexit is the sure route to a divided Britain', *Financial Times*, 11 January.

Tombs, Robert (2015), *The English and Their History* (London: Penguin).

Watt, Nicholas (2018), 'Brexit: Tory resentment of Irish power in the EU', *Newsnight*, 11 December.

Younger, Neil (2018), 'How Protestant was the Elizabethan Reformation?', *English Historical Review*, 133:564, pp. 1066–92.

2

'This is something which we know, in our bones, we cannot do': hopes and fears for a united Europe in Britain after the Second World War

Lara Feigel and Alisa Miller[1]

The title for this chapter takes us back to 1951. The initial plans for the European Coal and Steel Community were underway, and it remained to be seen whether Britain would play a part in it. The United States, worried that the Europeans would continue to destroy each other and would eventually call once again on America for aid, wanted Britain to join whatever European Federation might be about to emerge. In Washington the general hope was that Britain might act as a kind of sensible older sibling, preventing the tantrums of her European neighbours from escalating into violence that had drawn their partners, colonies and dominions into successive wars, resulting in enormous losses of life and riches.[2]

In January 1952, the British conservative politician Anthony Eden, who was about to take over as Foreign Secretary once again after the election later that year, used the occasion of accepting an honorary degree at Columbia University in New York to explain why US hopes were likely to be disappointed: 'The American and British peoples should each understand the strong points in the other's national character. If you drive a nation to adopt procedures which run counter to its instincts, you weaken and may destroy the motive force of its action' (Eden, 1953: 1156–7). 'You will realize', he continued, 'that I am speaking of the frequent suggestions that the United Kingdom should join a federation on the continent of Europe. This is something which we know, in our bones, we cannot do' (Eden, 1953: 1156–7). This quote captures the tone of debate in the early 1950s – and it is not a very different scene from the current one as we complete this chapter, though much has happened since. But of course then, as now, the political voices in Britain – though often arrogant about the nation's role in Europe and the broader world – were not unanimous.

In 1954 the civil servant Oliver Franks, then Chairman of Lloyds Bank, delivered the BBC Reith Lectures on 'Britain and the Tide of World Affairs'. The most controversial of these concerned Britain and 'The End of the Old World'. Opening this, Franks stated that 'I think most of you would be surprised if I suggested that August 10, 1952, was likely to be regarded as the most important date in the post-war decade of western Europe. But that is what I think. Why? It was the day on which the Schuman Plan became a reality' (Franks, 1954: 1).

Surveying the situation, Franks posited that the outlook of the majority of the people he spoke to was predominantly negative: 'I have met a good many men and women from different countries of western Europe and my conversations have left me with one clear impression: there are large numbers of people there who are living provisionally' (Franks, 1954: 2). The collective – and persistent – gloom born of a devastating war meant that there was no foundation on which to build. There were only three things that seemed to have life in them, and he thought that the people of Britain needed to be attentive to these. They were: communism (which offered hope for those in extreme poverty); Germany (which was by 1954 recovering far more speedily than anyone might have hoped a decade earlier); and the movement for European unity. About the latter, he said this:

> A great many of us feel the idea is so alien to our outlook that we are inclined to dismiss the movement as visionary and impracticable. But this is beside the point. The point is that nowadays the idea comes quite naturally to millions of people on the Continent. For in Europe the two world wars have been civil wars, tearing the fabric of life to pieces. The fact that they arose out of national quarrels and ambitions is an added reason why reasonable men are unable to stake their hopes for the future on the existing pattern of European society. They pin their hopes on the idea that a larger unity including their country with those of their neighbours might give a more enduring and better framework for life. (Franks, 1954: 2–3)

Franks was insistent that only this could ensure peace in Europe, and that Britain had to be a part of it. He went on to assert that: 'We have seen how Britain by taking a positive not a negative attitude, by recognizing the plain facts of her positive involvement in the life and security of her neighbours, has taken her place as a leader in western Europe' (Franks, 1954: 7). He was clear, however, that the nation could not take this self-described ascendency for granted. Political will and commitment were required, and if it was offered, Britain would shape the post-war world.

This was rousing stuff, but it begs the question: what exactly it would mean for Britain to lead, particularly if the nature of the emerging European project was predicated on the ideal of collective compromise and negotiation, as opposed to unilateral action? It also speaks to an important feature of the mid-century British debate. For all the emphasis on economic integration, arguably the most important and contested arena was cultural. At this point in history, we are suggesting, culture was not assumed to be just an adjunct, prettifying society, but was much more integral to politics. For Britain, Europe began as a cultural entity. Now, with Brexit looming, it looks like that might be all that we – the British and those living in the United Kingdom (or whatever remains of it) – will be left with. But that is a big all: an all that still has the power to keep us as Europeans and that the European Union would be wise to focus on as they do their best to survive the nationalism sweeping their con-stituent nations. Here we would like to look back to the moment when the notion of Europe as a cultural entity became a prevalent and powerful idea in Britain.

The appeal of union

The idea of a collective European culture had been developed for cen-turies across the countries now grouped within the EU, and was often linked with the idea of a politically federated Europe. Then as now, per-haps most enthusiastic were the Germans – think, for example, of Kant's 1795 proposal for an 'eternal peace congress' or Goethe's notion of 'world literature' (though this extended as far as the Orient) (Kant, 1795; qtd. in Eckermann, 1998). Influential French writers and philosophers also spoke of cultural bridges. In August 1848 at an international peace conference held in Paris, Victor Hugo announced: 'A day will come when France, Russia, Italy, England and Germany, all of the nations on the continent, will merge into a firm and superior unity ... A day will come when these two immense groups, the United States of America and the United States of Europe will be seen facing each other, stretching hands over the seas.'[3]

And in Britain too, there existed lone voices calling for a common European literature and for a European federation. One of the great spokespeople was William Stead, a British journalist who edited the *Review of Reviews* in the late nineteenth century. He toured Europe in 1898 and then wrote: 'And now this far-off, unseen event (a United States of Europe), toward which the whole Continent has been moving with a slow but relentless march, has come within the pale of practical politics, and on the threshold of the twentieth century we await this latest and greatest birth of time' (Stead, 1899: 30). Stead's emphasis on the inevitability of some form of integration reflects the relative optimism of the moment. Other tourists and subsequent witnesses to European battlefields (for example, the localised if exceptionally bloody clashes of the Risorgimento that introduced the illustrative word 'magenta' into the common language and helped to give birth to the International Red Cross) had seen enough to conclude that progress – cultural, humanitarian, technological, economic and political – demanded a federated future (Marwil, 2010: 184–5). This paralleled a broader desire for peace following the interminable Napoleonic wars and eventually culminating in the Entente Cordiale of 1904, which ran in parallel to the sense of a renaissance stemming from German unification and modernisation in the heart of the Continent.[4]

In the years leading up to the First World War, the calls for European integration were given a practical actuality in economic integration. The pre-conflict era was an increasingly globalised one with Europe at the centre of an interconnected imperial business system. Exports rose proportionally in Britain, France and Germany – although British trade and investment still mostly took place with its colonies and dominions – and general productivity and technology expanded, as did international investment, emigration and migrant labour. The increased revenues generated for national treasuries increased military spending, but this in turn – it was hoped – would actually deter conflict (Stevenson, 2004: 5).

Economic integration turned out not to be enough. The move towards European unity was brutally interrupted by war. Philip Larkin in his poem to commemorate 4 August 1914 turned to Roman numerals, 'MCMXIV', to 'lend a sense of time immemorial to the last moments of existence in history before the war'. He, like many other writers who fought in or grew up in the aftermath of the war, framed it as the 'watershed event in [the] archetypal story of lost "innocence"' (Sherry, 2013: 35–6). This lost innocence and the experience of graphic, mass death that caused it actually occurred in many 'foreign fields' – across the empire, at sea, at Gallipoli, in Africa and beyond – as identified by Rupert Brooke in his poem 'The Soldier', but the central theatre and focus of the war for the British metropolitan population was Belgium and France (Brooke, 1915). The conflict sucked lives and wealth in from across the imperial networks, and it imbued the Continent with a melancholy that was not soon shaken off.

Despite the war, some still spoke of a common bond. In the international context, some of the talk about European civilisation emerged as a counterpart to racist views and mounting fears about threats to white supremacy. In East Africa, for example, German officials assigned black soldiers to guard white settlers; this was considered by critics to be deeply undermining to the concept of 'European loyalty' (Steinbach, 2011: 154).

Other authors avoided racial arguments (at least on the surface): in 1916 the German writer Heinrich Mann wrote an article called 'The European', reminding the people of Europe of their common qualities.[5] British Romantic figures, and in particular Lord Byron, whose death in defence of freedom in Greece was taken to prefigure British engagement in a defensive war on the Continent, were presented as cultural touchstones during the war; their deep ties to European cultural movements were noted in articles in the popular newspapers and periodicals (Stock, 2010, 2011). When the poet-soldier Rupert Brooke died on the way to Gallipoli, the Belgian poet Émile Verhaeren wrote verses commemorating both his 'Englishness' and deep commitment to defending the common civilisation that the sacrifice – representing a broader Anglo-French brotherhood – entailed (Miller, 2017: 56–61). This spoke to a cultural bond underpinning the Allied cause but it was limited to certain nations: the enemy Germans and their *Kultur* was at this point broadly excluded from the brotherhood in Allied writings.

That said, some – including Brooke – were keen to point out that the picture of Germany as a hotbed of jingoistic nationalism only told half the story, championing its liberal qualities and pointing out the strengths of its strong Social Democratic movement, particularly when weighed against the repressions of Czarist Russia, a position Brooke outlined in a letter to Eileen Wellesley on 1 August 1914 (Brooke, 1916: 221; Keynes, 1968: 603). With an eye on both long-term progressive agendas and neutral publics the liberal public intellectual Charles Masterman, who became head of the British propaganda outfit at Wellington House, was keen to employ the novelist Ford Madox Ford to write as a 'cosmopolitan' and a 'European expert' and, in Ford's own words, 'a good German' who had much to say about the carefully woven web of cultural links that traversed the Continent (Saunders, 1996: 469–70). Less official British voices including the Bloomsbury artists and writers also helped to shield and nurture the European movement across the war years, affirming what Grace Brockington has described as their 'expectation of a new artistic, social and political renaissance' on the horizon (Brockington, 2010: 31). Diplomatically, David Lloyd George's government appeared to be moving towards integration with British engagement with – and indeed outsized influence on – the League of Nations, the Covenant of which contradicted the pre-war Concert of Europe's more formal approach to dispute resolution between signatories. The compromise between Wilson and the British resulted in a League that 'placed much faith in democracy' and relied on the idea that 'public opinion could restrain governments from going to war'. This was overly optimistic even in 1919 and 1920, with the memory of the First World War fresh: Lloyd George had to move with extreme caution to satisfy xenophobic voices at home that focused not on peace and integration but on reparations and the punishment of war criminals (Stevenson, 2004: 418–19).

Nonetheless, despite calls by some prominent British intellectuals for more substantive commitments, the main voices calling for a federated Europe between the two world wars were not, predominantly, from Britain.[6] A new journal, *Pan-Europa*, appeared in 1924. The political and economic construct proposed by its leader Count Coudenhove-Kalergi comprised an integrated conference of governments, a system of arbitration treaties and a customs union: a 'blend of the fashionable geopolitical calculation and an eclectic cultural anthropology'. It attracted support from many French and German writers in particular, among them Heinrich Mann's nephew (and Thomas Mann's son) Klaus Mann. The federated system was explicitly modelled on the American constitution and spoke to the international appeal of the idealism and rhetoric of Woodrow Wilson (Stirk, 2001: 26–7).[7] Arguments about common cultural inheritance had proved indispensable to the president in convincing political elites and ultimately the American public to militarily (and sentimentally) invest in the European war from 1917 (Dayton, 2018: 11–17). The proposed system appeared – at least for a time – resilient: the United States had only recently successfully rebuffed attempts by the then Great (European) Powers to pick off parts of their polity and resources and to impose a peace, even as they fought their own Civil War (Foreman, 2010).

Particularly as it became clear that the First World War was likely to be followed by another war, the search for a material expression of a common European culture became more urgent. If the various European nations could recognise that they shared both common roots and common ideals, then perhaps they would stop seizing territory from each other and periodically killing one another's citizens. Coudenhove-Kalergi's efforts initially had some impact. The French Premier and Foreign Minister Édouard Herriot called on his people in 1924 to 'create, if it is possible, a United States of Europe' (qtd. in Urwin, 1991: 6). And even in Britain, the first pan-European conference in 1926 received a positive response in some newspapers. The *Manchester Guardian* ran an editorial entitled 'The Oneness of Europe' in which it stated that '[t]he United States of Europe is no longer a dream; it has entered on the world of realities' (1926: 12). The historian Christopher Dawson – echoing the vague yet stirring language of civilisation and *Kultur* deployed by high-minded public intellectuals and politicians during the First World War – stated in 1932 that 'if our civilisation is to survive it is essential that it should develop a common European consciousness and a sense of its historic and organic unity' (Dawson, 1932: xxiii). Arguments that had been used to engage and cement relationships between Allies during war were now repurposed to promote an integrated system that – it was hoped – could stabilise national and colonial competition and help to maintain the peace.

Britain, Germany and Europe

The British writers who contributed to this discourse also had a brief moment of being taken seriously politically in the immediate aftermath of the Second World War – particularly T.S. Eliot, Stephen Spender, George Orwell and Storm Jameson. These writers came from quite different parts of the political spectrum in Britain, and worked to promote different political ends. But they all thought ultimately that national politics were less important than international co-operation and that even while countries were at war with each other, it was possible to remember what they had in common culturally and to use this as a basis for forming a stable peace. For all four of these figures – and much more broadly, for economists and politicians as well – the relationship between Britain and Germany was especially crucial here. Though these countries had been at war with each other for a decade by 1945, these writers were determined to argue that there was nonetheless as much uniting the British and the Germans as there was separating them. Furthermore after 1945 the ruins of Germany served as a tangible symbol for the need for a united Europe. These ruins in a sense formed the foundations of a new edifice of common suffering and a desire for collective construction that was to be cultural before it could be economic or political (Feigel, 2016).[8]

Politics

The politics of British integration in Europe were never straightforward. The moment when Britain looked set to be a major player in the early European Community, but ended up not being, provides a useful illustration of the complexities and internal divisions that dogged British Europeanists across the political spectrum. In the early days of the discussions about the European Coal and Steel Community treaty, it was expected that Britain as a major power and ally of the United States would play an important role. It did not, and this was largely the result of the actions and decisions of the Labour leader and Foreign Secretary Clement Attlee and Ernest Bevin in 1950, and subsequently of Conservatives Winston Churchill and Anthony Eden in 1951. The continuity between governments speaks to a common investment in 'Churchillism' predicated on the 'collaboration between capital and labour' as well as a reading of recent history that was essentially insular, centred on the culmination of the British imperial journey in the triumph of the 'Finest Hour', El Alamein as the 'Hinge of Fate' in the Second World War, and the 'Mother of Parliaments' (Calder, 1992: 270–1). The myth of a nation that 'stood alone' would wind its way through debates about the European community going forward.

As a result, in the early 1950s aloofness from Europe received consistent political support, despite potential rewards for direct engagement. The French diplomat Jean Monnet said later: 'I never understood why the British did not join this, which was so much in their interest. I came to the conclusion that it must have been because it was *the price of victory* – the illusion that you could maintain what you had, without change.'[9] This was to some extent true. In the immediate postwar period, British politicians and the public were largely complacent about Britain's role in the world. Conservatives remained (over) confident about the role that would be played by the Commonwealth even as they were preoccupied with the challenges posed by a dwindling empire. Labour leaders were first and foremost concerned with the construction of the welfare state at home. Despite the intervening experience of another war, political formulations lagged behind the fledgling economic and cultural arguments for a closer union that some were beginning to advance. In a sense both parties accepted the original formulation proposed by Coudenhove-Kalergi with respect to the 'division of the world into competing blocs of continental dimensions', with Britain and its empire forming a separate entity to the European core (Stirk, 2001: 27). Neither of the major parties saw immediate value in focusing on Europe at the expense of their orthodox priorities. Justifications for the aloof British position ranged from the geopolitical to the anecdotal. Sir Frank Roberts, a senior diplomat at the time, recalled Eden saying that he had constituents with relatives in Canada or Australia or New Zealand or South Africa, but that none of them talked about their relatives on the continent of Europe.[10] Apparently this meant that Europe must be less close to his constituents' hearts.

Both Eden and Churchill hoped that Britain could somehow direct discussions in Europe without directly joining in or committing resources or political capital. This resulted in mixed messages, which must have been as confusing for Europeans as the mixed messages they are receiving from post-referendum Britain as this chapter is being written and Brexit negotiations continue. At the University of Zurich in September 1946, Churchill sent a strong message of support to the burgeoning idea of a federated Europe, rising against a backdrop of ruination, anxiety and tentative idealism:

> What is the plight to which Europe has been reduced? Some of the smaller states have indeed made a good recovery, but over wide areas a vast quivering mass of tormented, hungry, care-worn and bewildered human beings gape at the ruins of their cities and homes, and scan the dark horizons for the approach of some new peril, tyranny or terror. Among the victors there is a babel of jarring voices; among the vanquished, the sullen silence of despair.
>
> Yet all the while there is a remedy which, if it were generally and spontaneously adopted, would as if by miracle transform the whole scene, and would in a few years make all Europe, or the greater part of it, as free and as happy as Switzerland today. What is this sovereign remedy? It is to recreate the European family, or as much of it as we can, and provide it with a structure under which it can dwell in peace, in safety and in freedom. We must build a kind of United States of Europe. (Churchill, 1946)

Hearing this typically dramatic and sentimental speech,[11] it would be reasonable to assume that Churchill is pledging his support not merely to the United States of Europe existing, but to Britain being a part of it and hence taking on a leading role in standing against 'tyranny or terror' as a – it can be assumed – leading member of the 'European family' (Churchill, 1946). He was not. In 1950 the British Cabinet decided not to participate in Schuman Plan discussions.

It is also interesting to consider what exactly would have been required to push the Cabinet to join the deliberations, given rising unease among British cultural elites about French post-war cultural and political resurgence and resistance to Washington's increasingly paternalistic, directive tone (Calder, 1992: 252–3). The French government had insisted that all parties partaking in the conversation should sign up in advance to being a part of the plan, without knowing quite what they were signing up to. This seemed to the British representatives unreasonable, and the Minister of State pleaded with the French to let the British join in on different terms, with the understanding that they would join the project if it seemed feasible to do so, after the initial formal discussions. The French refused this, leading to retrospective arguments that it was either their mishandling of diplomacy or their explicit wish that the British be kept out of the European project at this stage (O'Toole, 2018).[12] However it is as possible that, had the British government been allowed to contribute to the discussions on their own terms, they still would not have joined, preferring to influence the organisation rather than commit to becoming a member of it.

British representatives believed that even though they were not members they were managing to influence the developing institutions without committing geopolitical capital. When Edmund Hall-Patch retired as representative of the United Kingdom on the Organisation for European Economic Cooperation (OEEC) in July 1951, he reflected proudly if somewhat misguidedly that 'the Europeans look to us for leadership; they are delighted when we are able to give it; they respond to it in a remarkable manner' (Hall-Patch, 1951). Churchill concurred. Later that year, having returned to power, he was explicit in disassociating himself from the political and economic implications of his Zurich speech: 'I never thought that Britain or the British Commonwealth should, either individually or collectively, become an integral part of a European federation.' While he welcomed the Schuman Plan and thought it was a shame – if for no other reason than prestige – that Britain had not contributed directly to the discussions, he was clear that by no means would he want the nation to join the project as an equal partner to the other European states, and was determined to resist American pressure on this count.

Returning to the familiar rhetorical territory of defence of the island nation, Churchill concluded that none of the other committed states 'have the advantages of the Channel, and [they] were consequently conquered'. He went on to reiterate the broad, established goals of his government. 'Our first object', he stated, 'is the unity and consolidation of the British Commonwealth and what is left of the former British Empire. Our second, the "fraternal association" of the English-speaking world; and third, United Europe, to which we are a separate, closely – and specially – related ally and friend' (Churchill, 1951a). This all becomes even more explicit in a Foreign Office memorandum of 12 December 1951: 'The United Kingdom cannot seriously contemplate joining in European integration.' There was simply too much to lose with respect to the sterling area and the Commonwealth. But neither would they take an explicit stance against the formation of the bloc, for 'while it is neither practicable nor desirable for the United Kingdom to join the integration movement, there would seem to be an advantage in encouraging the movement without taking part in it' (Churchill, 1951b). The British government officially assumed the right to be both a benevolent balancer in the world order and a natural beneficiary of any continental integration.

Even those who did want to be part of it were unsure that the British ought to take on the responsibility of an equal player. Franks in his Reith Lecture quoted earlier went on to say that he thought the British ought to have country membership rather than ordinary membership – taking his idiom from the language of the British gentlemen's club, where there were different memberships for those who lived in London and those who lived outside it: 'We pay our subscription and take on our obligations, but not the full subscription, or all the obligations of the regular members, our continental neighbours' (Franks, 1954: 6). The language reflects a deeper truth about the entrenched ideals at the core of the British establishment and how it framed its political and economic policies (Stone & Fawtier Stone, 1984),[13] even as the ancient regime shifted to embrace some Labour principles and lost its hold on an international empire.

British writers and Germany

Broadly speaking this was the political picture with respect to the British political establishment, but what of its writers? During the Second World War, writers had been more anxious than many politicians to engage with a nuanced view of their European counterparts, and in particular with respect to the enemy to distinguish between Germans and Nazis – between good and bad Germans. Stephen Spender, during the war, had published articles in *Horizon* on German literature, urging British readers to read Hölderlin and Goethe and to see them as influences on British writers they admired. Together with T.S. Eliot, he also extolled the work of the German literary critic E.R. Curtius, who had been a mentor for him in the 1930s. Curtius himself had made the great case for reading the literatures of Europe collectively in his introduction to *European Literature and the Latin Middle Ages*. Here he insists on the impossibility of interpreting any of our 'national literatures' in artificial isolation from each other: 'European literature is an "intelligible unit" which disappears from view when it is cut into pieces' (Curtius, 1990 [1953]: 14–15). He went on to advance the idea of the ' "timeless present" which is an essential characteristic of literature', which meant that the 'literature of the past can always be active in that of the present. So Homer in Virgil, Virgil in Dante, Plutarch and Seneca in Shakespeare, Shakespeare in Goethe … There is here an inexhaustible wealth of possible interrelations' (Curtius, 1990 [1953]: 14–15).

   In January 1945 George Orwell mocked the simplicity of the British anti-German fervour in two of his regular columns in the socialist magazine *Tribune*. Reading a copy of the *Quarterly Review* from the Napoleonic wars, he was impressed to find French books respectfully reviewed at a time when Britain was fighting for its existence in a bloody and exhausting war. He complained that no such reviews of German literature could appear in the press now, although the situation was very similar. In fact, as Orwell well knew, the situation was very different; any works of literature to come out of Nazi Germany would be endorsed by the fascists. The Allies were fighting partly in the name of all the German cultural figures who had been persecuted by the Nazis. But Orwell's complaints the following week were more convincing. Visiting a London exhibition of waxworks illustrating German atrocities, he was sickened by captions inviting people to '[c]ome inside and see real Nazi tortures, flogging, crucifixion, gas chambers' and advertising a children's amusement section at no extra charge. Nazi-hating was being used to justify sadist pornographic voyeurism: 'If it were announced that the leading war criminals were to be eaten by lions or trampled to death by elephants in the Wembley Stadium, I fancy the spectacle would be quite well attended' (Orwell, 1945a: 19).[14] Writers who took this kind of position tended to emphasise that what they were fighting for was not to destroy Germany, but to create a new, united Europe.

Storm Jameson, who was president of English PEN, the international society for writers, published a pamphlet in 1941 called 'The End of This War'. Here she said that although they were fighting so that National Socialism could be 'discredited and broken', the Allies should not hope for total victory. They should not simply destroy Germany and restore pre-war Europe, or even pre-Hitler Europe. Europe before Hitler was better than the present but it was not in itself desirable: 'In any event we cannot restore it: we can only neglect our duty to begin creating a unified Europe, and so come to a bad end' (Jameson, 1941a). They needed to convince the nations of Central and Eastern Europe to co-operate, to restore half-destroyed countries, and to convince German citizens of the evils of pan-Germanism. And here she set out plans for a European federation, arguing specifically that culture can lead the way in creating political unity: 'The German nation can and must be educated to take its place in Europe. In a Europe reorganised on a dual principle. A) that no nation is able to concentrate sufficient military power to overrun the rest of Europe ... B) that no nation is tempted to assault Europe by the economic instability of the greater numbers of their countries' (Jameson, 1941a).

She rejected a relativistic reading of how the German people and nation had so debased themselves, and posited the British as those best placed to direct their collective reinvention within a European whole:

while it is childish to pretend that the Germans are savages, it is equally childish not to realise that they are politically backward, and to draw the necessary conclusions. Our hope lies in being able to re-educate them, in being able to make good Europeans of them. Europe was once a cultural entity, and at a time when national cultures were diverse and lively. To live, it must become an economic entity, with whatever diversity of

political needs. Security with freedom. Can we offer this to Europe?
Nothing less is worth the cost we are paying for the chance. Nothing less
offers any hope of peace. (Jameson, 1941a: 31–2)

Ironically, for Jameson, the Nazis had begun this process – they had
demonstrated energy and vision in creating their New Order, even if it
was demonic energy. Now the Allies needed to display the same kind of
energy in saving Europe.

Later that year she made explicit in her speech at the PEN Congress
that she was also calling on the British to see themselves as Europeans. The
'English writer', she said here, has two duties. One was to remind the reconstruction commissions that the unit of value in the world was the single
human being – that a German child therefore needed the same chance as a
British child. The other duty was 'to persuade the English that we are responsible to Europe, and cannot out of indifference or modesty evade our responsibility. The responsibility is to the future of every child: this includes every
English child' (Jameson, 1941b: 16). She did not make light of the challenge
implicit in the project: 'Only a fool would make light of the immense difficulties of creating a new European order: only Englishmen who are ignorant, or
tired, or discouraged, will refuse to try' (Jameson, 1941b: 16).

Ruins

After the war, some of these writers visited Germany, and what they found
there contributed specifically to their vision of a federated Europe. This
was also the case for some politicians who went to Germany, but they had
to temper their enthusiasm with a consciousness of the prevailing views
among the public at home. George Orwell visited Germany in April 1945
and wrote a series of articles for the *Observer*, describing the destruction.[15] Afterwards in London, waiting to return to Europe, he wrote an
article for the *Observer* insisting that a rural slum of the kind envisaged by
Morgenthau would not help Europe. Germany was Europe's problem and
the rest of Europe had to realise that the impoverishment of one country
would impact unfavourably on the world as a whole. He thought it was
absurd to debate the ethics of bombing – 'war itself is inhumane' – and
the important question concerned the ethics of reparations versus reconstruction (Orwell, 1945b: 5).

A few months later, Orwell wrote an essay called 'Toward European
Unity' for the *Partisan Review*. Here he said that if he was a bookmaker,
he would give the odds of the survival of civilisation within the next few
hundred years as low. It seemed very likely that the atom bomb would
destroy everything. He thought the only way to avoid this was through a

federated socialist Europe. They needed to present 'somewhere or other, on a large scale, the spectacle of a community where people are relatively free and happy and where the main motive in life is not the pursuit of money or power. In other words, democratic Socialism must be made to work throughout some large area' (Orwell, 1947: 5). This could only be Europe and therefore Europe must be federated.

These ideas received greater and fuller consideration in the work of Stephen Spender, who visited Germany for two long stretches in 1945 and then wrote a book, *European Witness*, describing his impressions of post-war Germany and France. This book explores many of the ideas that resonate in cultural debates about Britain and Europe today. What is particularly interesting is the way that Spender sees the destruction of the war itself as an act of European scientific collaboration that in some way sets the scene for a new form of creative collaboration.

He begins the book with the destruction of the ruined cities that shocked everyone in Germany. Devoting several pages to Cologne, where the people resemble 'a tribe of wanderers who have discovered a ruined city in a desert and who are camping there, living in the cellars and hunting amongst the ruins for the booty, relics of a dead civilisation' (Spender, 1947 [1946]: 22), he goes on to write how '[t]he great city looks like a corpse and stinks like one also, with all the garbage which has not been cleared away, all the bodies still buried under heaps of stones and iron' (Spender, 1947 [1946]: 22–3). The act of devastation and its implicit violence is embodied in the ruins: 'In the destroyed German towns one often feels haunted by the ghost of a tremendous noise. It is impossible not to imagine the rocking explosions, the hammering of the sky upon the earth, which must have caused all this' (Spender, 1947 [1946]: 23).

This is where Spender suggests that the destruction itself is an act of collaboration, and that it is a collaboration that offers itself to one form of philosophy: 'The destruction is *serious* in more senses than one. It is a climax of deliberate effort, an achievement of our civilisation, the most striking result of co-operation between nations in the twentieth century. It is the shape created by our century as the Gothic cathedral is the shape created by the Middle Ages' (Spender, 1947 [1946]: 23–4; emphasis in original). After this, Spender describes his own feeling of nausea, which grew as he spent more time in Germany. What depressed him most was a 'potentiality in my environment, as vivid as the potentialities of Nazism in 1931. This was the potentiality of the ruin of Germany to become the ruins of the whole of Europe: of the people of Brussels and Paris, London and New York, to become herds wandering in their thousands across a continent, reduced to eating scraps and roots and grass'. As he walked along the streets of Bonn with a wind blowing the disgusting smell of dust out of the ruins, he thought that the whole of their civilisation could be blown down in a day like this city had been. There were now two possibilities: creation and destruction. And the more constructive one required 'resolution, unity, will' (Spender, 1947 [1946]: 68).

So what was this constructive solution and who was going to achieve it? In Spender's view, the kind of creation that was going to redeem Europe was going to be best achieved by artists: 'We are confronted with this choice between creation and destruction immediately after a period in our history when it had seemed that morals were simply an affair of private conduct and that no necessity of making a moral choice confronted the whole of society' (Spender, 1947 [1946]: 92). For a long time, as technology had multiplied, society had become more automatic. It had been accepted that books could not change very much because society was no longer run by a few individuals; it had become an automaton. In Spender's view, 'All the arts could do was to save a few individuals from becoming as mechanically minded as other people in the age in which they lived by opening their eyes to other kinds of reality'. With the war, however, everything had changed. The social automatism had developed a means of destroying itself – the end result of technology was the atom bomb. So a new pattern of world society 'designed for the end of securing peace' had to come into being, and this involved 'a majority of the peoples of the world' assuming 'complete and conscious responsibility for the future pattern of the world' (Spender, 1947 [1946]: 92).

That use of 'conscious' is important, because for Spender the most conscious people were likely to be writers or artists, and therefore the solution was at least in part humanist and, hence, cultural. 'We have got to set the whole *human* interest in front of the existing power-and-wealth interests, at a time when we have almost abandoned thinking of politics in terms of humanity'; they would do this by uniting Europe (Spender, 1947 [1946]: 93; emphasis in original).

He went on to provide a useful metaphor, writing that 'one might compare the countries of the world to-day to clocks. Each country registers a different time, but outside their time there is one time for the whole world, registered on one clock, with a time-bomb attached to it. Unless the countries of the world can synchronise their time and their sense of reality, that time-bomb is likely to explode' (Spender, 1947 [1946]: 96). The world was now truly global: everyone needed to see this:

all the time, behind London, Paris, Prague, Athens are those shadows, those ghosts, the destroyed towns of Germany which are also the part of the soul of Europe which has collapsed visibly into chaos and disintegration. Their ruin is not just their ruin, it is also pestilence, the epidemic of despair spreading over and already deep-rooted within Europe, the black foreshadowing of the gulf which already exists in us – the gulf which we can still refuse. (Spender, 1947 [1946]: 97)

Here a finite entity – a federated Europe – provides an answer to existential anguish. It is inevitable that this solution should be built on cultural principles, because the fundamental malaise it is addressing is psychological as much as it is political and economic.

This response to Germany was not of course limited to the British. It seems telling that it was directly after visiting Germany in conjunction with a production of his play *The Flies*, that Jean-Paul Sartre wrote an article in *Politique Etrangère* demanding that the cultural unity of Europe should be transformed into political unity. He began here by talking about culture: 'Can French culture be defended as such?' he asked.

> To this, I answer simply: No ... Is there some other way of saving the essential elements of that culture? Yes. But on condition that we attack the problem in an entirely different manner, and that we understand that today there can no longer be a question of a French culture, no more than of a Dutch, a Swiss, or a German culture. If we want French culture to survive, it must be integrated within the framework of one great European culture. (Sartre, 1949: 245)

Sartre added political conclusions almost as though it was against his will: 'Naturally, this cultural unity cannot be constituted of itself. To be sure, we can even now ask governments, associations, private individuals to inaugurate a cultural policy; to be sure, we can have cultural interchange, more translations, personal contacts, we can draw up a program for books, for international newspapers.' He addressed the frailty of such efforts: 'All this was tried before the 1939 war. Such attempts, though very interesting, would be fruitless today, because they would create a superstructure for cultural unity, which would not be matched by any unity in the infrastructures. Therefore we must conceive – and I shall stop here because I wish to avoid the political question – European cultural unity as the only one capable of saving what is valid in each country's culture.' The rewards would be both specifically national and collective: 'By striving for a unified European culture, we will save French culture. However, a unified culture would have no meaning, would be a purely verbal achievement unless set within the framework of far more profound efforts to bring about Europe's political and economic unity' (Sartre, 1949: 247).

Sartre's unwillingness to take responsibility for the political implications of his cultural argument were shared by T.S. Eliot and articulated – if not resolved – in 'The Unity of European Culture', which he delivered as a series of lectures on German radio in 1946. Eliot distinguished here between Europe as a political organisation (a union to be created) and Europe as a cultural organisation (an existing entity). In defining the unity of European culture he began with language, suggesting that English was the richest language for poetry, largely because it comprised Germanic, Scandinavian, Norman French, French Latin and Celtic influences. As a result of these influences, and cross-fertilisations, he thought that poetry only flourished when the languages were able to cross-pollinate; this was a particular problem during the war when writers were cut off from each other and this was true of the other arts as well.

For years, there had been a fraternity of artists, based partly upon a sense of this interdependency, which had enabled them to come together and discuss ideas collectively whatever differences of national loyalties and political philosophy they had. The problem now was that this situation had reversed: 'nowadays we take too much interest in each other's domestic politics, and at the same time have very little contact with each other's culture'. This made nations intolerant of other cultures. It meant that Germany had wanted to create a world state with a uniform world culture. There was a danger that in calling for a unified Europe, politicians even in 1946 were calling for yet another version of this totality. Eliot thought this was dangerous – and his language here recalls Spender's – because it turned the world into a machine, and incorporated culture within it. In fact, though, 'culture is something that must grow; you cannot build a tree, you can only plant it' (Eliot, 1949: 196).

So Eliot's European federation had to retain its sense of differentiation as well as become a political machine – and it was not clear whether or not he was prepared to accept that political machine or not:

> The Western World has its unity in this heritage, in Christianity and in the ancient civilisation of Greece, Rome and Israel, from which, owing to two thousand years of Christianity, we trace our descent. I shall not elaborate this point. What I wish to say is, that this unity in the common elements of culture throughout many centuries, is the true bond between us. No political and economic organisation, however much goodwill it commands, can supply what this culture unity gives. If we dissipate or throw away our common patrimony of culture, then all the organisation and planning of the most ingenious minds will not help us, or bring us close together.
>
> This unity of culture, in contrast to the unity of political organisation, does not require us all to have only one loyalty: it means that there

will be a variety of loyalties. It is wrong that the only duty of the individual should be held to be towards the State; it is fantastic to hold that the supreme duty of every individual should be towards a Super-State. (Eliot, 1949: 201)

There is something quite evasive here – because what would a unity of culture mean without political unity? What does it require of writers and artists and how are they going to achieve anything practical? Eliot seems actively to resist this possibility at the same time as he offers it up as the only hope for the future.

Brexit

It is unclear where this would have left Eliot in relation to the current Brexit crisis, but it is helpful nonetheless in 2019 to look back at this mid-century cultural moment. To many the developments in Britain in the time since the referendum of June 2016 have been both shocking and existential: the vote itself, the shallowness of the debate that preceded it, and the self-righteous racism and isolationism that has followed.

The Remainers, however, must take their share of the blame. We were too busy taking our European links for granted to read the books where we could find, laid out fairly explicitly, the dissatisfaction that was brewing with the European Union. In 2014 a book published by Daniel Beddowes and Flavio Cipollini called *The EU: The Truth About the Fourth Reich – How Adolf Hitler Won the Second World War* claimed that the European Union had been Hitler's idea and that it had been a success for him because the only country it was benefitting was Germany: 'It was [Walther] Funk who predicted the coming of European economic unity. Funk was also Adolf Hitler's economics minister and his key economics advisor … The Nazis wanted to get rid of the clutter of small nations which made up Europe and their plan was quite simple. The EU was Hitler's dream' (Beddowes and Cipollini, 2014).[16] In Britain there has been a steady stream of statements, articles and speeches – provided by the likes of the UKIP MEP Gerard Batten and the Conservative MP Boris Johnson – to this effect for years (Bennett, 2014; Stone, 2016). As construed by prominent Brexiteers, the 'new German invasion, cloaked in the guise of peaceful co-operation, is more damnable [than the imagined Nazi invasions of the past] because it does not give the English Resistance a proper physical target' (O'Toole, 2018: 52). It introduced a new form of 'vassalage' encrusting the former colonial masters: to quote the Irish journalist and critic Fintan O'Toole, Brexit 'may be the last stage of imperialism – having appropriated everything else from its colonies, the dead empire appropriates the pain of those it has oppressed' (O'Toole, 2018: 151, 21).

This feels a useful moment, then, to look at the dissenting voices from the past – to see that the scepticism has always been there. It is also a useful moment to look at what motivated the most passionate proponents of European federation in Britain – to see that it was the spectacle of the ruins of Germany. We can see from Spender's writing that the enthusiasm for the EU was fundamentally born out of war – and out of the Manichean world it conjured. This was a generation who had seen what hell looked like and knew that they had to prevent it from spreading its flames across the Continent. They also accepted, and even yearned for, a European Union that the cultural historian James Sheehan has described as a 'super *civilian* state' as opposed to a superpower; an entity that is fundamentally concerned with preserving civilian institutions and individual well-being as opposed to compelling its citizens to 'kill and die' (Sheehan, 2009: 220–1; emphasis in original). It was therefore easy to sacrifice some self-determination, though not everyone in Britain was prepared to do so.

If European federation was supported by cultural figures at this point, it seems to have been both because culturally the sense of a common foundation was already strong, and because they were more likely to have been exposed to the images of destruction overseas – to have visited or at least directly confronted the physical and psychological ruin that was post-war Germany. But it was also because the move towards a conception of Europe that excluded nationalism was itself a vision compatible with culture, with its focus on the value both of the individual and of collective, rather than of the nation state. Spender argued that art itself mattered again – and here we could think of the constitution of UNESCO (another organisation that Britain is in the midst of leaving), suggesting that if wars began in the minds of men it was in the minds of men that the defences of peace would be constructed.[17] For Spender, in order to create a society where life itself is valued, the arts had to be mobilised again.

This perhaps is something to reflect on again now: the dreams that motivated European idealists in the mid-century. For those who dreamt then of an integrated Europe that included Britain, culture and mainstream politics and economics came together to a greater extent than they appear to do now. Perhaps it's still possible to reignite the dream of cultural unity. Certainly, the Remain campaign could have tried harder to promote a positive image of Europe, rather than simply talking pessimistically about the perils of leaving. Or perhaps in the end we need simply to accept that those who are still enthusiastic about European unity are culturally motivated. Either way, we need to do all that we can to keep the European project alive as a cultural vision.

Notes

1 lara.feigel@kcl.ac.uk and alisa.m.miller@kcl.ac.uk. This chapter has been made possible by funding from the European Research Council (ERC) for the project 'Beyond Enemy Lines: Literature and Film in the British and American Zones of Occupied Germany, 1945–1949' [FP7/2007–2013; grant agreement No. 335101]. Many thanks also to Dr Anne Chapman of the Centre for Modern Literature and Culture at King's College London for her assistance in preparing the chapter for publication.

2 Much has, of course, been written about the complex geopolitical, diplomatic and economic evolution of the European project. With particular attention to the United States and its attempts to direct the Anglo-European relationship in the immediate post-war period, see for example Urwin (1991), Gillingham (2004), Ellwood (2014) and Scott-Smith (2003) the latter of which takes a particular cultural-political angle in its analysis of the Congress for Cultural Freedom. For a succinct, historical analysis of European integration against a backdrop of political and cultural scepticism see Crespy and Verschueren (2009) and specifically of Britain as the 'awkward partner' see Ludlow (2018).

3 The conference at which Victor Hugo spoke was convened in Paris from 21 to 24 August 1848. Hugo's speech was published in Hugo (1937: 68–9), quoted in Pegg (1983: 5).

4 For an expansive study of Germany's nineteenth-century renaissance and the role this played in advancing calls for a common European culture, see Watson (2011).

5 His writings on the topic were later collected and published in Mann (1960), cited in Schonfield (2012: 260).

6 See for example Peter Wilson's work on individuals including the English classicist Gilbert Murray – with his emphasis on the integration liberalism stemming from a common Hellenic heritage – and Leonard Woolf's attitude towards the League of Nations (Wilson, 2011, 2015).

7 For further discussion of the influence of the United States on post-First World War discourses, and in particular of the spread of Wilsonian rhetoric and its international influence during and after the First World War, see Manela (2007).

8 For a portrait of the British in Germany in this period, an analysis of the meaning of the ruins of Germany for politicians and writers throughout the world in 1945 and for a discussion of the ideas of Spender and Orwell, see Feigel (2016) and see also the Beyond Enemy Lines project (www.beyondenemylines. co.uk) for which this chapter is an output. For another perspective on Anglo-German 'Kulturpolitik' see also Clemens (1994).

9   Monnet quoted in Charlton (1983: 307; emphasis in original) as part of a retrospective oral history project, with no exact date provided.

10 Roberts was speaking on the WideVision Productions/Channel 4 television series, *What Has Become of Us?* for its third programme entitled 'The Last Roar' that was later broadcast on 11 December 1994. Cited in Hennessy (2006: 681).

11 It is interesting to note that another Second World War leader seeking a return to power, Charles de Gaulle, mirrored Churchill in his invoking of a language of desolation that was potentially an even more alarmist vision of the future, in January 1951 in Nimes speaking of the potential destruction of Notre-Dame in Paris and the Colosseum in Rome destroyed by bombs in a future world war, should some new way forward not be located (with him at the helm of national politics). Charles de Gaulle quoted in Jackson (2018: 422).

12 For an analysis of reactions to this period and how they echoed through British discourse about Europe, see in particular 'The Pleasures of Self-Pity' (O'Toole, 2018: 1–25).

13 For a history of the landed English establishment and its legacy see Stone (1984) and Clark (1985).

14 For an assessment of Orwell's ideas on post-war Germany and Europe, see Feigel (2016: 175–6). For a broader discussion of how various writers and critics contemplated German culture in the immediate post-war and subsequently over the course of the second half of the twentieth and early twenty-first centuries, see Rau (2013).

15 For a discussion of Orwell's visit to Germany and his impressions of the country in April 1945 see Feigel (2016: 51).

16 Sections of Beddowes' and Cipollini's arguments were subsequently reprinted verbatim and reported on in the right wing British daily the *Express* (Bennett, 2014), thereby reaching a significant readership.

17 It is both cheering and depressing to take note of one of the winners of the 2017 English Pen Award: see Åsbrink (2017), which speaks eloquently about the themes of Europe, war, and individual and collective trauma.

References

Åsbrink, Elisabeth (2017), *1947: When Now Begins* (London: Scribe).

Beddowes, Daniel J. and Flavio Cipollini (2014), *The EU: The Truth about the Fourth Reich: How Adolf Hitler Won the Second World War* (London: Andrew Books).

Bennett, Owen (2014), 'The EU was HITLER'S idea and it proves Germany WON the Second World War, claims new book', *Express*, 17 April. www.express. co.uk/news/world/470967/The-EU-was-HITLER-S-idea-and-it-proves-Germany-WON-the-Second-World-War-claims-new-book (last accessed 14 February 2019).

Brockington, Grace (2010), *Above the Battlefield: Modernism and the Peace Movement in Britain, 1900–1918* (New Haven: Yale University Press).

Brooke, Rupert (1915), *1914 and Other Poems* (London: Sidgwick & Jackson).

(1916), 'An usual young man', in *Letters from America* (London: Sidgwick & Jackson), pp. 173–80.

Calder, Angus (1992), *The Myth of the Blitz* (London: Pimlico).

Charlton, Michael (1983), *The Price of Victory* (London: British Broadcasting Corporation).

Churchill, Winston (1946), 'United States of Europe', *International Churchill Society: Resources: Speeches: 1946–1963* (19 September). https://winstonchurchill. org/resources/speeches/1946–1963-elderstatesman/united-states-of-europe/ (last accessed 13 February 2019).

(1951a), Public Records Office, CAB 129/48, C. (51) 32 (29 November).

(1951b), Foreign and Commonwealth Office, *Documents on British Policy Overseas (DBPO)*, Series II, vol. I, no. 414 (12 December).

Clark, J.C.D. (1985), *English Society 1688–1832: Ideology, Social Structure and Political Practice During the Ancient Regime* (Cambridge: Cambridge University Press).

Clemens, Gabriele (1994), *Kulturpolitik im besetzten Deutschland, 1945–1949* (Stuttgart: Franz Steiner Verlag).

Crespy, Amandine and Nicolas Verschueren (2009), 'From Euroscepticism to resistance to European integration: an interdisciplinary perspective', *Perspectives on European Politics and Society*, 10:3, pp. 377–93.

Curtius, Ernst Robert (1990 [1953]), *European Literature and the Latin Middle Ages*, trans. Willard R. Trask (Princeton: Princeton University Press).

Dawson, Christopher (1932), *The Making of Europe: An Introduction to the History of European Unity* (London: Sheed & Ward).

Dayton, Tim (2018), *American Poetry in the First World War* (Cambridge: Cambridge University Press).

Eckermann, Johann Peter (1998 [1836]), *Conversations of Goethe*, trans. John Oxenford (New York: Da Capo Press).

Eden, Anthony (1953), 'Extract from a speech of the Secretary of State for Foreign Affairs, The Right Hon. R.A. Eden, delivered at Columbia University, on Britain's attitude to European Federation and the Atlantic Community', 11 January 1952, in Nicholas Mansergh (ed.), *Documents and Speeches on British Commonwealth Affairs, Volume 2, 1931–1952* (London: Oxford University Press), pp. 1156–7.

Eliot, T.S. (1949), 'The Unity of European Culture', in T.S. Eliot, *Christianity and Culture: The Idea of a Christian Society and Notes towards the Definition of Culture* (New York: Harcourt, Brace & Co.), pp. 187–202.

Ellwood, David W. (2014), *Rebuilding Europe: Western Europe, America and Postwar Reconstruction* (London: Routledge).

Feigel, Lara (2016), *The Bitter Taste of Victory* (London: Bloomsbury).

Foreman, Amanda (2010), *A World on Fire: An Epic History of Two Nations Divided* (London: Allen Lane).

Franks, Oliver (1954), 'The end of the old world', 28 November 1954, *Reith Lectures: Britain and the Tide of World Affairs*, pp. 1–7. http://downloads. bbc.co.uk/rmhttp/radio4/transcripts/1954_reith1.pdf (last accessed 13 February 2019).

Gillingham, John (2004), *Coal, Steel and the Rebirth of Europe, 1945–1955: The Germans and French from the Ruhr Conflict to Economic Community* (Cambridge: Cambridge University Press).

Hall-Patch, Edmund (1951), Foreign and Commonwealth Office Papers, *DBPO* Series II, vol. I, no. 466 (July).

Hennessy, Peter (2006), *Having it So Good: Britain in the Fifties* (London: Allen Lane).

Hugo, Victor (1937), *Oeuvres complètes: Actes et paroles, Volume 1* (Paris: Albin Michel).

Jackson, Julian (2018), *A Certain Idea of France: The Life of Charles de Gaulle* (London: Allen Lane).

Jameson, Storm (1941a), *The End of This War* (London: Allen & Unwin).

(1941b), 'The Duty of the Writer', in Herman Ould (ed.), *Writers in Freedom: A Symposium based on the XVII International Congress of The P.E.N. Club held in London in September 1941* (London: Hutchinson & Co.), p. 16.

Kant, Immanuel (1795), *Perpetual Peace: A Philosophical Essay*, trans. M. Campbell Smith (London: George Allen & Unwin).

Keynes, Geoffrey (ed.) (1968), *The Letters of Rupert Brooke* (New York: Harcourt, Brace & World).

Ludlow, N. Piers (2018), 'The historical roots of the "awkward partner" narrative', *Contemporary European History* 28:1 (February), pp. 35–8.

Manela, Erez (2007), *The Wilsonian Moment: Self Determination and the International Origins of Anticolonial Nationalism* (Oxford: Oxford University Press).

Mann, Heinrich (1960), *Essays* (Hamburg: Claassen Verlag).

Marwil, Jonathan (2010), *Visiting Modern Warn in Risorgimento Italy* (New York: Palgrave).

Miller, Alisa (2017), 'England and France in the First World War: translating the myth of the poet soldier' in Nicolas Bianchi and Toby Garfitt (eds), *Writing the Great War / Comment écrire la Grande Guerre?* (Oxford: Peter Lang), pp. 49–64.

'The oneness of Europe', *Manchester Guardian*, 5 October 1926, p. 12.

O'Toole, Fintan (2018), *Heroic Failure: Brexit and the Politics of Pain* (London: Apollo).

Orwell, George (1945a), 'As I please', *Tribune*, 12 January, p. 19.

(1945b), 'Future of a ruined Germany', *Observer*, 8 April, p. 5.

(1947), 'Toward European unity', *Partisan Review*, July/August, p. 5.

Pegg, Carl, H. (1983), *The Evolution of the European Idea, 1914–1932* (Chapel Hill: University of North Carolina Press).

Rau, Petra (2013), *Our Nazis: Representations of Fascism in Contemporary Literature and Film* (Edinburgh: Edinburgh University Press).

Sartre, Jean-Paul (1949), 'Défense de la culture française par la culture européenne', *Politique Etrangère* 14:3, pp. 233–48.

Saunders, Max (1996), *Ford Madox Ford: A Dual Life, Volume 1: The World Before the War* (Oxford: Oxford University Press).

Schonfield, Ernest (2012), 'The Idea of European Unity in Heinrich Mann's Political Essays of the 1920s and Early 1930s' in Mark Hewitson and Matthew D'Auria (eds), *Europe in Crisis: Intellectuals and the European Idea, 1917–1957* (New York: Berghahn Books), pp. 257–70.

Scott-Smith, Giles (2003), *The Politics of Apolitical Culture: The Congress for Cultural Freedom and the Political Economy of American Hegemony, 1945–55* (London: Routledge).

Sheehan, James J. (2009), *Where Have All the Soldiers Gone? The Transformation of Modern Europe* (London: Mariner Books).

Sherry, Vincent (2013), 'First World War Poetry: A Cultural Landscape' in Santanu Das (ed.), *The Cambridge Companion to the Poetry of the First World War* (Cambridge: Cambridge University Press), pp. 35–50.

Spender, Stephen (1947 [1946]), *European Witness* (London: Hamish Hamilton).

Stead, William T. (1899), 'The United States of Europe on the eve of the Parliament of Peace', *Review of Reviews*, p. 30.

Steinbach, Daniel (2011), 'Challenging European Cultural Supremacy: The Internment of "Enemy Aliens" in British and German East Africa during the First World War' in James Kitchen, Alisa Miller and Laura Rowe (eds), *Other Combatants, Other Fronts: Competing Histories of the First World War* (Newcastle upon Tyne: Cambridge Scholars), pp. 153–76.

Stevenson, David (2004), *Cataclysm: The First World War as Political Tragedy* (Cambridge, MA: Basic Books).

Stirk, Peter M.R. (2001), *A History of European Integration* (London: Continuum).

Stock, Paul (2010), *The Shelley-Byron Circle and the Idea of Europe* (New York: Palgrave Macmillan).

(2011), ' "Almost a separate race": racial thought and the idea of Europe in British encyclopaedias and histories, 1771–1830', *Modern Intellectual History* 8:1, pp. 3–29.

Stone, Jon (2016), 'Nazis created "basic plan" for European Union, Ukip MEP Gerard Batten says', *Independent*, 16 May. www.independent.co.uk/news/uk/politics/eu-referendum-nazis-created-basic-plan-for-the-european-union-ukip-mep-gerard-batten-says-a7032221.html (last accessed 14 February 2019).

Stone, Lawrence and Jeanne C. Fawtier Stone (1984), *An Open Elite? England 1540–1880* (Oxford: Oxford University Press).

Urwin, Derek W. (1991), *The Community of Europe: A History of European Integration since 1945* (London: Longman).

Watson, Peter (2011), *The German Genius: Europe's Third Renaissance, the Second Scientific Revolution and the Twentieth Century* (London: Simon & Schuster).

Wilson, Peter (2011), 'Gilbert Murray and international relations: Hellenism, liberalism and intellectual cooperation as a path to peace', *Review of International Studies* 37:2, pp. 881–909.

(2015), 'Leonard Woolf, the League of Nations and peace between the wars', *Political Quarterly* 86:4, pp. 532–9.

3

EU enlargement and the freedom of movement: imagined communities in the Conservative Party's discourse on Europe (1997–2016)

Marlene Herrschaft-Iden

Introduction

The so-called 'Eastern' enlargement of the EU was decided upon at the Luxembourg European Council in December 1997 and came into force in 2004, with ten new members joining. Because the UK had not imposed transitional controls, large numbers of immigrants originating from these new EU member states came to live and work in the UK (Blockmans, 2015: 131). Since then, this development saw 'the issue of immigration from newly acceding EU member states rising to the top of the agenda in the UK' (Blockmans, 2015: 132). It was a hotly debated topic both in the general election campaign in 2015 and in the in/out referendum campaign in 2016 and remains so until today, when the legal status of EU citizens living and working in the UK hangs in the balance while the Conservative government negotiates the new terms of the EU–UK relationship. While UKIP has always been calling for an exit from the EU, thus ending the free movement of people, and while the Leave campaign chose the equally unambiguous slogan 'Take back control of our borders', the role of the Conservative Party in the discourse on enlargement is less easy to classify. Following the enlargement process in their role of Official Opposition from May 1997 and in government since May 2010, Conservative Party leaders maintained the policy to support enlargement of the EU throughout, including the entry of Bulgaria and Romania in 2007 and Croatia in 2013.

This chapter shows how the rise of immigration to the top of the political agenda over the years was addressed by Conservative Party leaders and how this chimes with references to political communities in parliamentary discourse. To this end, I will trace back the Conservative Party's discourse on enlargement since 1997, looking for images of the British nation as either distinct from other EU membership candidates, or sharing similarities with them that warrant their inclusion. It will be argued that although the support for enlargement did not waver across the years, there were nevertheless significant changes in the discourse: a shift from the promise of economic and strategic gains in the British national interest to an increasing concern with migration in the wake of enlargement.

Theoretical framework and methodology

Chilton argues that language is used by people to 'exchange mental pictures of the world' (Chilton, 2004: xi) and that 'language and politics are intimately linked at a fundamental level' (Chilton, 2004: 4). With regard to shared 'mental pictures' of communities, I argue that the political is very much part of culture and vice versa, and in this context the language–identity nexus is especially worth considering. Indeed, Anderson defines a nation as 'an imagined political community – and imagined as both inherently limited and sovereign' (Anderson, 1991: 6), while Barker claims that a nation is a 'system of cultural representation by which national identity is continually reproduced through discursive action' (Barker, 2012: 259). A closer look at the political discourse in the UK thus promises insights into how politicians imagine the communities they deem relevant. Anderson adds that '[c]ommunities are to be distinguished, not by their falseness/genuineness, but by the style in which they are imagined' (Anderson, 1991: 6). This chapter explores the style in which the British nation and the new member states in an enlarged European Union were imagined and verbally represented, with a focus on enlargement and the freedom of movement.

Fairclough and Fairclough argue that political speeches consist mainly of argumentation, seeking to justify proclaimed goals and that in the description of events and arguments used, underlying values can be found (Fairclough and Fairclough, 2012: 1–15). The justifications for supporting enlargement offered by Conservative Party leaders were therefore included in the analysis. Contributions to debates in the House of Commons serve as primary sources because of parliament's central role in political discourse in the UK. Speeches held 'on the floor of the House' are also directed at a large audience outside parliament (TV broadcasting and media reporting securing this further outreach and impact). I searched the online archive (*Hansard*) for all contributions by Conservative

Party leaders from May 1997 until June 2016. This includes the time the Conservative Party was in opposition during the Labour governments from 1997 to 2010 and the Conservative-Liberal Democrats coalition government from 2010 to 2015. Additionally, I included the remaining months of David Cameron's term of office as prime minister (PM) until his resignation on the day after the EU referendum (24 June 2016). To find the relevant speeches in the large corpus of all oral contributions to parliamentary debates by the party leaders in the researched period, a lexical search for the keywords 'enlargement', 'freedom of movement', 'free mov*' and 'transitional control*' was conducted. Table 3.1 summarises where and when the search terms were found.

Table 3.1   List of analysed Conservative leaders' speeches on enlargement

Party leader	Title of debate	Date	Code
John Major	European Union	09.06.1997	'enlargement'
John Major	European Council (Amsterdam)	18.06.1997	'enlargement'
William Hague	NATO Summit	09.07.1997	'enlargement'
William Hague	European Council	15.12.1997	'enlargement'
William Hague	European Council (Cardiff)	17.06.1998	'enlargement'
William Hague	European Council (Vienna)	14.12.1998	'enlargement'
William Hague	European Commission	16.03.1999	'enlargement'
William Hague	Berlin European Council and Kosovo	29.03.1999	'enlargement'
William Hague	Special European Council (Tampere)	19.10.1999	'enlargement'
William Hague	Helsinki European Council	13.12.1999	'enlargement'
William Hague	European Council	21.06.2000	'enlargement'
William Hague	Government Annual Report	13.07.2000	'enlargement'
William Hague	Nice European Council	11.12.2000	'enlargement'
Iain Duncan Smith	European Council (Seville)	24.06.2002	'enlargement'
Iain Duncan Smith	European Council	28.10.2002	'enlargement'
Iain Duncan Smith	European Council (Copenhagen)	16.12.2002	'enlargement'
Iain Duncan Smith	Engagements	21.05.2003	'enlargement'
Michael Howard	Debate on the Address	26.11.2003	'enlargement'
Michael Howard	European Council	15.12.2003	'enlargement'

(continued)

Table 3.1   (*cont.*)

Party leader	Title of debate	Date	Code
Michael Howard	Engagements	04.02.2004	'transitional controls' + 'free movement'
Michael Howard	Engagements	11.02.2004	'transitional controls'
Eastern enlargement comes into force			
Michael Howard	European Council	20.06.2005	'enlargement'
David Cameron	EC Budget	19.12.2005	'enlargement'
David Cameron	European Council	19.06.2006	'enlargement'
David Cameron	European Council	23.06.2008	'enlargement'
David Cameron	European Council	21.06.2010	'enlargement'
David Cameron	Engagements	09.11.2011	'transitional controls'
David Cameron	EU Council	12.12.2011	'enlargement'
David Cameron	European Council	05.03.2012	'enlargement'
David Cameron	European Council	26.11.2012	'enlargement'
David Cameron	European Council	17.12.2012	'enlargement' + 'transitional controls'
David Cameron	Engagements	19.12.2012	'transitional controls'
David Cameron	Afghanistan and EU Council	02.07.2013	'transitional controls'
David Cameron	EU Council	28.10.2013	'transitional controls'
David Cameron	Engagements	27.11.2013	'transitional controls'
David Cameron	G7	11.06.2014	'transitional controls'
David Cameron	European Council	30.06.2014	'transitional controls'
David Cameron	Engagements	03.09.2014	'transitional controls'
David Cameron	European Council	30.10.2015	'transitional controls'

Findings

The leaders of the Conservative Party in the period in question were John Major, who briefly stayed on as leader after having lost the 1997 general election, and was followed by William Hague on 19 June 1997, who stayed in office until 13 September 2001. His successor was Iain Duncan Smith, who was replaced by Michael Howard on 6 November 2003. David Cameron took over on 6 December 2005. While in opposition from 1997 to 2010, twenty-three contributions by Conservative Party leaders in opposition contained the word 'enlargement'. Only one of them contained the term 'free movement', namely the one on 4 February 2004. In two more debates, 'transitional controls' were discussed, bringing the total up to twenty-five speeches. The term 'freedom of movement' was not mentioned at all in this period. The picture changed when the Conservative Party became part of the coalition government with the Liberal Democrats from 2010 to 2015; enlargement was mentioned five times in this period, whereas transitional controls were mentioned ten times, resulting in fourteen relevant debates in total (one overlap).

1997–2004: before the Eastern enlargement

After the decision to confer candidate status to the ten countries had been made in December 1997, negotiations for the 'Eastern' enlargement of the EU were formally opened in March 1998 and concluded in 2002, with accession coming into force in May 2004. As PM, John Major had argued in favour of EU enlargement and had maintained that the EU 'cannot possibly be complete' (Official Report, 9 June 1997; vol. 295, col. 810) without the prospective candidate countries during his remaining days as party leader.

William Hague

William Hague commented on enlargement during eleven separate parliamentary debates as party leader. To begin with, Hague repeats Conservative support for enlargement, and calls for the inclusion of even more 'central and eastern European nations' (Official Report, 9 July 1997; vol. 297, col. 939) than the ten already involved in the accession process, thus creating the impression of the EU as a group of nation states which happen to be in close geographical proximity to one another. The British nation is apparently seen as belonging to that group. He also refers to the 'future stability of Europe' which can only be safeguarded by further enlarging this group, implying that this stability is at risk; his mention of a possible NATO enlargement in the next sentence (Official Report, 9 July 1997; vol. 297, col. 939) points to Russia. Against the background of these security concerns, EU enlargement, like NATO enlargement, appears as a means to extend the Western sphere of influence to the former communist states in Eastern Europe.

Commenting on the decision made during the Luxembourg European Council 'to press ahead' with enlargement, Hague uses the adjective 'historic' (Official Report, 15 December 1997; vol. 303, col. 21), emphasising the importance of the Central and Eastern European countries' transition from communism to democracy and market economy as candidates for EU membership. Additionally, the national interest is brought up when Hague speaks of enlargement as 'a long-standing British objective' (Official Report, 15 December 1997; vol. 303, col. 21), thus justifying Conservative support for this policy. Further on, Hague nevertheless suggests that 'European Union costs will escalate as a result of enlargement' (Official Report, 15 December 1997; vol. 303, col. 21). Hence, the costs for the UK as a net contributor to the EU budget on the accession of new members (all with economies that cannot match the UK's) are mentioned here while possible economic benefits to the UK are not. This creates the impression that the UK is not seeking an economic advantage, but is letting the candidates join for other, more magnanimous reasons.

During the following nine debates, Hague repeatedly calls for reform of EU policies like the Common Agricultural Policy (CAP) (Official Report, 17 June 1998; vol. 314, col. 370–371 / Official Report, 29 March 1999; vol. 328, col. 734 / Official Report, 11 December 2000; vol. 359, col. 353) and EU institutions (Official Report, 16 March 1999; vol. 327, col. 889) before enlargement occurs. He thus links enlargement with reform proposals the Conservatives favour, namely giving more power to the nations making up the EU membership: 'Is it not in the interests of Britain and of Europe to argue the case for a more flexible Europe of nation states co-operating together?' (Official Report, 19 October 1999; vol. 336, col. 255). In line with this, he insists that he does not want the UK to be 'run by the European Union' (Official Report, 13 December 1999; vol. 341, col. 25). Hague therefore argues that enlargement is positive when used as a lever to change the overall make-up of the EU, something he repeats later on (Official Report, 11 December 2000; vol. 359, col. 353). Significantly, there is no fundamental opposition at this point against an Eastern enlargement of the EU.

Iain Duncan Smith

Following this, Duncan Smith brings up enlargement in four separate debates. In the first, he takes up his predecessor's demands for reform, criticising the fact that a reform of the CAP is still lacking (Official Report, 24 June 2002; vol. 387, col. 614). During the debate on the following European Council meeting in October 2002, Duncan Smith says that

[e]nlargement is a great prize that is worth fighting for. The 10 new countries seeking membership of the EU will bring 70 million customers for British goods and services in a single market extending from the Atlantic to the Baltic. The prospect before us is of a new Europe built on co-operation between stable democratic nations and the prosperity of open markets. (Official Report, 28 October 2002; vol. 391, col. 543–4)

Remarkably, Duncan Smith describes an enlarged EU as 'a prize' – and he proceeds to explain its worth: the new members are 'customers for British goods'. This unashamedly points to the mainly mundane motives for supporting enlargement: he obviously hopes for a boost to the British economy, which justifies Conservative support for enlargement. There is no mention of possible consequences for British workers in case the anonymous '70 million customers' not only want to buy British goods but come to the UK and work there as well (nor of the fact that British jobs might be lost because it is cheaper to employ people in the new member states). In short, all the resentment and fear of too many migrants that the Conservatives will emphasise some years later is completely absent from the debate at this moment in time.

Also notable is the geographical description of a single market – and thus, I argue, a sphere of influence – 'extending from the Atlantic to the Baltic'. This introduces a geopolitical dimension suggesting that Duncan Smith is advocating EU enlargement as a strategic measure to extend influence. Finally, Duncan Smith puts into words the vision of a future Europe that he approves of: 'a new Europe built on co-operation between stable democratic nations and the prosperity of open markets'. From a political point of view, this is a decidedly intergovernmental make-up with no supra-national elements mentioned (or needed, apparently), all based economically on 'open markets'. The Conservative leader's argument thus remains macro-economic and basically reduces the enlargement of the EU to the enlargement of the single market – a development that allegedly will only benefit British business, completely ignoring the people living in the new member states. The UK appears as a successful trading nation that is not otherwise connected to the rest of the EU member states.

Two months later, after the accession date has been agreed upon at a European Council meeting, Duncan Smith concludes: 'This historic summit is a tribute to the long, hard and sometimes lonely battles fought by successive British Governments to extend the benefits of EU membership to the former communist states of central and eastern Europe' (Official Report, 16 December 2002; vol. 396, col. 539). The illuminating use of the metaphor 'battle' to describe a long negotiation resulting in the accession of ten new members to the EU shows how the Conservative leader frames the co-operation with other EU members. Consequently, the other EU members are seen as enemies on a battlefield rather than as partners or fellow members of a group of like-minded countries. Even allies seem to have deserted or betrayed the British, for the battle is not only described as 'long' and 'hard', but also 'lonely'. What is more, it is not a battle fought for British interests, but one to allow the 'former communist' states to share the benefits of EU membership. The attribute 'historic' and the mention of 'successive governments' united in the endeavour show that here, a community comprising generations of British politicians is imagined, to the exclusion of other European nations. Consequently, the summit becomes a 'tribute' to the British governments who have not only prevailed in the end but have also been leading the way; and all that chivalrously, for the sake of others, it would seem. The British nation is framed as a 'limited' community united by the virtues of persistence and strength which guarantee its triumph when pitted against other nations pursuing diverging objectives.

Furthermore, Duncan Smith criticises the duration of the accession process: '13 years of excluding central and eastern European countries from western European markets, all because Brussels insisted on full compliance with social legislation' (Official Report, 16 December 2002; vol. 396, col. 539). After having been the victims of communism, the new member states are portrayed as passive victims again; this time subject to the EU denying them access to the club due to the importance attached to social rights for the candidate countries' inhabitants. These rights are thus portrayed as dispensable or at least secondary. Using 'Brussels' as a metonymy for the EU institutions that are instrumental in this decision serves rhetorically to exclude British commissioners, government leaders and MEPs from the EU, which by implication becomes a stern foreign authority denying the former communist countries the timely participation in all the benefits of free markets. This logic and the portrait of these nations as being at the mercy of foreign powers or ideologies – here first communism and then the inflexible EU run from Brussels – recall discourses of empire, where the subaltern – in this case the candidate countries – cannot speak for themselves and are not considered active players in the game. The British nation, in contrast, seems to have their best interests at heart and appears as a heroic advocate of the weak and wronged.

Michael Howard

Surprisingly, Duncan Smith's successor Howard is the first Conservative Party leader to discuss the issue of the freedom of movement, voicing concern about potential migration to the UK during Prime Minister's Questions (PMQs):

> On 1 May, 10 countries – including Hungary, Slovakia, Poland and the Czech Republic – will join the EU. We welcome that. However, Britain, unlike almost every other EU country, has imposed no transitional controls on the free movement of citizens from the accession countries of eastern Europe ... If other countries have controls and we do not, will not people from the accession countries be much more likely to come to Britain? (Official Report, 4 February 2004; vol. 417, col. 753)

And one week later, again during PMQs, Howard raises the issue again: 'Will he impose transitional controls on immigration from the accession countries or not?' (Official Report, 11 February 2004; vol. 417, col. 1405–6). Since PMQs are the format where parliamentary proceedings receive most public and media attention, it can be assumed that this insistence on curtailing the new EU citizens' freedom of movement is a conscious attempt to set an agenda for further public debate where possible immigration following EU enlargement would be cast as negative. It is surprising, however, that Howard only refers to this shortly before the actual entering into force of the Eastern enlargement on 1 May 2004, which creates the impression that the Conservative Party leadership only then turned their attention to the fact that enlargement is not only about markets, but about people and their rights, too. In view of their often-repeated support for enlargement as such, it becomes clear for the first time that their position on allowing the new EU citizens to make full use of their rights, including the right to live and work in any EU member state, is quite the reverse. This marks a distinctive shift in the discourse. The UK is suddenly no longer portrayed as a strong trading nation benevolently sharing the gift of prosperity and benefiting from enlargement, but as a nation incapable or unwilling to welcome immigrants, who are clearly not seen as a desirable consequence of enlargement by Howard.

2004–16: from enlargement to the Brexit referendum

Michael Howard

Nevertheless, Howard asks the PM one year later to 'confirm that ... Britain will continue to support EU enlargement – including sticking to the timetable for Romania and Bulgaria to join, and starting talks on Turkey's future accession' (Official Report, 20 June 2005; vol. 435, col. 526) after the accession of the ten countries has been implemented. Howard also speaks out against pleading the need for internal reform of EU institutions as justification to delay further enlargement, thus partly revising his predecessors' stance and singling out enlargement as desirable in its own right. While other EU members oppose Turkey's potential accession, the Conservative leader not only supports it but wants to bring it about as soon as possible. It is notable that unlike previously, the issue of internal EU migration is left unaddressed here, when some years later, it will dominate the news and decide election outcomes UK-wide.

David Cameron

Cameron talked about enlargement of the European Union three times during his time as leader of the Opposition and in fifteen more debates after he became PM in May 2010, a strongly increased frequency showing the rising topicality of the issue. While the first instance in 2005 is concerned with costs attributed to enlargement (Official Report, 19 December 2005; vol. 440, col. 1566), Cameron advocates further enlargement of the EU to the East and South-East to 'eventually include all the western Balkans, Ukraine and, perhaps, even Belarus' (Official Report, 19 June 2006; vol. 447, col. 1068) one year later. This is justified with the claim that EU membership is a means to achieve the following goals: 'co-operation, trade, stability and democracy on our continent' (Official Report, 19 June 2006; vol. 447, col. 1068). Clearly, the UK is seen as a proponent and shining example of these characteristics, but the EU is acknowledged as the best way to achieve them on a larger scale, namely 'on our continent'. Notably, the UK is thus framed as part of this community. Cameron does not mention cultural/religious differences or intra-EU migration at all, however. In his role as opposition leader, Cameron only refers to enlargement once more when he rejects the claim made by the Labour government that the Treaty of Lisbon is a prerequisite for further enlargement (Official Report, 23 June 2008; vol. 478, col. 27).

As PM, Cameron refers to Iceland's application to join the EU in the context of the global financial crisis and once more repeats the general stance that '[t]his country should be ... a strong supporter of continued EU enlargement' (Official Report, 21 June 2010; vol. 512, col. 36–7). He justifies this as follows:

> It struck me ... just what a positive difference enlargement has made, particularly in relation to members from central and eastern Europe, who, on many issues, take a similar view to us and can be very useful allies. This is an agenda that we want to push forward. In terms of

maintaining stability and peace in the western Balkans, anchoring those countries into the European Union is a thoroughly positive thing to do. (Official Report, 21 June 2010; vol. 512, col. 45)

Cameron clearly sees the gain of 'useful allies' as a further advantage of enlarging the EU. Although the British national interests and strategic advantages for the UK itself are foregrounded, the newer member states are acknowledged as like-minded countries. Additionally, he repeats foreign policy goals like stabilising the Balkans region, once more presenting EU enlargement as the means of choice to achieve them. Like ships arriving in a safe haven, EU membership guarantees their stability in Cameron's metaphor. He obviously sees the UK as a prominent guarantor of peace and stability, painting a positive image of a strong nation and a force for good extending its blessings to others in need. In conclusion, he seems to see no downsides and summarises that 'enlargement has been a success for the United Kingdom, in terms of being able to drive our national interests forward' (Official Report, 21 June 2010; vol. 512, col. 45).

Turning to the issue of intra-EU migration for the first time as PM, Cameron criticises Labour as 'a party that trebled immigration, let an extra 2.2 million people into our country [and] allowed everyone from eastern Europe to come here with no transitional controls' (Official Report, 9 November 2011; vol. 535, col. 278) in a debate in 2011. It becomes very clear that he seeks to distance himself from these policies, which include the free movement of people from Eastern European countries having joined the EU. Obviously, the Conservative Party leader is now anxious to appear to be taking a tough stance on immigration of any kind, even if he claims that he continues to support enlargement as such. This is essentially a hypocritical approach to enlargement: Cameron does not want to accept that EU citizenship comes with certain rights, or at least wants to curtail them while on the other hand still wanting to profit from new political alliances to further British national interests (and certainly from the market access to the new member states) straight away.

One year later, Cameron argues in favour of enlargement, describing it as one 'of the key successes for the European Union in recent years' and claiming that it was a 'British initiative' (Official Report, 26 November 2012; vol. 554, col. 43). He also shows a willingness to pay for the integration of 'those countries that joined the EU as part of enlargement' in order for them to be 'connected with the rest of the EU, when, of course, some of them have had previous economic connections heading in other directions' (Official Report, 26 November 2012; vol. 554, col. 43). A strategic element comes into play here, and Cameron obviously thinks it worth a lot of money to replace former ties to Russia with EU connections. He repeats his position one month later: 'in terms of the level of payments we make, we have to accept the fact that in an enlarged European Union – and we support enlargement – we are going to see a greater percentage of those structural funds go to the relatively poorer countries of eastern and southern Europe' (Official Report, 17 December 2012; vol. 555, col. 571–2).

Cameron continues by setting out his vision for the ultimate extension of the EU in 2012:

> I would argue in favour of, as some would put it, a Europe that extends from the Atlantic to the Urals and includes all those countries that are currently applying ... One of the European Union's greatest successes has been that countries wanting to join have entrenched their democracy and their belief in open and free markets ... Britain has always argued for enlargement and we should continue to do that. We should always put in place transitional controls, which I am afraid the last Government failed to do. (Official Report, 17 December 2012; vol. 555, col. 577)

The union is thus again envisioned as a community of democratic nations (this can be counted as a shared characteristic and value) which have market economies (a further similarity). However, this basic definition would apply to many other nations and states in the world. So, the only characteristic which makes the EU unique is the fact that the member countries are located in the same geographical area which is called Europe. The existence of an 'imagined community' of European nations sharing a common culture or values is thus not present in Conservative discourse (although human rights are mentioned as a shared value in another debate in 2012).

The next debate contribution for the first time connects the end of the transitional controls for the latest accession countries with possible welfare fraud – Cameron promises to do everything he can to 'restrict access to benefit' for nationals of these countries moving to the UK (Official Report, 19 December 2012; vol. 555, col. 846). This discursive connection is repeated half a year later, when he introduces the term 'benefit tourism' and announces transitional controls for any new EU members (Official Report, 2 July 2013; vol. 565, col. 768). He thus frames the British national community as a target of fraudulent behaviour which is laid at the door of migrants from Eastern European member states, who are thus cast as undesirable outsiders.

Later in the same speech, however, he defends the UK government's support for enlargement despite these alleged dangers by pointing out the expected economic advantages: 'It is in Britain's interests that the EU continues to enlarge and expand. Croatia has been added to what is already the world's largest single market, and Britain as a trading nation will have all sorts of opportunities to increase our trade with and investment in Croatia' (Official Report, 2 July 2013; vol. 565, col. 769). It thus becomes very clear that a distinction is made between securing 'opportunities to increase our trade', i.e. profiting from business with the new member states, and the freedom of movement of Romanian and Bulgarian citizens in particular, who are described as potentially fraudulent benefit claimants and not as an advantage for the imagined community of British nationals. This is implied in the pronoun 'our (trade)' – clearly, it is the British nation that is meant here, and the 'others' are undesirable immigrants from the newer EU member states. This impression is further underlined when, concerning Romanian and Bulgarian citizens moving to the UK, Cameron has to defend his policy against calls for prolonging the transitional controls from within his own parliamentary party: 'We have kept the transitional arrangements for as long as we possibly can' (Official Report, 28 October 2013; vol. 569, col. 676).

Emphasising this more and more unambiguously negative attitude towards EU citizens, Cameron accuses the former Labour government of having committed a 'shameful dereliction of duty' when they 'decided in 2004 to have no transitional controls at all. They predicted 14,000 Polish people would arrive to work in Britain; in the event, the number was over 700,000' (Official Report, 27 November 2013; vol. 571, col. 259). Moreover, the right of free movement is thus only acknowledged to be rebutted immediately; the number of EU citizens using it is framed as problematic. Consistently, Cameron insists he tried everything to deny it to Romanians and Bulgarians: 'Of course there are benefits of free movement within the EU, but there should be proper transition controls. We increased the transition controls on Bulgaria and Romania from five years to seven years when we became the Government' (Official Report, 27 November 2013; vol. 571, col. 259).

Cameron mentions pressure felt due to the public's perception of immigration and eroding trust as reasons for the increasingly tough stance on free movement in 2014 (Official Report, 11 June 2014; vol. 582, col. 561). Later that month, while he acknowledges that 'the enlargement process has been successful in driving the development and improving the democracy and governance of many of these [recently acceded] countries', thus justifying his continued support for enlargement, he nevertheless calls for 'a totally new approach to transitional controls' (Official Report, 30 June 2014; vol. 583, col. 605). These seem now a regular feature of any debate on enlargement.

A few months later, even the mere imposition of transitional controls and restricting the access to benefits for some EU citizens coming to the UK does not seem enough anymore. Cameron now suggests transitional controls should only be lifted when certain conditions are met: 'We should … ensure they will not have full access to our markets until their economies are of a radically different size and shape' (Official Report, 3 September 2014; vol. 585, col. 279). This statement shows a clear sense of Us and Them when he talks about 'our markets' which are vastly superior to 'their economies'. He thus makes a one-sided demand which apparently proposes unlimited access to the aforementioned new markets and the related trade opportunities for the UK, but limited access to the UK itself for citizens of poorer EU countries.

Moving into the year 2015, with the renegotiations prior to the announced referendum on British membership of the EU already under way, Cameron highlights that he is pushing for changes in the way enlargement works and obviously wants to have the right to deny the 'unfettered rights' including free movement to other EU citizens. Emphasising national particularities of the UK like having opted out of the Schengen agreement, Cameron demands special treatment by the other EU partners (Official Report, 10 October 2015; vol. 600, col. 668). This can be interpreted as a visible alienation from the EU as an imagined political community of equals possessing the same rights that the other member states want to uphold. Moreover, he stresses that 'we have borders', thus discursively creating an exclusive British community that needs to be protected from outsiders by 'border controls'. After this contribution in October 2015, shortly after the general election when the Conservative leader had become PM again, this time with an absolute parliamentary majority after promising an in-out referendum, neither the term 'transitional controls' nor 'enlargement' was mentioned by Cameron up until his resignation on 24 June 2016.

Conclusion

To conclude, the inquiry yields a result that may appear paradoxical: although the Conservative Party was in opposition from 1997 to 2010 and adopted a decidedly Eurosceptic stance in these years, every mention of EU enlargement, except two during the entire time, was positive about the policy itself. The justification for this support was threefold: a macroeconomic argument based on the assumption that free trade would automatically lead to more prosperity both for the UK and the countries concerned formed the basis for Conservative support of enlargement. The Conservative Party leaders did not, however, specify how exactly or how much they thought British citizens would benefit from enlargement, and they remained equally silent about the fact that extending the free market, just like any other increase of globalisation, might have negative consequences for low-skilled workers in the UK. Second, strategic foreign policy aims were put forward, namely withdrawing the Eastern European accession countries from Russia's sphere of influence as well as ensuring peace and stability in the region, especially in the Balkans. A third line of argument linked enlargement with calls for internal reform of EU institutions and policies, like the CAP. In a nutshell, the entire pro-enlargement discourse centred around trade opportunities, strategic foreign policy aims, and the vision of a less deeply integrated EU. And even afterwards, during the period of the coalition government and beyond, the goal of enlarging the EU even further, to include not only Croatia and the Balkan countries but Turkey and Ukraine as well, was not retracted by David Cameron.

A further striking result is that the freedom of movement, which played such a key role in the in/out debate and continues to be an issue in the current Brexit negotiations, was only explicitly mentioned twice in the period from 1997 to 2010, even though the Conservative Party was in opposition and could have used the issue to attack the Labour governments. It was Howard who first brought up the issue at all, and it was also he who pointed out, somewhat belatedly in two sessions of PMQs in February 2004, that the UK had not imposed transitional controls. Otherwise, however, the topic seems to have been largely ignored. Indeed, the Conservative opposition discourse on enlargement does not feature human beings as actors at all, except in these two instances, and possible implications of EU migration for domestic issues such as jobs and welfare were not even hinted at. This only changed in November 2011, when intra-EU immigration was mentioned by David Cameron for the first time. Transitional controls have continued to be a regular feature of the Conservative discourse on enlargement since December 2012, and in July 2013, the term 'benefit tourism' was introduced in connection with free movement, linking EU migration to abuse of the British welfare system. The Conservative Party thus reacted to a shift in the public mood, not least expressed by the fast-growing support for UKIP, since their own line of argument during the decades leading up to this point had not addressed migration in connection with EU enlargement. This may be seen as the residue of an imperial mindset, since the long-term non-representation of a possible exchange of people is reminiscent of the handling of immigration from former colonies – first, the colonies were seen as markets and passive recipients, but when many people from the Commonwealth started to come to the UK to live and work there, this triggered a strong public and political reaction – Enoch Powell's dire predictions in his Birmingham speech of 1968 cannot easily be forgotten.

Finally, it must be kept in mind that the Conservative Party leaders did not engage in a decidedly anti-immigration discourse in connection with EU enlargement while they were in opposition. Their stance only became more critical of the implications of free movement once they were in government (and could arguably leave the positive arguments to their pro-European coalition partner, the Liberal Democrats). This coincided with a 'sharp increase in the volume of newspaper coverage relating to migration' (Allen, 2016: 1) in the already largely Eurosceptic British press (e.g. Daddow, 2012: 1219) and sat awkwardly with their continued support for every possible enlargement of the EU. This created a dilemma that Cameron sought to solve by (unsuccessfully) renegotiating the applicability of the freedom of movement and equal rights for all EU citizens in the UK before the in/out referendum in June 2016.

The UK as a political community was for a long time imagined as a strong and proud trading nation successfully securing its national interests as well as making it its mission to extend the blessings of its (superior) economic model to less fortunate countries – a stance that distinctly recalls imperial discourses. Additionally, the British nation was portrayed as a patron of peace, stability and democracy whose benefits it helps to spread across the European continent, using EU membership as a vehicle. As long as enlargement remained a largely foreign and trade policy issue, this position was upheld in the party leaders' contributions to the debate. Only briefly did they mention migration before 2011, when it enters into Cameron's vocabulary, and the image of the British nation changes to a poorly defended and endangered community at risk of being ripped off by fraudulent migrants from other EU countries, which are thus framed as unwanted outsiders.

Consistently, the EU itself was described as a group of co-operating nation states in one geographical area, which is of course quite a minimal definition that may apply to many other intergovernmental co-operations. The EU was largely imagined not as a political community of people who share the same values, like a nation, but a group of independent countries united only by largely technical characteristics such as similar economic and political systems as well as strategic foreign policy objectives. As far as intra-EU migration is concerned, the Conservative discourse thus did nothing to promote a common identity with fellow Europeans.

On the contrary, the Conservative Party leaders resisted the idea of a cultural closeness between the British and other European nations, arguing instead that the important factors characterising the European community were market democracy and location.

In a nutshell, there were two major shifts in the Conservative discourse on EU enlargement: Eastern European member states had initially been framed as useful and like-minded allies before the issue of free movement was foregrounded in 2011. Ever since, they have been described as a source of unwanted or even criminal migrants. And while the British nation was for a long time acknowledged to be a part of the European project, this equally changed when national particularities were foregrounded that allegedly required borders closed to the rest of the EU.

References

Primary sources

Contributions to parliamentary debates by John Major

Official Report, 9 June 1997; vol. 295, col. 810–11.

Contributions to parliamentary debates by William Hague

Official Report, 9 July 1997; vol. 297, col. 939.
Official Report, 15 December 1997; vol. 303, col. 21.
Official Report, 17 June 1998; vol. 314, col. 370–1.
Official Report, 16 March 1999; vol. 327, col. 889.
Official Report, 29 March 1999; vol. 328, col. 734.
Official Report, 19 October 1999; vol. 336, col. 255.
Official Report, 13 December 1999; vol. 341, col. 25.
Official Report, 11 December 2000; vol. 359, col. 353.

Contributions to parliamentary debates by Iain Duncan Smith

Official Report, 24 June 2002; vol. 387, col. 614.
Official Report, 28 October 2002; vol. 391, col. 543–4.
Official Report, 16 December 2002; vol. 396, col. 539–40.

Contributions to parliamentary debates by Michael Howard

Official Report, 4 February 2004; vol. 417, col. 753.
Official Report, 11 February 2004; vol. 417, col. 1405–6.
Official Report, 20 June 2005; vol. 435, col. 526.

Contributions to parliamentary debates by David Cameron

Official Report, 19 December 2005; vol. 440, col. 1566.
Official Report, 19 June 2006; vol. 447, col. 1068.
Official Report, 23 June 2008; vol. 478, col. 27.
Official Report, 21 June 2010; vol. 512, col. 36–7; 45.
Official Report, 9 November 2011; vol. 535, col. 278.
Official Report, 26 November 2012, vol. 554, col. 43.
Official Report, 17 December 2012; vol. 555, col. 571–2; 577.
Official Report, 19 December 2012; vol. 555, col. 846.
Official Report, 2 July 2013; vol. 565, col. 768–9.
Official Report, 28 October 2013; vol. 569, col. 676.
Official Report, 27 November 2013; vol. 571, col. 259.
Official Report, 11 June 2014; vol. 582, col. 561.
Official Report, 30 June 2014; vol. 583, col. 605; 617.
Official Report, 3 September 2014; vol. 585, col. 279.
Official Report, 10 October 2015; vol. 600, col. 668.

Secondary sources

Allen, William L. (2016), 'A Decade of Immigration in the British Press', *Migration Observatory Report, COMPAS*. University of Oxford.

Anderson, Benedict (1991), *Imagined Communities: Reflections on the Origin and Spread of Nationalism*, revised and extended edition (London: Verso).

Barker, Chris (2012), *Cultural Studies: Theory and Practice*, 4th edition (London: SAGE).

Blockmans, Steven (2015), 'Enlargement' in Michael Emerson (ed.), *Britain's Future in Europe: Reform, Renegotiation, Repatriation or Secession?* (Brussels: Centre for European Policy Studies (CEPS)), pp. 127–31.

Chilton, Paul A. (2004), *Analysing Political Discourse: Theory and Practice* (London: Routledge).

Daddow, Oliver (2012), 'The UK media and "Europe": from permissive consensus to destructive dissent', *International Affairs* 88:6, pp. 1219–36.

Fairclough, Norman and Isabela Fairclough (2012), *Political Discourse Analysis* (London: Routledge).

4

The discursive role of Europe in a disunited kingdom

Klaus Stolz

Introduction

In the referendum on 23 June 2016, British citizens voted 52 to 48 per cent for the United Kingdom to leave the European Union, a result that showed Britain deeply divided on a number of different levels. In addition to major differences across age, social class and education, the four different constituent nations of the UK also voted in quite different ways: while England and Wales were in favour of leaving, Northern Ireland and, even more strongly, Scotland voted to remain part of the EU – a clear split across the constituent nations of the UK that was immediately seen as the most apparent sign of an increasingly 'disunited Kingdom' (Seldon, 2016). But beyond throwing into relief existing major faultlines of the British constitutional settlement, the referendum poses a new major threat to the unity and integrity of the British state. On the morning after the referendum, Nicola Sturgeon, Scottish First Minister and leader of the Scottish National Party (SNP), announced that now 'a second [independence] referendum must be on the table' (Sturgeon, 2016). At the same time, the late Martin McGuinness, then-deputy First Minister of Northern Ireland, called for an immediate referendum on Irish reunification. Since then, the twists and turns of the Brexit negotiation process have been keenly observed in both nations, with nationalists ready to capitalise on the conflicts of interest.

The Brexit referendum and the reactions to it clearly show continental Europe to be inextricably intertwined with the internal British constitutional debate. In fact, while Brexit and Scottish independence are fairly recent issues, the general idea that Europe, the EU and the European integration process crucially influence, structure or even determine the constitutional order of the British state has been with us for decades (if not for centuries). In this chapter I will trace how different political actors and different commentators have made different use of Europe in a predominantly domestic debate about the constitutional, and especially the territorial order of the United Kingdom. The argument is structured mainly in chronological order, highlighting major turning points in this discourse. Furthermore, it is strongly focused on the Scottish Question (Mitchell, 2014), since the union between England and Scotland is not only at the heart of the United Kingdom, but also seems to be the most contested of its relationships.

I will start with a look at the role Europe played in the process of British nation-building in the eighteenth and nineteenth centuries as described by Linda Colley. This classical historical account of how Europe as the quintessential 'Other' helped forge the British nation (Colley, 1992) forms the basis of an exploration of three more recent periods in which the role Europe played in the territorial integration of the United Kingdom became much more variable and contested. The first section is concerned with the British accession to the European Economic Community in 1973 and the related debates in which Europe was perceived as a hostile centralising force by British nationalists as well as by sub-state nationalists from the peripheral nations of the UK. The second period under scrutiny comprises the eighteen years of Conservative rule in the 1980s and 1990s coinciding (though not at all incidentally) with a noticeable Europeanisation of the domestic constitutional debate. The last stage of my analysis deals with the role of Europe in the most recent constitutional dispute between Scotland and the United Kingdom, marked by the Scottish independence referendum in 2014 and the Brexit referendum in 2016. My inquiry into Europe's role up to the present in the domestic constitutional discourse will finish with a cautious outlook regarding the territorial integrity of the United Kingdom outside the European Union.

Forging the British nation in the eighteenth and nineteenth centuries: Europe as the Other

The United Kingdom is a unique formation: it is a union of four different constituent nations which have been integrated into the British state at different times, under different circumstances and conditions. The diverse ways in which England, Wales, Scotland and Ireland (later Northern Ireland) came together to form a unitary state, though, begs the question as to whether, and to what extent they came to form a new British nation distinct from its constituent parts. In *Britons: Forging the Nation 1707–1837*, Linda Colley famously delineates the favourable conditions of this state and nation-building process in the eighteenth and early nineteenth centuries (Colley, 1992). Among the most important of these factors are the early industrialisation and the subsequent economic success of Britain and its territorial expansion across the world via the British Empire. In both of these developments all four nations had their stake in creating not only a common interest but also a new form of loyalty to the British union, though in Ireland, this loyalty was clearly restricted to the protestant elite.

According to Colley, however, another cultural factor was crucial in this nation building process: it was the perception of Europe – in particular France – as the Other, more than anything else that provided shared meaning among Britons and thus helped forge the British nation. While the newly bundled together British ruling classes of the early eighteenth century remained 'in some respects ostentatiously unBritish' (Colley, 1992: 165) as they were influenced both by their various Celtic and Continental European roots, dynastic relations, and cultural practices (especially from France and Italy), they consciously adopted a more patriotically British stance in order to consolidate their own social and political position. Hence:

> By the time of Waterloo, a generation of patrician Britons had grown up for whom Continental Europe was more a cockpit for battle, and a landscape of revolutionary subversion, than a fashionable playground and cultural shrine. Out of necessity, therefore, as well as for reasons of prudence and patriotic choice, members of the ruling order were encouraged to seek out new forms of cultural expression that were unquestionably British. (Colley, 1992: 167)

In this period Europe was not only perceived and portrayed as hostile to Britain's economic, political and military interests, but also as culturally different, in particular with regard to religion. As Colley writes: 'At odds in so much of their culture and secular history, the English, the Welsh and the Scots could be drawn together – and made to feel separate from the rest of Europe – by their common commitment to Protestantism' (Colley, 1992: 18). Although Colley's seminal interpretation of Europe as the Other has since been qualified by other historians (see Hilton, 2006; Neisen, 2004; Wilson, 2004), the essence of the argument still stands, since there is plenty of evidence that during the eighteenth and nineteenth centuries, Europe provided a kind of unity and cultural cohesion to an otherwise quite heterogeneous United Kingdom – a unity that supported the state structure and arguably even forged a British nation. Needless to say, the centrality of Protestantism to this 'imagined community' (Anderson, 1991) clearly excluded the best part of the Irish population. Catholic Ireland with its violent colonial history was never really accommodated in the British state and did evidently not form part of this British nation-building.

The 1970s accession debate: European integration as a centralising force

British attitudes towards Europe in the twentieth and twenty-first centuries have clearly been conditioned by the central role Europe played in the foundation of the British nation and state. By the mid-twentieth century the Othering of Europe had been even further amplified by two gory world wars started by continental forces. Thus, when the European integration process commenced in the immediate post-war period, Britain took up the role of a benevolent observer and sponsor (see Churchill, 1946) rather than that of an active partner. The common wartime experience had also further welded Britain's constituent nations closer together. As a consequence, post-war general elections exhibit high levels of territorial integration (Stolz, 2018: 168–9). Politics textbooks of the 1960s generally portray Britain (often still called England) as territorially homogeneous (see Blondel, 1963; Pulzer, 1967 and Bogdanor even in 1983). Blondel, for example, writes: 'Britain is essentially a homogeneous nation, in which distinctions are not based on geography, but on social and economic conditions' (Blondel, 1963: 26).

By the 1970s, though, the situation had changed. Britain's relative economic decline had turned into a full-blown economic crisis in conjunction with increasing social polarisation. This development gave rise to two inter-related processes: a rapprochement towards Europe and the ascent of sub-state nationalism. Both of these processes, European integration and British disintegration, directly challenged the unitary British state and its central constitutional doctrine of absolute sovereignty resting in the Westminster Parliament. In the public discourse that accompanied British accession to the EEC in 1973 and the build-up to the 1975 referendum, the two most unlikely bedfellows, British nationalism and sub-state nationalism in Britain, fell closely in line with each other in their opposition to European integration. A look at the parliamentary debates of that time shows anti-EEC advocates at Westminster mainly concerned with the 'loss of sovereignty', 'the bureaucratic rigidities' of the Common Market and its 'undemocratic form of administration' (HC Debate, 1971, 809, col. 1079–220). These concerns were shared by all three sub-state nationalist parties, the SNP in Scotland, Plaid Cymru in Wales and Sinn Féin in Northern Ireland, who campaigned vigorously and – in contrast to the major British parties – almost uniformly against British entry. They perceived the EEC as an additional layer of political decision-making on top of the British parliamentary system, even more remote than Westminster itself and thus as a further renunciation of Scottish, Welsh or Irish sovereignty. European integration, it was suspected, would make Scotland, Wales and Northern Ireland even more peripheral than they already were.

In a rhetoric not unlike that of former UKIP leader Nigel Farage, then-SNP leader Billy Wolfe claimed that the EEC would throw Scotland into 'a political dark age of remote control and undemocratic government' (*Scotsman*, 22 May 1975, quoted in Saunders, 2014). On a different occasion he even linked the EEC and its advocates with communism, perhaps the most damaging comparison possible in the days of the Cold War: 'The Common Marketeers of today are as much doctrinaire centralists as their opposite numbers in the Kremlin in Moscow' (Wolfe, 1973: 139). In a party brochure the SNP even claimed that 'Centralisation – Common Market style – could be a death blow to our very existence as a nation' (SNP, 1974: 12, quoted in Tarditi, 2010: 12). The SNP's rejection of the EEC was thus largely based on ideological opposition to European integration. However, the EEC referendum debate also provided an opportunity to score points in the domestic constitutional battle over Scotland's position in the United Kingdom – and this opportunity was eagerly seized. In the run-up to the EEC referendum, opinion polls suggested that the Scottish electorate could be on course to reject British accession (Hepburn, 2010: 72; Mitchell, 1996: 141). As the only party in Scotland with a clear anti-EEC stance, the SNP was thus in a position to champion anti-Common Market sentiments in Scotland and to project itself as the authentic voice of Scotland. This marked contrast between Scotland's supposedly anti-European attitude and the much more positive mood in England also seemed to offer an additional opportunity to capitalise on English-Scottish divergence. The SNP secretly hoped for a referendum result that would show that Scotland had been led into the European Community by the British government against its expressed will, simply on the basis of an English majority (Tarditi, 2010: 12–13). Such a result would have provided the party with additional ammunition in its quest for Scottish independence (just like the reverse situation did in 2017; see below).

In the event, the Scots – just like all the other constituent nations – voted in favour of EEC membership (58.4 per cent in favour), although with significantly lower levels of support than England (68.7 per cent) and Wales (64.8 per cent). While the referendum result can be seen as a defeat for Scottish and Welsh nationalists, the EEC accession debate as such clearly helped to establish them on the British political map. Nationalist pressure finally made the Labour government hold a referendum on devolution for Scotland and Wales in 1979. The referendum failed for a number of reasons, not least of all the unpopularity of the Labour government at that time. In the referendum campaign Europe and the EEC hardly featured at all, as it was still perceived as a rather centralist project that had nothing to do with the self-government aspirations of Britain's peripheral nations. The abortive devolution referendum of 1979, though, proved to be the last stage in the renegotiation of the British territorial order in which Europe and European integration did not play a significant discursive role.

The 1980s and the 1990s: the Europeanisation of the British constitutional debate

During the long reign of the Conservatives in Britain from 1979 to 1997, the image of the European Community and the expectations with regard to its influence on the structure of the British state changed fundamentally. This had to do with the nationalist, little-Englander sentiment of the Thatcher government in Britain and with the new dynamics in the European integration process in the run-up to the Maastricht Treaty (1992). As Keating and Jones once put it: 'Class, sectoral, partisan, and territorial oppositions have … moved from hostility to the Community to seeing it as a means of outflanking a centralizing, right-wing UK government' (Keating and Jones, 1995: 98–9). This was true for Labour and the British left as well as for intellectuals and reformers in England (e.g. Charter 88), but even more so for the broad self-government movements that emerged in Scotland and in Wales. For Scotland, Lindsay Paterson depicted the mood of the time as follows: 'The old Scottish preference for an assimilationist nationalism now seems to be focused on Europe. In the new Scottish culture of the 1980s and 1990s, to be European has been equated to being progressive and democratic, in almost the same way as being British was in the eighteenth and nineteenth centuries; and to be British has been tantamount to being anachronistic' (Paterson, 1994: 176). This new pro-European attitude heavily influenced the debate about the British state and its territorial order. It found its concrete expression, though, in two very different visions: the first looked at Europe as a decentralising force that would strengthen the position of Scotland, Wales and Northern Ireland inside the United Kingdom in the context of European attempts to establish a so-called 'Europe of the Regions'. The second accepted the European Community as a member state-based organisation, albeit as one that offers favourable conditions for small European states and thus as a potential home for Britain's peripheral nations after a break-away from the UK.

British decentralisation in a 'Europe of the Regions'

From the 1990s onwards, the 'Europe of the Regions' rhetoric took hold in Britain. Academics, often belonging to Scottish and Welsh autonomy movements, advocated the so-called sandwich hypothesis: the nation state squeezed between a regional and a supra-national (European) level. The establishment of a Committee of the Regions, the recognition of the subsidiarity principle and the expansion of European Regional Policy meant that Europeanisation was now seen as being inextricably linked to decentralisation in Britain. Paterson, Brown and McCrone, for example, argued that 'it is this European dimension, moreover, that continues to make Scottish self-government highly likely in the medium term: powers will probably continue to move from the old states, upwards to Brussels and, by reaction, also downwards. Eventually the UK will have to join this process, however reluctantly' (Paterson *et al.*, 1992: 638). While this functionalist argument somehow depends on an 'invisible hand' to produce the expected (and strongly desired) outcome, others detected 'a legitimate Community interest in the architecture of "internal" British governance' (Scott *et al.*, 1994: 62). The prospect of proactive European intervention into the British constitutional order is even more explicit in Christopher Harvie's account of that time, where he states: 'Scots increasingly see their future in a settlement in which European authority imposes a devolution of power' (Harvie, 1994: 219). And indeed, only a couple of years later, in 1999, Tony Blair's New Labour government finally established regional parliaments and assemblies in Scotland, Wales and Northern Ireland. This new devolution settlement in which Westminster handed down legislative competencies to regional representative bodies can be seen as 'the most radical constitutional change … since the Great Reform Act of 1832' (Bogdanor, 1999: 1).

Contrary to the stipulations quoted above, however, devolution in the UK can hardly be seen as a direct result of European integration and as a verification of the sandwich hypothesis. It was neither initiated nor actively supported by any European organisation or actor. Instead, it was first and foremost a British solution to a British problem. Its pragmatic and piecemeal development and its highly asymmetric structure (with different degrees of autonomy for the three peripheral nations and no representative body for England) was all but European, following a traditional British model of territorial order instead (see Stolz, 1999, 2000).

This is not to say that Europe did not play any role at all, though this European influence happened mainly on the discursive level. The 'Europe of the Regions' idea spilled over into the British political debate in the early 1990s and was taken up by regionalists and devolutionists, especially within the Labour Party and the Liberal Democrats, which by then had started working together on a new attempt to establish devolution in Scotland and Wales. The 'Europe of the Regions'-shibboleth was also quite popular in the Welsh nationalist party, Plaid Cymru, which aimed at 'full national status for Wales' in a Europe in which sovereign states were seen to be withering away (Elias, 2006). Contrary to the devolution debates in the run-up to the 1979 referendum, Europe thus provided a new framework, support and imagery to the self-government movements that gave their campaigns additional momentum. Now, the establishment of a regional tier of government could not only be portrayed as a potential answer to a domestic constitutional problem, but also as a modern, almost inevitable development in line with the general thrust of European politics.

Independence in Europe

Yet, Europe did not only feature in the campaign of devolutionists who wanted to reform the domestic territorial order of the UK. Rather, Europe affected the whole self-government movement including its separatist forces. In the late 1980s even the SNP, which had been so strongly opposed to the European Community in the 1970s, came to embrace European integration. At the party conference of 1988 it proclaimed its new slogan 'Independence in Europe'. Membership in the European Community has since been at the heart of its self-government vision for Scotland.

For the SNP, Keating and Jones' 'outflanking' of a hostile UK government (see above) had a very specific meaning. According to Isobel Lindsay, sociologist and SNP executive member at that time, Europe seemed to offer three different escape routes from the impediments of the domestic constitutional battle (Lindsay, 1991: 91). First, European institutions and even European states were (rather naively) seen as potential allies in getting international recognition in the event that Westminster would not accept an electoral majority as sufficient mandate for Scottish secession. Second, the increasing importance of the European dimension meant that Scotland and its self-government movement could escape its fixation with England as the central object of reference. Comparing Scotland to other small yet independent European countries such as Norway, Denmark and later Ireland was meant to increase Scottish aspirations and self-confidence. Finally, and perhaps most importantly, membership in the European Community allowed the Scottish nationalists to break out of the separatist corner. The European Community provided Scotland with the opportunity to leave the United Kingdom for an alternative, and supposedly more benevolent, 'external support system' (Keating, 2004: 369) and thus to dissociate fears of insecurity and isolation from the Independence trademark.

This policy change was also a clear and public reflection of the ideological modernisation of the SNP. Accepting that even as an independent state Scotland's capacity to pursue its own policy preferences would be restricted by global and European forces was a clear break with some of the more fundamentalist sections of the party who still held on to the vision of absolute sovereignty. It was a step towards what the Scottish sociologist David McCrone (1991) termed 'post-nationalism' at that time. Full membership for Scotland inside the European Union has since been consolidated as the central plank of SNP policy by two simultaneous processes: the further deepening (EU, monetary union etc.) and widening (enlargement) of European integration, and the frustrating experience of Scotland's newly established regional institutions in their attempts to influence the still member state-dominated EU structures. While its European enthusiasm has clearly cooled since the European debt crisis in 2009, the overall pro-European policy has never been seriously challenged.

The referendum years of 2014 and 2016

The close link between the domestic constitutional debate and the European question can finally be shown when looking at the 2014 Scottish independence referendum and the 2016 Brexit referendum. While the question of direct membership to the European Union played an important role in the first one, the apparent electoral divergence between the UK's constituent nations in the latter may well be seen as final indicator for an increasingly disunited kingdom.

The 2014 Scottish independence referendum

Devolution has fundamentally changed the Scottish political arena. Establishing institutions exclusively focused on Scotland clearly benefited Scottish nationalists. After two legislative periods in opposition, the SNP took over the Scottish government as minority administration in 2007. In government, the SNP immediately started to prepare to fulfil its major policy commitment: a referendum on Scottish independence. At the subsequent election in 2011 it won an overall majority and thus a mandate to hold the referendum. After negotiations with the UK government, the Scottish government won permission to hold the referendum before the end of 2014.

Very early in the referendum campaign, the question of Scotland's EU membership became a major bone of contention. The SNP had long argued that an independent Scotland would automatically remain part of the EU. In its White Paper in November 2013, the Scottish government altered this position. It now envisaged accession via an 'internal enlargement' process on the basis of Article 48 of the European Treaties which, according to the Scottish government, would have provided 'a suitable legal route to facilitate the transition process, by allowing the EU Treaties to be amended through ordinary revision procedure before Scotland becomes independent, to enable it to become a member state at the point of independence' (Scottish Government, 2013: 241). Even more explicitly it stated: 'There is no Treaty provision that would require Scotland to leave the EU on independence' (Scottish Government, 2013: 457). This position was roundly rejected by the UK government. Instead, Prime Minister David Cameron stated that Scotland would have to queue up behind Serbia, Montenegro and others before it could be admitted to the EU (McTague and Groves, 2014) – a position that was also supported by EU officials. In his contentious intervention, EU Commission President Barroso claimed that secession would place Scotland automatically outside the EU and Scottish EU membership would thus have to come via Article 49, the normal route to accession. According to him, this would make it 'extremely difficult, if not impossible' for Scotland to secure EU membership at all (BBC, 2014). As all member states would have a veto on the decision, the main obstacle was often seen in the potentially dismissive attitude of the Spanish government, which has its own problems with separatist movements.

Despite major disagreement among experts, unionist activists from the major British parties, the Conservatives, Labour and the Liberal Democrats, and the official 'Better Together' campaign organisation utilised this perspective, advising the pro-European Scottish public that only a vote to remain inside the UK would keep Scotland inside the EU. Doubts about the post-secession status of Scotland vis-à-vis the European Union allowed them to scare off independence-leaning voters with prospects of 'a literal and figurative border' (Home Secretary Theresa May, quoted in Riley-Smith, 2014) between England and Scotland and possible mass immigration to Scotland (Berbéri, 2016). On 18 September 2014 the Scottish voters opted 45 to 55 per cent to remain inside the United Kingdom. It is difficult to evaluate the exact impact of the EU question on this result. Polls before the referendum suggest, though, that it could have skewed the final outcome by a few percentage points, as the lack of clarity with regard to EU membership was one issue that may have prevented Scots from voting for Scottish independence.

The 2016 Brexit referendum

In the last days of the Scottish independence referendum, increasingly close poll results had led Prime Minister Cameron and the leaders of the two other unionist parties to offer the Scots a completely new deal should they vote to stay inside the United Kingdom (*Daily Record*, 2014). The first test case for this famous 'Vow' came when the Conservative UK government announced to hold a referendum on British withdrawal from the European Union. Anticipating Scottish divergence from the English position (and thus most probably from that of the UK), Scotland's First Minister, SNP leader Nicola Sturgeon, demanded a veto for all constituent nations to a possible exit from the EU. At that time Prime Minister Cameron, though, made it quite clear that despite all promises about the future accommodation of Scotland, the United Kingdom remained a unitary state and that this decision would thus be taken by a majority of UK citizens, no matter what the result in each of the constituent nations would be. To make matters worse, during the Brexit referendum campaign many of those who had advised Scotland to vote to stay in the UK in order to remain part of the European Union in 2014 now openly campaigned for the UK – including Scotland – to leave the EU. Thus, in Scotland, the Brexit referendum campaign felt like a betrayal from the very start.

The uneven distribution of votes at the referendum itself further confirmed the divisive force of the European question for the domestic constitutional debate in Britain. The most dramatic repercussions in this respect have been experienced and still are to be expected in Northern Ireland and Scotland. In Northern Ireland, Brexit is a fundamental challenge to the Good Friday Agreement (GFA), especially to its North–South provisions. A 'hard Brexit', i.e. withdrawal not only from the EU but also from its Common Market and its Customs Union, is commonly seen as incompatible with the open border policy that is enshrined in the GFA. The potential erection of a hard border (physical infrastructure and customs control) between Ireland and Northern Ireland, though, would not only be contrary to an international treaty, it would also reopen the constitutional question in Northern Ireland and would quite possibly endanger the still fragile peace process. Amazingly, the Northern-Irish dimension had hardly been considered during the referendum campaign.

Predictably, this changed dramatically when the Brexit negotiations began, as both the EU and the Irish government demanded a solution to this problem from the UK government. The most obvious solution would have been to grant exceptional status to Northern Ireland entailing continued regulatory alignment with the Republic of Ireland. Such an arrangement, however, was made impossible by the staunch opposition of the DUP, the major party of Protestant unionism in Northern Ireland, threatening to terminate their vital parliamentary support for the minority Conservative government. Their fear was that any special status for Northern Ireland would effectively move the hard border to the Irish Sea and would thus constitute a first step to Irish reunification. The Withdrawal Agreement finally endorsed by Theresa May and the EU, though, stipulated a different mechanism: during a transition period, the UK would remain both in the Customs Union and in the European Single Market. After that period a backstop arrangement would commit the whole of the UK (including Northern Ireland) to enter a 'single customs territory' with the EU and Northern Ireland to remain aligned to selected regulations of the European Single Market until other solutions to avoid a hard border are found. As this backstop arrangement cannot be revoked unilaterally, it could mean that the Northern Ireland border problem would effectively tie the whole of the UK to a 'soft Brexit', while still stipulating regulatory differences between Northern Ireland and Great Britain. For many, this is the worst of all worlds, and cross-party opposition ensured the repeated rejection of this 'deal' in parliament.

In Scotland, the British Brexit decision against the expressed will of a majority in Scotland has revived the constitutional debate in a number of ways. Immediately after the referendum the Scottish government floated ideas about possible Brexit exemptions for Scotland. In an inverse Denmark/Greenland scenario (Greenland is part of Denmark yet not part of the EU) it was argued that Scotland could remain part of the EU (and the UK) even after Britain left it. The least the UK government could do to reflect the pro-European position in Scotland, the Scottish government argued, was to negotiate the preservation of direct access to the Common Market for Scotland. The UK government, though, rejected any special status for Scotland on the grounds that this would be legally impossible or at least too complicated in its implementation. In contrast to its plans for Northern Ireland, the UK government also made it clear that it was not prepared to compromise the unity of its Brexit approach in Scotland. Hence, the issue was finally dead before negotiations with the EU even started.

A second field of Scottish–UK conflict has unfolded with the pending repatriation of legislative competencies from the EU to the UK. As many of the policy fields currently regulated by the EU (such as agriculture, fisheries etc.) are devolved to the legislative bodies in Scotland, Wales and Northern Ireland by British domestic law, the devolved governments demanded that, after Brexit, they should return to this level. The UK government, though, wants to replace the European Single Market with a new British Single Market, necessitating repatriation to Westminster rather than to the devolved legislatures. The subsequent legal battle between Westminster and the Scottish Parliament, as both had legislated in their own favour, finally had to be settled by the Supreme Court. Unsurprisingly, the court ruled any modification of the UK Withdrawal Act by the Scottish Bill invalid. The ruling made it clear that despite an existing convention to the contrary (the so-called Sewel convention), the UK Parliament may not only legislate on devolved matters, but it may even do so against the expressed will of devolved parliaments. Highlighting the subordination of the devolved parliaments to the sovereign parliament in Westminster, this ruling exposed the British devolution settlement again as essentially unitary in character and, thus, further undermines the idea of the United Kingdom as a union of equal partners.

By far the most dramatic potential consequence of the Brexit decision for the United Kingdom, though, would be a second Scottish independence referendum. As stated above, the Scottish government has already stated that it considers Brexit to constitute 'a significant and material change in the circumstances in which Scotland voted against independence in 2014' and thus to constitute a clear mandate to hold another referendum (Sturgeon, 2016). The Scottish Parliament's request for legislative permission to hold such a referendum, though, was rejected by Prime Minister May until the end of the Brexit negotiations ('now is not the time'). Due to its considerable losses at the 2017 general election, the SNP was persuaded to put the project on hold. However, there should be no doubt that any Brexit deal short of remaining inside the European Single Market will again push the issue to the fore. Being taken out of the EU and its common market by an English majority against the expressed will of its own population and against promises made during the independence referendum will add significantly to Scottish political grievances with and in this United Kingdom. On the other hand, a 'hard Brexit' would arguably further weaken the economic argument for an independent Scotland, as Scottish secession would now (in contrast to the situation in 2014) entail a hard border between Scotland and England. In any case, the prospect of another independence referendum clearly confirms the old assumption that 'Europe might still become the trigger of Scotland's constitutional future' (Stolz, 2000: 69), if not for the break-up of the United Kingdom.

Conclusion

Brexit has underlined once more what has become increasingly clear over the last decades: the European political order and the internal political order of the United Kingdom (and that of any other European state) are inextricably linked. As shown, during the nineteenth century common opposition to Europe strengthened centripetal tendencies within the UK. The increasing rapprochement with Europe during the second half of the twentieth century, by contrast, helped to unleash its centrifugal forces. The Brexit referendum of June 2016 can finally be seen to fulfil a double role: on the one hand, it serves as an indicator for an ongoing process of domestic disintegration, manifested in the diverging attitudes of the UK's constituent nations towards Europe. On the other hand, Britain's withdrawal from the EU may in turn also prove to become a major catalyst in this process – a process that might finally result in the break-up of the United Kingdom.

Europe may thus come to play an important role both in forging the British nation and in its final deconstruction/dismantling. In contrast to some of the notions presented above, though, Europe does not have a uniform or unidirectional effect on Britain's domestic development. Instead, Europe's effect is highly contingent upon the state and the development of the European integration process itself, the specific British context of the time and the way concrete actors make use of Europe in domestic discourse. The European Union has become a major additional framework in which the territorial politics of its member states are played out. These institutions and the European integration process have produced, and will produce, windows of opportunity for actors to introduce, advocate or reject particular constitutional notions and models. In Britain, the EU has provided arguments for devolutionists, separatists and die-hard unionists alike. The same actors have used Europe in different ways at different times. Scottish separatists, for example, have come full circle from an outright rejection of European centralism to making membership in the EU their primary goal.

The current process of dismantling Britain's EU membership is a time of major constitutional upheaval. Disentangling the various British–EU relationships provides ample opportunity for those who want to break up an already highly fragile United Kingdom. However, whether the UK will survive and in what form it may survive will not be determined by any European automatism at work, even though the relationship to the Continent can never be disregarded. Ultimately, the territorial integrity of the United Kingdom depends, as it has always depended, on the capacity of unionist forces to adapt their territorial politics creatively in order to provide the UK's constituent nations with a new and attractive balance of autonomy and participation. On this question, though, the jury is still out.

References

Anderson, Benedict (1991), *Imagined Communities: Reflections on the Origins and Spread of Nationalism* (London: Verso).

BBC (2014), '"Extremely difficult" for Scotland to join EU – Barroso', *Andrew Marr Show*, 16 February. www.bbc.com/news/av/uk-politics-26215579/extremely-difficult-for-scotland-to-join-eu-barroso (last accessed 8 December 2017).

Berbéri, Carine (2016), 'The impact of Scotland's prospective membership of the EU on the 2014 referendum debate: concerns over borders', *Études écossaises* 18, pp. 11–28.

Blondel, Jean (1963), *Voters, Parties and Leaders* (London: Penguin).

Bogdanor, Vernon (1983), *Multi-Party Politics and the Constitutions* (Cambridge: Cambridge University Press).

(1999), *Devolution in the United Kingdom* (Oxford: Oxford University Press).

Churchill, Winston (1946), 'Speech delivered at the University of Zurich', 19 September. https://rm.coe.int/16806981f3 (last accessed 5 December 2017).

Colley, Linda (1992), *Britons: Forging the Nation 1707–1837* (New Haven and London: Yale University Press).

Daily Record (2014), *The Vow*, 16 September.

Elias, Anwen (2006), 'Europeanising the Nation: Minority Nationalist Party Responses to European Integration in Wales, Galicia and Corsica', unpublished PhD thesis (Florence: European University Institute).

HC Debate (1971), 809, cc 1079–220.

Harvie, Christopher (1994), *Scotland and Nationalism: Scottish Society and Politics 1707–1994* (London and New York: Routledge).

Hepburn, Eve (2010), *Using Europe: Territorial Party Strategies in a Multi-Level System* (Manchester: Manchester University Press).

Hilton, Boyd (2006), *A Mad, Bad and Dangerous People? England 1783–1846* (Oxford: Oxford University Press).

Keating, Michael (2004), 'European integration and the nationalities question', *Politics and Society* 32:3, pp. 367–88.

Keating, Michael and Barry Jones (1995), 'Nations, Regions and Europe: The UK Experience' in Barry Jones and Michael Keating (eds), *The European Union and the Regions* (Oxford: Oxford University Press), pp. 65–114.

Lindsay, Isobel (1991), 'The SNP and the Lure of Europe' in Tom Gallagher (ed.), *Nationalism in the Nineties* (Edinburgh: Polygon), pp. 84–101.

McCrone, David (1991), 'Post-nationalism and the decline of the nation-state', *Radical Scotland* 49, pp. 6–8.

McTague, Tom and Jason Groves (2014), 'Leave Britain and you join the back of the EU queue but stay and get FULL control of your taxes, Cameron tells Scotland', *Mail online*, 2 June. www.dailymail.co.uk/news/article-2646334/Leave-Britain-join-EU-queue-stay-FULL-control-taxes-Cameron-tells-Scotland.html#ixzz50wbe0Ty4 (last accessed 11 December 2017).

Mitchell, James (1996), *Strategies for Self-Government: The Campaign for a Scottish Parliament* (Edinburgh: Polygon).

—— (2014), *The Scottish Question* (Oxford: Oxford University Press).

Neisen, Robert (2004), *Feindbild, Vorbild, Wunschbild: Eine Untersuchung zum Verhältnis von britischer Identität und französischer Alterität 1814–1860* (Würzburg: Ergon Verlag).

Paterson, Lindsay (1994), *The Autonomy of Modern Scotland* (Edinburgh: Edinburgh University Press).

Paterson, Lindsay, Alice Brown and David McCrone (1992), 'Constitutional crisis: the causes and consequences of the 1992 Scottish general election result', *Parliamentary Affairs* 45, pp. 627–39.

Pulzer, Peter (1967), *Political Representation and Elections in Britain* (London: Allen & Unwin).

Riley-Smith, Ben (2014), 'Britons "would need passport to visit an independent Scotland"', *Daily Telegraph*, 14 March. www.telegraph.co.uk/news/uknews/scottish-independence/10699069/Britons-would-need-passport-to-visit-an-independent-Scotland.html (last accessed 11 December 2017).

Saunders, Robert (2014), '"An auction of fear": the Scotland in Europe referendum, 1975', *Renewal: A Journal of Labour Politics* 22:1/2, pp. 87–95.

Scott, Drew, John Peterson and David Millar (1994), 'Subsidiarity: a "Europe of the Regions" v. the British constitution', *Journal of Commons Market Studies* 31, pp. 47–67.

Scottish Government (2013), *Scotland's Future: Your Guide to an Independent Scotland* (Edinburgh: The Scottish Government).

Seldon, Anthony (2016), 'A disunited Kingdom ... why Brexit-Britain is as divided as Europe in 1914', *Telegraph*, 26 June.

Stolz, Klaus (1999), 'Labour and British Territorial Politics: (Lots of) Continuity and (Maybe Some) Change' in Hans Kastendiek, Richard Stinshoff and Roland Sturm (eds), *The Return of Labour: A Turning Point in British Politics* (Berlin and Bodenheim: Philo), pp. 221–36.

—— (2000), 'The European myth in Scotland and the Scottish model in Europe', *Journal for the Study of British Cultures* 7:1, pp. 61–73.

—— (2018), 'The 2015 General Election: The End of Britain?' in Klaus Detterbeck and Klaus Stolz (eds), *The End of Duopoly: The Transformation of the British Party System* (Augsburg: Wißner Verlag), pp. 162–79.

Sturgeon, Nicola (2016), 'Statement on Brexit-Referendum at Bute House', BBC, 26 June. www.bbc.com/news/uk-scotland-36620375 (last accessed 4 December 2017).

Tarditi, Valeria (2010), 'The Scottish National Party's changing attitude towards the European Union', Sussex European Institute Working Paper No. 112.

Wilson, Kathleen (2004), *Culture, Identity and Modernity in Britain and the Empire, 1660–1840* (Cambridge: Cambridge University Press).

Wolfe, Billy (1973), *Scotland Lives: The Quest for Independence* (Edinburgh: Reprographia).

Part II

British discourses of Europe in literature and film

5

'Extr'ord'nary people, the Germans': Germans as aliens in post-war British popular culture

Judith Vonberg

In May 1955, West Germany was incorporated into NATO, an event welcomed and in part instigated by the British government under Winston Churchill. Exactly a decade after the end of the Second World War, Germany was joining Britain as part of an international alliance that stood against the Soviet bloc. At the same time, countless post-war fictions continued to peddle a narrative of tyrannical, violent Germanness.[1] As Sonya Rose argues, war is a time for demarcating the national self from others, for asking what makes 'us' different from 'them' (Rose, 2003: 72). But with regard to the perception of Germans in Britain, the demarcation lines drawn in the early 1940s lingered on into the 1950s and beyond. In this chapter, I will argue that by continuing to locate Germanness as the alien 'Other' to Britishness in the post-war period, Britons could counter what Tony Judt calls 'the loss of national direction' (Judt, 2010: 301) and bolster a sense of British unity.

Many post-war British novels, films and comic strips depicted Germans as alien to all humanity – often literal embodiments of the 'inhumanity' revealed with the discovery of the concentration camps in April 1945. But a second group of texts posited Germanness as the direct and specific opposite to Britishness. Implicit in this construct was a much older understanding of 'alien' as a person of foreign origin, an understanding that accrued fewer neutral associations towards the end of the nineteenth century as the concept of the 'alien friend' was eroded and 'alien' came to signify difference and threat. Previously welcomed, aliens were now often objects of hostility and suspicion, subject to the 1905 Aliens Act and to the whims of the newly created immigration department (Dummett and Nicol, 1990: 102–4). As Dummett and Nicol argue, it was fictional accounts of German invasion, rooted in contemporary paranoia, that fed that paranoia and generated popular support for the Aliens Restriction

Act of 1914, passed again in 1919 'on a wave of anti-German hatred' and not repealed until 1971 (109). What Petra Rau calls 'the anxious notion of the foreign' (Rau, 2009: 43), which pervaded Britain in the pre-First World War period, developed at a time when the foreigners believed to represent the greatest cause for anxiety were Germans. Although concern regarding aliens in the post-1945 period was largely focused on non-white immigration, developments in the earlier part of the century had forged a link between Germanness and alien threat, which, combined with the renewed threat of invasion experienced during the recent conflict, the insistence during that conflict on German alterity and the perceived need to shore up British identity, led to the resurfacing of the trope. In this chapter, I will use close readings of two post-war films – *Sink the Bismarck!* (1960) and *The One That Got Away* (1957) – to explore both the trope and its ambiguities in the post-war setting.

Visions of chaos and unity

'We live at opposite poles. We have not a main idea in common.'

The 1950s was a period of overall decline and fragmentation for Britain, with economic growth lagging behind that of other European countries, most notably West Germany, and burgeoning class, racial and generational conflicts. Despite the hopes that accompanied Labour's welfare reforms and what Jim Tomlinson calls the 'vista of rising prosperity' (Tomlinson, 2003: 63), epitomised in Prime Minister Harold Macmillan's famous declaration in 1957 that 'most of our people have never had it so good', Britain's relative economic and real political decline was soon obvious to many. More intangible fears regarding the fractures within British society were growing too. As Kathleen Burk puts it, 'the national identity was, as historians began to say, contested' (Burk, 2003: 12).

Divisions within British society had troubled many public figures during the recent war too. As Rose argues, wartime Britain was a nation with 'deep class divisions' populated by people with 'heterogeneous pastimes' (Rose, 2003: 4). Churchill's speeches did not give voice to an existing unity, but were instead 'ruthless in their search' for it (Colls, 2002: 126). The 'othering' of the German nation had long been used as a means of stabilising a sense of British identity and was used by figures as politically diverse as Lord Vansittart and J.B. Priestley in the years preceding and during the Second World War with the same aim. 'We live at opposite poles', wrote Vansittart of Britons and Germans, 'We have not a main idea in common' (Vansittart, 1941: 26). One recurring element of this opposition was the 'German' suppression (and the corresponding 'British' celebration) of diversity, individuality and individual freedom. In a scathing attack on Hitler's Germany written in 1935, Leonard Woolf disparaged the absolutist German state, which demands unity, obedience and loyalty from its citizens, who are conceived of not as individuals but only 'in their relation to the state' (Woolf, 1935: 76). Images and reports from 1930s Germany seemed to corroborate this link. Recalling a parade of German storm troopers in Berlin in January 1933, a *Daily Express* journalist noted that they seemed to be 'lacking the uniformity and discipline of real troops' ('Hitler declares against war for Germany', 1933). Uniforms varied or were non-existent and their marching was 'poor'. By September, their uniforms 'were spotless and brand new', their goose-stepping 'strong and rhythmic' and their responses to the cheering crowds always 'in chorus' and 'always the same' ('Hitler declares against war for Germany', 1933). Propaganda films of rallies and parades – thousands of Germans raising their arm in the Hitler salute – made their way into British newsreels of the period, reinforcing this image of uniformity. Outward signs of heterogeneity and individuality had been purged in a visual display of inward homogeneity of belief and character.

The image of German uniformity was particularly useful in turning the undeniable and potentially problematic heterogeneity of Britain into a strength. A homogenous society is a Germanic society, so the thinking went, therefore its opposite should be celebrated. It is difficult to perceive 'that the whole nation has a single identifiable character', wrote George Orwell in a 1940 essay in which he explicitly conflates Britain and England. 'Are we not 46 million individuals, all different?' he asks. 'And the diversity of it, the chaos!' (Orwell, 1953: 193). In a 1941 pamphlet, J.B. Priestley took an even more celebratory tone, praising 'the people', a word that for him conjured up 'a confused but lively vision of a hundred faces and a hundred voices', and disparaging 'the masses', which he described as 'bundles of instincts and appetites' and 'units of man-power' (Priestley, 1941: 18). For the Nazis, too, 'the people' ('das Volk') were desirable and 'the masses' ('die Massen') undesirable. Yet the Nazi understanding of the terms was the exact inverse of Priestley's. While Priestley (and Orwell) celebrated the disordered, multifarious nature of 'the people', the Nazis decried this same quality in the 'Masse', understood as chaotic, uncontrolled and potentially rebellious. The 'Volk', equivalent to Priestley's description of the mass as 'units of man-power', was perceived as the desirable result of the imposition of a structure of domination on the mass, which becomes the ordered and oppressed subject of the oppressor (Theweleit, 1978: 102–14).

From this perspective, diversity and 'chaos!' could, paradoxically, become the means of unifying Britain against the rigid, inflexible enemy. As Gill Plain explores in her survey of the decade's literature, 'unity forged out of diversity' quickly became the central theme of many fictional stories depicting British military triumphs (Plain, 2013: 115). These 'group hero narratives', such as W.E. Johns' *Spitfire Parade* (1941) featuring the ace pilot and adventurer Biggles and his 'Gimlet' series of novels (1943–54), revolved around a heterogeneous group of British characters who worked together, while maintaining their individuality, to defeat the Germans (Plain, 2013: 115–16). Post-war fictions such as *Sink the Bismarck!* – explored in detail next – drew on similar tropes of Britishness and Germanness for the same purpose: to turn the growing, and potentially threatening, diversity of Britain into the means by which it could be united.

A war of national characters? Sink the Bismarck!

Lewis Gilbert's 1960 film *Sink the Bismarck!* epitomises the post-war trend described above. The frequent cuts inviting comparison between diverse British and clichéd German characters, the incorporation of documentary footage, the black-and-white film and the truth-based narrative are elements repeated in numerous films of the period, all of which establish images of Britishness and Germanness congruent with the dominant wartime tropes. Significantly, in all of these films, the German characters are established as primarily German rather than Nazi, inviting the post-war audience to read the representation of Britain's erstwhile enemy as relevant to a post-war understanding of the German nation. In *Bismarck*, this is achieved by the Germans' own rhetoric. In a speech to his crew, Admiral Lütjens declares, 'We are faster, we are unsinkable and we are German!' and, 'never forget that you are Germans, never forget that you are Nazis'. His words instil a pride and self-belief that are rooted firstly in national identity (Germanness), and only secondly in ideology (Nazism). A close reading of this film will reveal how the portrayal of British unity through diversity is countered and strengthened by the depiction of German disunity disguised by uniformity.

    Sink the Bismarck! tells a partly fictionalised story of the sinking of the German battleship *Bismarck* by the Royal Navy in 1941. Derided by critics, one of whom described it as an 'incredibly old-fashioned film; almost as though one were watching a 1940 piece of flag-waving instead of a 1960 piece of drama' (P.G.B., 1960), it was nevertheless the second highest box-office earner in Britain that year and was also financially successful in North America (Billings, 1960). Fictional character Captain

5.1   Documentary footage of the launch of the battleship *Bismarck* in Hamburg, 1939 from *Sink the Bismarck!* (1960), dir. Lewis Gilbert.

Jonathan Shepherd (Kenneth More) is assigned to co-ordinate the attempt to hunt down and destroy the ship. Much of the action takes place in the Admiralty War Room, with regular cuts to scenes on the *Bismarck* and on the British ships involved in the mission. The crew of the *Bismarck* is headed by Admiral Lütjens (Karel Štěpánek) and Captain Lindemann (Carl Möhner), the film's central German characters.

The two opening scenes establish the contrast between the British and German characters and establishments. The film opens with real documentary footage of the launch of the battleship *Bismarck* in Hamburg, 1939 (see figure 5.1). Tens of thousands of German citizens raise their arms in a Nazi salute to Hitler. High-angle shots dwarf and dehumanise the massed crowds (depicted as 'units of man-power'), already dwarfed by the vast ship, while only Hitler and his entourage are granted close-ups. This short documentary scene both binds the subsequent narrative and the depictions of Germans therein closer to fact and provides an image of national homogeneity that contrasts starkly with the visual display of Britishness encompassing heterogeneity and individuality that follows immediately afterwards.

In this second scene, which takes place behind the credits, the camera follows Captain Shepherd as he walks to work through Trafalgar Square, his coat hung casually over his arm. More was a very popular actor with British audiences in the 1950s, his role in *Doctor in the House* (1954) described by Christine Geraghty as 'resolutely British' (Geraghty, 2000: 93), a phrase that could equally be applied to his portrayal of Richard Hannay in the 1959 adaptation of John Buchan's *The 39 Steps*. This 'Britishness' is characterised by a cheerful, breezy attitude and modest self-confidence. His prominent position on the billing for *Sink the Bismarck!* would therefore arouse certain expectations for his role. This expectation, combined with the juxtaposition of the first two scenes, establishes Shepherd's first appearance as a display of British – as opposed to German – identity. As he walks through the square, his manner is self-possessed but relaxed, authoritative but not authoritarian. He passes other Londoners, some in military and others in civilian clothing, each differentiated by their appearance, stance and gait in their brief moment on screen. Their paths criss-cross as each figure or pair of figures chooses their own route across the square. After an initial bird's eye view, eye-level shots dominate the sequence, allowing each figure – female or male, civilian or military – to be perceived as an individual and symbolising the equal worth of each.

The first scene inside the Admiralty War Room confirms all of these initial impressions. As Shepherd sees one man without his regulation jumper, another eating a sandwich on duty and a third addressing a female officer by her first name, he is told by the outgoing chief of operations, 'We're quite informal here about some things'. This is the manifestation of what Jeremy Paxman, in an entertaining and rigorously researched study of 'the English', calls the 'society of individuals', a key facet of English/ British identity in his analysis (Paxman, 1999: 139). There is room for flexibility, informality and individuality and the challenge of superiors is permitted, even welcomed. Shepherd, however, is displeased and demands that rules are strictly adhered to without exception. His attitude changes by the end of the film, however, in an affirmation, as will shortly be explored, of the desirability of 'British' flexibility and heterogeneity as opposed to 'Germanic' rigidity and uniformity.

The first scene set on the *Bismarck* establishes the grounds for the contrast between the nationalities that were implied in the film's opening. In a visual motif borrowed from the crime genre, Lütjens is first seen sitting in a chair with his back to the camera casting a dark shadow on the wall next to him (see figure 5.2). His posture is rigid and he faces away from his interlocutor, responding to him in a formal monotone. Turning to the camera, he reveals a smug, hard face, pleased at an opportunity lent by the poor weather conditions to outwit the British. Just as More was expected to portray admirable Britishness, Štěpánek, a Czech actor who fled to Britain from Austria in 1940, was known for playing Teutonic villains in films such as *Escape to Danger* (1943), *The Captive Heart* (1946) and *The Cockleshell Heroes* (1955). This scene both alludes to and re-affirms this extradiegetic association, as well as immediately confining the character within a cliché that allows for no individuality or malleability in a further reinforcement of the notion that Germanness meant the eradication of the individual. We are fed a series of visual and aural cues that declare Lütjens

5.2   In a visual motif borrowed from the crime genre, Lütjens is first seen sitting in a chair with his back to the camera casting a dark shadow on the wall next to him. From *Sink the Bismarck!* (1960), dir. Lewis Gilbert.

to be a typical German villain who will only affirm existing assumptions about the brutality, coldness and, significantly, uniformity of the German national character.

The following conversation with Captain Lindemann, who is deferential and flatters his superior, is also revealing. Unlike the cinematic portrayal of the British establishment, where rank is preserved but respect given equally and meaningful interaction encouraged, the German military hierarchy is depicted dividing and isolating individuals. But this is not the self-determining individualism in which the British took pride. Instead, Lütjens is rigidly defined by his rank, inhabiting a cabin full of cigars, crystal goblets, ornamental wood panelling, gilt-framed portraits and gleaming trophies, symbols of luxury that communicate Lütjens' role, not his individual personality, which we never glimpse. He does not resent this enforced existence, but relishes the individual glory he could achieve. There can be 'glory for us' in this voyage, he tells Lindemann, who responds ingratiatingly, 'For you, sir. You are the Fleet Commander'. Lütjens is visibly pleased with this response. Later, he is portrayed making individual decisions for personal gain, a trait that is echoed further down the ranks when the *Bismarck* is on the verge of sinking in the film's final scenes. Having heard about a dangerous fire in the forward magazines of the ship, the officer in charge gives the order to flood the magazines, an action that he knows will cause the death of many men. In contrast to Shepherd's decision to make a British troop convoy vulnerable to attack, depicted as an agonising choice in which ethical considerations are paramount, this order is given in aggressive tones and without any regard for the human lives that will be lost. The scene cuts to the men below as they struggle to escape. An earlier shot of the crisply uniformed, visually homogeneous crew ('units of man-power') lining up to hear Lütjens' rousing speech is exposed as a chimera. Now we see men clambering over each other, those higher up the ladder pulled back down by those below – a visual manifestation of what Priestley described as 'bundles of instincts and appetites'. Unable or unwilling to work as a team – 'a society of individuals' – to ensure the survival of some, they are instead depicted as a group of disparate persons driven by an instinctive and personal urge for survival. The individualism displayed by them and their superiors is not the kind celebrated by Orwell and Priestley, but an indication of deep-seated disunity. In contrast, frequent cuts between the Admiralty War Room and various characters – military and civilian, young and old – with diverse personalities on British ships counter the depiction of German selfishness with one of British teamwork and unity. This is certainly not a nation that has 'a single identifiable character', the film asserts, but it is in this diversity – rather than in German uniformity – that true unity is to be found.

Yet, as I mentioned earlier, the film is not merely a static portrayal of two divergent and stereotyped national identities. We witness the British protagonist pulled between two character types and confronting a choice between – as this film posits it – Germanic and British traits. The more disciplined, formal regime – to be read as anti-British and Germanic – that Shepherd introduces in the Admiralty Operations Room threatens the emotional and professional solidarity that exists in the informal atmosphere as he finds it. Furthermore, Shepherd's strict professionalism and emotional distance from his colleagues echo the same (but far more extreme) tendencies in Lütjens. His behaviour is portrayed as a threat to the meaningful interaction between ranks depicted in this and other postwar naval films, interaction that indicates the unity that exists between disparate British individuals but that is absent from the German ranks. Unlike Lütjens, however, he is not devoid of empathy and is portrayed feeling deep and ordinary human emotions that he chooses to disguise. These are implied in brief, silent signals – a heavy sigh or a hand passed over the face. His mildly 'Germanic' traits remain just that and are soon revealed as the result of the unhealthy suppression of grief after the death of his wife in an air raid. A return to a more emotionally open, informal relationship with his colleagues is depicted both as a return to Britishness and a return to emotional health.

While the British characters in *Bismarck* show diversity, development and depth, qualities celebrated as key to Britain's wartime victory, the German characters are depicted either as stereotypes or en masse. For despite the film's opening documentary segment, *Bismarck* is not a realistic account of a real wartime event: the German characters are clichés and the informality among the British ranks is far-fetched. Rather it replays a wartime narrative – invoking idealised images of diverse but unified Britons and demonised images of seemingly homogeneous but disunified Germans – in an attempt to stabilise post-war British identity.

The (only) *One That Got Away*: Britain's ambivalent response to Hardy Krüger

Alien or akin? Ambiguity in the British view of the Germans

'Put yourself, if you can, in the average German's place', Victor Gollancz urged his readers in a 1945 pamphlet, *What Buchenwald Really Means* (Gollancz, 1945: 9). You hear rumours about the camps, but you know that if you start to probe, you will be signing your own death warrant and that of your family, he argued. '*Will* you do this?' For Gollancz, an ardent socialist, Britons and Germans were linked not only by their shared habitation of the planet – 'we are all brothers and sisters' – but by a particular bond (Gollancz, 1945: 10). 'If there is something wrong with German "blood" there is something wrong with English "blood"', he declared, 'for the two are, in large measure, one and the same' (Gollancz, 1945: 12).

For many Britons in 1945, the last thing they wanted to do was to put themselves 'in the average German's place' or to acknowledge any form of kinship with that nation. Yet there were films including the 1957 box-office hit *The One That Got Away* that demanded that very identification from their audience. The close reading that follows will show how empathetic depictions of Germans who were akin rather than alien to Britons embodied ambivalence and aroused an equally ambivalent response among Britons wary of suggestions of Anglo-German kinship.

Franz von Werra: an 'exceptional German'?

'What a story! Everyone wants it! *John Bull* secures first world serial rights! Film and radio rights sold before publication!' declared a full-page advert in the *Daily Express* on 2 October 1956. The story in question was *The One That Got Away*, a book by Kendal Burt and James Leasor. 'UNUSUAL ... AUDACIOUS ... ENTHRALLING' was how the *Express* described it, 'The War's Most Incredible Escape Story' (1956). The book tells the story of Franz von Werra, one of only two members of the German armed forces who successfully escaped back to Germany during the Second World War having been held as a POW by the British. Shot down over England in

1940, he was interrogated before being sent to a POW camp in the Lake District. An ingenious escape plan succeeded and he was hunted for five days before being captured and sent to a different camp. He immediately began digging a tunnel and escaped with four other men. Pretending to be a crashed Dutch pilot, part of a secret 'Special Bomber Squadron', he bluffed his way to an RAF base and into the cockpit of a Hurricane. He was caught once more and sent to Canada where he escaped through a train window and trekked through blizzards and across a frozen lake to reach the United States, a neutral country. He eventually returned to Germany and wrote, somewhat fancifully, about his escapades. Leasor and Burt's book was based partly on von Werra's account and partly on other documentation and witness accounts. Both the BBC radio adaptation that followed in November 1956 and the 1957 film, directed by Roy Ward Baker, were based closely on the book, serialised in late 1956 in *John Bull*. My analysis will focus on the film, as this was the version that aroused the most critical interest, both at the time and in subsequent scholarship, not least because of leading actor Hardy Krüger and his tempestuous relationship with the British press and public.

Krüger's brief British career, beginning with *The One That Got Away*, was superbly analysed in a 2006 article by Melanie Williams. She argues that Krüger's astonishing transformation from *persona non grata* to national heartthrob and unofficial ambassador can be attributed to a concurrence of factors, including improving Anglo-German political relations and Krüger's charisma and good looks (Williams, 2006: 85–107). Yet the transition was complex and controversial, and was mirrored in conflicting responses to *The One*. As Williams notes, 'the fact that the film encouraged the spectator to identify with a German protagonist did not go unquestioned' (Williams, 2006: 90). Isabel Quigly, writing for the *Spectator*, was particularly perturbed: 'The film's attitude seems to be that this was just somebody rather like us, only he happened to be on the other side: which, one cannot say often or loudly enough, isn't necessarily true' (Quigly, 1957). What initially seems to be a powerful rejection of the premise that Germans might be 'rather like us' and an acceptance of the essentialist arguments addressed earlier in this chapter becomes, through the qualifying word 'necessarily', far more ambivalent. The desire to maintain a distinction between Britons and Germans – and the fear that this distinction was weakening – is palpable in the clause 'one cannot say often or loudly enough', yet the final phrase implies that many Germans may indeed be 'rather like us'. Williams shows how the film itself manifests a similar ambivalence, arguing that it 'treads a tightrope in trying to make us identify with the German while still retaining a critical distance from his exploits'. I will take this argument further by showing how the ambivalent British response to both von Werra and Krüger is echoed within the film itself, in which three conflicting understandings of what this German wartime hero should mean for Britain compete for supremacy.

The first of these is established in the opening scene. A German plane has been shot down and is making a crash landing. A British cook, hard at work in an outdoor kitchen a short distance away, looks up and yells, 'Another Jerry!' before running towards the plane, cleaver in hand. The phrase invites us to see the downed pilot, before he has appeared on the screen, as simply one more German in a long and uniform list. The scene cuts to von Werra as he jumps out of his plane and, realising he will soon be a prisoner, burns his documents. A series of eye-level, medium close-up shots acquaint the audience with this particular Jerry. Yet his appearance only affirms the impression of generic Germanness. He is broad-faced, square-jawed and blond-haired – blue-eyed too, although this is disguised by the black and white film (see figure 5.3). Indeed, it was his striking 'resemblance to the Aryan ideal', as Williams puts it, that dominated his initial reception in Britain. 'In appearance', the *Times* noted, Krüger was 'the Nazi dream come true' ('The One That Got Away', 1957), while Krüger was met with accusations of Nazism at his first British press conference based on his 'sportliche Gestalt' ('athletic shape'), '*arische* Form des Schädels' ('*Arian* shape of skull'), blond hair and blue eyes (Krüger, 1998: 255–6).

5.3   Hardy Krüger in *The One That Got Away* (1957), dir. Roy Ward Baker.

There was a desire to categorise this German, whose presence in the British film world was undesired by many and aroused anxiety. He was one of the Aryan masses, alien to Britons and a potential threat. Just as von Werra's presence on British soil in reality and in the film is a cause for defensive actions and ever greater vigilance, so too was Krüger's presence in Britain and in British culture often characterised by metaphors of bombardment and invasion. An article in *Picturegoer* published on 19 September 1959, titled 'The German Invasion' argued, 'It seems that what Hitler failed to do by way of invasion here during the war, German stars are determined to make up for – by getting plum roles in our pictures' ('The German invasion', 1959). The playfulness of the rhetoric cannot disguise an underlying anxiety about Krüger's presence, generated partly by the post-war drive, based on wartime myths, to characterise Germans as antithetical and hostile to Britons. The media simply did not know what to do differently with this strikingly Aryan German who used to think – by his own admission – that Hitler was 'a terrific person' ('The magic of Hardy Krüger', 1958). The opening segment of *The One* affirms the validity of this attitude. Von Werra, if not Krüger – who has no dialogue that could individualise him – is just 'another Jerry', one of 'them' posing a threat to 'us', who must be disarmed and carefully guarded.

Yet this impression is quickly undermined. His first interrogation, during which he spouts generic Nazi rhetoric that foreshadows Lütjens' nationalistic pronouncements in *Bismarck* – 'we are stronger in every respect', 'the German people are as one man' – is followed by a telephone conversation between his interrogator and a colleague at Air Defence Intelligence. The latter asks of von Werra and the interrogation, 'usual sort of thing, I suppose?' The former responds thoughtfully, 'Not quite the usual. All the routine jargon of course, but he doesn't believe a word of it … The only thing von Werra believes in is von Werra'. Following the opening scene, in which he is 'another Jerry', von Werra quickly emerges as 'a rebellious individualist', as Richard Falcon aptly describes him in a brief discussion of the film (Falcon, 1995: 80). He uses irony to mock his stoical British escorts, shows audacity in his repeated demand to be moved to a POW camp, mischievousness, when he discovers the hidden microphone in his cell and starts talking directly to the RAF, and an extraordinary amount of pluck and ingenuity in his three escape attempts. As he recites 'the routine jargon' in his first interrogation, it is clear to the audience, not just the interrogator, that, unlike Lütjens, von Werra does not ascribe to the ideology he represents. His voice is unusually monotonous and his manner apathetic as he delivers a set of phrases obviously learned for this purpose.

This individualism itself sets him apart from the other Germans in this fictional world. The RAF staff member transcribing von Werra's first interview remarks dismissively, 'same old claptrap', while the ADI officer expects nothing other than 'the usual sort of thing', his question barely a question at all. The implication is that captured Germans have so far shown little diversity in character or ideology, an impression borne out by the prisoners we later meet. Although, unlike in many post-war films, they are individualised by appearance, their behaviour and dialogue is undifferentiated. We know neither their names nor their stories. They lack von Werra's imagination, humour or courage, dutifully following his instructions to enable his or their escape and joining together in a rousing chant of 'Sieg Heil!' before starting their journey to Canada. Amongst these Germans, von Werra is not only unusual, but also unique. The protagonist's signet ring and rigid forefinger are invoked visually and in dialogue several times to draw attention to von Werra's singularity, while his choice of pet – a lion cub – only underscores his anomalous nature. Indeed, the whole premise of the film and its marketing was based on von Werra's virtual uniqueness amongst all German prisoners held by the British during the Second World War. He is 'the one who got away', one of only two Germans who escaped from British captivity and made it back to Germany. The *Daily Express* could not have described his story as 'fantastic', 'amazing' and 'incredible' if he were just 'another Jerry', a representative German whose escapes were commonplace. Britain's reaction to Krüger directly echoed these two attitudes – was he a generic German or an anomalous German whose existence proved the rule? Following his transition from figure of hate to heartthrob, the suggestion that he was representative of his nation acquired a positive spin. In February 1960, *Films and Filming* published a very optimistic article by Austrian actor Karlheinz Böhm, who claimed that after seeing Krüger in his British films, audiences 'saw the average German in a different light, taking Krüger as being typical of his people' (Böhm, 1960). Almost two decades later, however, and having observed Krüger's astonishing success from afar, Chancellor Helmut Schmidt cautioned him against viewing that success as particularly significant for Anglo-German relations: 'Die späte Zuneigung [hat] Ihrer Person gegolten … Nicht uns. Nicht dem Volk auf der anderen Seite des Ärmelkanals. Denn ein einziger Film kann nicht zwei Weltkriege vergessen machen' (Krüger, 1998: 260).[2] Especially, he could have added, when that film was set during one of those wars. Furthermore, the 'affection' shown towards Krüger was rooted partly in the perception of his non-German traits as belonging to the post-war image of Britishness, not least his plucky individualism, stoical response to adversity and sense of humour. As Rau argues:

> The British audience took to Krüger's rugged good looks and cheered the plucky underdog in the same way in which it would respond to *The Great Escape* a few years later … What made such characters appealing to a British audience (irrespective of the actors' nationalities or the characters' ideological affiliations) was that they embodied what the audience understood to be Anglo-Saxon virtues. This turned them into exceptional Germans; at least it de-politicised them. (Rau, 2013: 132)

Von Werra is depoliticised early in the film, implicitly by his rebellious individualism and explicitly by the interrogator's remark, 'The only thing von Werra believes in is von Werra'. This made it possible, easy even, for a British audience to identify with the German protagonist, who shared neither the ideology nor the character perceived in wartime and in many post-war representations of the war as representing a threat to Britain and Britishness. This identification was encouraged by numerous medium close-up and close-up eye-level shots of von Werra that invite us to put ourselves in this German's place. This is indeed 'somebody like us', the film suggests, but this fact need not be as problematic as Quigly's review suggests. He is an 'exceptional German' in both senses – an unusual spe-cimen of his nationality and unusually superior, due, we are invited to conclude, to his 'British' traits, which enable him and no other German to escape so successfully from British imprisonment. From being perceived or depicted as 'another Jerry', easily categorised as antithetical and hostile to Britons, both von Werra and Krüger became accepted as an 'excep-tional German' displaying British traits of individualism and spontan-eity. Krüger himself describes being accepted by the British public as 'eine[r] der Ihren' and expected to agree with them and to show that he 'für England eintrete' (Krüger, 1998: 261–2).[3] Von Werra's escapes from British captivity and his ability to outwit bumbling Britons along the way did not therefore threaten the wartime myth of superior Britishness but instead bolstered it. Britishness was vindicated – through the depiction of a foreign hero displaying British characteristics, through his capture by the British on both occasions and through the multiple allusions to von Werra's uniqueness: the only German to have successfully escaped was one who displayed supposedly British traits.

Thus, despite asking Britons to put themselves in the place of a German, the film did not present nearly as powerful a challenge to the idea that Germans were 'unlike other peoples' as the initial furore suggests. An anomalous German with British traits, von Werra is divested of any

5.4   Hardy Krüger in *The One That Got Away* (1957), dir.
Roy Ward Baker.

metonymic power. Yet there are two segments in the film that stand out
for their refusal to locate von Werra as either 'another Jerry' or an 'exceptional German'. The first occurs just after his escape from Grizedale Hall
and the second on his trek towards the Canadian/American border. On
both occasions, we see him as a man battling nature – terrain, weather
and darkness. He struggles to find food and shelter and becomes soaked,
frozen and exhausted. As he flees through the Lake District, extreme
long shots highlighting von Werra's vulnerability are interspersed with
medium shots and close-ups that reveal his dirtied, rain-streaked face
and unkempt hair (see figures 5.4 and 5.5). He has no dialogue in this
sequence that would identify him as belonging to a particular nationality
and, having removed the identifying badges from his jacket, he is devoid
of any signs of allegiance: he is simply a man battling the natural elements
for his own survival.

An uninterrupted twelve-minute sequence of film following von
Werra's escape from the train travelling through Canada echoes and
builds on this earlier series of scenes. The snow-covered terrain, freezing
temperatures and vast distances make this battle even more gruelling. In
this long sequence, we see only von Werra and do not hear him speak. His
battle to reach neutral territory and, even more fundamental, his battle
to survive are told through his facial expressions, his body language and
the film's soundtrack – universal languages that do not distinguish by
nationality. Extreme close-up shots register his grimaces of pain, despair
or exhaustion and his beaming smiles of delight or relief (see figures 5.6

5.5   Hardy Krüger in *The One That Got Away* (1957), dir.
Roy Ward Baker.

5.6   Hardy Krüger in *The One That Got Away* (1957), dir.
Roy Ward Baker.

and 5.7), while medium and long shots reveal his hunched shoulders as
he trudges determinedly across the vast frozen river and his slumped,
exhausted form lying in a boat that carries him to the American shore
of the river. Shots of von Werra trekking across the hostile terrain are
accompanied by orchestral music in a minor key that conveys the per-
ilous nature of his quest. His arrival at the river heralds a crescendo, a

5.7   Hardy Krüger in *The One That Got Away* (1957), dir.
Roy Ward Baker.

transition to a major key and a sequence of soaring, uplifting strings that
provides the perfect aural accompaniment to the smile that spreads across
von Werra's face. As he jumps up and down with glee, the tempo picks up
and echoes his frolicking. Williams argues that 'the film has attempted to
depict him as an admirable but almost superhuman escape machine' and
it is only his 'euphoric little jig' as he reaches America that 'humanizes
the hero' (Williams, 2006: 92). I contend instead that this is the culmination of a humanising process that begins soon after the first scene and
finds fulfilment in the long sequence just addressed. In this sequence,
more closely related to the adventure than the prisoner of war genre, and
narrated through visual and aural cues that render nationality invisible
and irrelevant, von Werra is a human being answering to the universal
challenge to survive. This is not just 'somebody like us', which implies a
'them' elsewhere who are not like 'us', but a human being akin to all others.

In the context of films such as *Bismarck*, it certainly was a mark of progress to depict a German as a hero and find such resounding box-office
success. Yet, as I have shown, this depiction was less straightforwardly
positive than it first appears. The ambivalent response to both von Werra
and Krüger is epitomised in two readers' letters published in *Picturegoer*
on 4 January 1958. 'Heroism is heroism whatever the nationality', wrote
Stephanie Horne of Sheffield. Mrs Owen in Coventry disagreed. 'Why
glorify a callous and sadistic enemy?' she demanded ('Letters', 1958).

A close look at Krüger and the post-war political and cultural context
of which he was a part shows that, more than a decade after the end of

the war, the ordinariness – the humanness – of Germans could not yet be acknowledged in British popular culture without a corresponding urge to depict such figures as anomalous. The drive to preserve the depiction of Germans as, in the words of James Stern's father, 'extr'ord'nary people', alien to Britons, remained strong (Stern, 1990: 58).

Notes

1   These include the novels *Green Hazard* (1945), *The Fifth Man* (1946) and *Now or Never* (1951) by Manning Coles, *Dark Wanton* (1948) by Peter Cheyney, *The Search* (1958) by Roy Farran and *Hands of the Devil* (1959) by Tony Faramus, and the films *The Echo Murders* (1945), *Night Boat to Dublin* (1946), *Counterblast* (1946), *Snowbound* (1948), *Carve Her Name With Pride* (1958), *The Treasure of San Teresa* (1959) and *The Quiller Memorandum* (1966).
2   'Their affection was directed at you. Not at us. Not at the people across the channel. Let's face it, a film can't make people forget about two world wars.'
3   '[O]ne of their own'; 'speak out in favour of England'.

References

Billings, Josh (1960), 'It's Britain 1, 2, 3 again in the 1960 box-office stakes', *Kinematograph Weekly*, 15 December, pp. 8–10.
Böhm, Karlheinz (1960), 'The world before us', *Films and Filming*, March, pp. 11–13.
Burk, Kathleen (ed.) (2003), *The British Isles since 1945* (Oxford: Oxford University Press).
Colls, Robert (2002), *Identity of England* (Oxford: Oxford University Press).
Dummett, Ann and Andrew Nicol (1990), *Subjects, Citizens, Aliens and Others: Nationality and Immigration Law* (London: Weidenfeld & Nicolson).
Falcon, Richard (1995), 'Images of Germany and the Germans in British Film and Television Fictions' in Cedric Cullingford and Harald Husemann (eds), *Anglo-German Attitudes* (Aldershot: Avebury), pp. 67–89.
Geraghty, Christine (2000), *British Cinema in the Fifties: Gender, Genre and the New Look* (London: Routledge).
'The German invasion' (1959), *Picturegoer*, 19 September, p. 5.
Gollancz, Victor (1945), *What Buchenwald Really Means* (London: Gollancz).
'Hitler declares against war for Germany' (1933), *Daily Express*, 4 September, p. 7.
Judt, Tony (2010), *Postwar: A History of Europe since 1945* (London: Vintage).
Krüger, Hardy (1998), *Wanderjahre: Begegnungen eines jungen Schauspielers* (Hamburg: Gustav Lübbe Verlag).
'Letters' (1958), *Picturegoer*, 4 January, p. 3.

'The magic of Hardy Krüger' (1958), *Picturegoer*, 23 August, p. 5.

'The One That Got Away' (1957), *The Times*, 14 October, p. 3.

Orwell, George (1953), *England, Your England and Other Essays* (London: Secker & Warburg).

Paxman, Jeremy (1999), *The English: A Portrait of a People* (London: Penguin).

P.G.B. (1960), 'Sink the Bismarck!', *Films and Filming*, March, p. 23.

Plain, Gill (2013), *Literature of the 1940s: War, Postwar and 'Peace'* (Edinburgh: Edinburgh University Press).

Priestley, J.B. (1941), *Out of the People* (London: Heinemann).

Quigly, Isabel (1957), 'Gun happy' (includes review of *The One That Got Away*), *Spectator*, 18 October, p. 20.

Rau, Petra (2009), *English Modernism, National Identity and the Germans 1890–1950* (Aldershot: Ashgate).

(2013), *Our Nazis: Representations of Fascism in Contemporary Literature and Film* (Edinburgh: Edinburgh University Press).

Rose, Sonya (2003), *Which People's War? National Identity and Citizenship in Britain 1939–1945* (Oxford: Oxford University Press).

Stern, James (1990), *The Hidden Damage* (London: Chelsea Press).

Theweleit, Klaus (1978), *Männerphantasien, vol. 2: Männerkörper – zur Psychoanalyse des weißen Terrors* (Frankfurt: Roter Stern).

Tomlinson, Jim (2003), 'Economic Growth, Economic Decline' in Kathleen Burk (ed.), *The British Isles since 1945* (Oxford: Oxford University Press), pp. 63–89.

Vansittart, Robert Gilbert (1941), *Black Record: Germans Past and Present* (London: Hamish Hamilton).

'The war's most incredible escape story' (1956), *Daily Express*, 2 October, p. 8.

Williams, Melanie (2006), ' "The most explosive object to hit Britain since the V2!": The British films of Hardy Kruger and Anglo-German relations during the 1950s', *Cinema Journal* 46:1, pp. 85–107.

Woolf, Leonard (1935), *Quack, Quack!* (London: Hogarth).

6

'I don't want to be a European': the European Other in British cultural discourse[1]

Menno Spiering

Them or Us

The arguments for and against 'Brexit' have by now been repeated end-lessly. Outwardly, it seems to have been all about costs and benefits, about sovereignty and immigration and, of course, border control. How will leaving the European Union profit the country? How will an exit affect the refugee crisis? Will the Calais jungle move to Folkestone, or will a new Iron Curtain keep them on the Continent? It is worth noting that in the British media, and in British discourse in general, the refugee issue is often referred to as a 'European crisis', meaning it is seen as a problem of and for 'the Europeans', and less so for the British.[2] It is 'Them', 'the Europeans', on the one hand, and 'Us', 'the British', on the other. In this spirit, a pre-referendum BBC series on Britain and Europe, presented by Nick Robinson, was called *Them or Us*. All this indicates that the European-question-debate is also driven by a discourse of differentness. At heart it is about a perceived divergence between the national Self and the European Other; it is about cultural exceptionalism.[3]

Of course, contrastive self-definition is not unique to the British. The Self only acquires meaning in relation to an Other. In fact, the closer cul-ture groups live together (as is the case in Europe), the more they seem to feel the need to stress their perceived dissimilarities. In his *Civilization and its Discontents*, Sigmund Freud called this phenomenon 'the narcis-sism of small differences'. The point is that the British feel different not just from the French, Germans or other nations, they feel different from the Europeans *en masse*. The Europeans collectively can be, and often are, seen as the Other. In 1941 George Orwell observed: 'it is quite true that the so-called races of Britain feel themselves to be very different from one another ... But somehow these differences fade away the moment that any two Britons are confronted by a European' (Orwell, 1941: 25). Almost forty years later Robert Blake echoed these thoughts by claiming: 'England is no doubt in one sense part of Europe, but the differences between the English cultural, political and social heritage and that of any other European country are far greater than the differences within mainland Europe itself' (Blake, 1982: 25).

This perception of Europe as the Other makes British Euroscepticism special and powerful. Yes, there is considerable overlap between British and other Eurosceptic parties and opinions. There is a shared concern about costs, sovereignty, national identity, democracy and immigration. But non-British Eurosceptic parties do not contrast their nation with 'the Europeans', as in the slogan 'I am British not European' which is bandied about by many UKIP supporters on the Internet. The non-British parties are anti-European in the sense of being against the EU or the 'European idea', that is, the idea of an 'ever closer union'. But they would not, and could not, call themselves non-European in an existential sense. In the run-up to the referendum, the Leave campaign reported that the 'investor' Richard Tice was strongly backing exit. 'A two-year stint in Paris in the 1990s convinced him Britain and continental Europe have fundamentally different cultures – and that his country has nothing to lose from going its own way' (Tice, 2015). For a French or German Eurosceptic there would be no logic in making a similar claim about a fundamental difference between their own and 'European' culture, the one is part of the other. In British national discourse, exceptionalism vis-à-vis 'the Europeans' is so ubiquitous that it forms, in fact, part of a 'banal nationalism' that is so pervasive as to be no longer noticed. At the Channel Tunnel terminal in Folkestone drivers are greeted by a sign 'Stop! Are You Ready to Drive in Europe?' Evidently, travellers must be reminded that the tunnel leads to a place called 'Europe' where they do things differently. British media and politicians habitually compare their country and nation to Europe and the Europeans. Often the comparison is not in Europe's favour, but that is to be expected in any identity discourse. The British are of course by no means alone in regarding the Self a touch better than the Other.

Cultural exceptionalism formed part of the British European debate right from the start. In the early 1960s, when the UK first applied for membership of the European Economic Community (EEC), people frequently argued that they did not understand or care about the economic issues. What they wanted to flag up were the differences between Britain and Europe. In 1961 the poet W.H. Auden claimed 'if I shut my eyes and say the word Europe to myself, the various images which it conjures up have one thing in common; they could not be conjured up by the word England' (Auden, 1963: 53). In serious academic discourse, the idea of an

Anglo-European dichotomy can also easily be spotted. An older example would be the Oxford history curriculum which for many years required students to prepare three papers on 'English history' and two more on 'European history' (Ludlow, 2002: 102). In recent times, in spite of quite a few revisionist works that argue for treating English and European history as one, plenty of examples can be found of academics who continue to see an essential difference. Alan Macfarlane, in his famous book *The Origins of English Individualism*, actually berates himself for ever having flirted with fashionable relativism. Of course, the English are unlike the Europeans. 'England as a whole is different from the rest of Europe'. 'England stands alone' (Macfarlane, 1991: 5). In 1982 Robert Blake simply declared that England's 'cultural, political and social heritage is distinct from mainland Europe' (Blake, 1982: 25). Another case in point is the book *Convergence or Divergence?* by Jeremy Black, which abounds with phrases such as 'Continental ideology', 'Continental society', 'Continental ideas and cultural idioms' (Black, 1994: 2, 67, 265).

Causes

So what causes are mentioned to explain the differences between Britain and Europe? The most popular one today is that living on an island makes the British different and special in relation to the Europeans of the Continent. References to 'the island people' are found in great abundance in academic works, BBC series, popular books and political speeches. In his book *The English*, Jeremy Paxman almost immediately starts to define his subject as 'the island nation' (Paxman, 2007: 30). Part one of the 2016 BBC series *Them or Us* is entitled 'An Island Apart', and in his speeches David Cameron more than once praised the 'island character' of the British. As he announced his fateful decision to call an 'in-out referendum' he told his audience: 'We are special, different, unique. We have the character of an island nation' (Cameron, 2013).

The popularity of the 'island story' is due to its relative innocuousness. It is not about class, race, gender or ethnicity. And it sounds so logical. Surely, the environment shapes our character? Mediterraneans are more passionate than cold Scandinavians, and the Swiss character is supposed to be 'forged by the daily confrontation with the difficult mountainous environment of the Alps', giving 'those who inhabit it a sense of dignity and grandeur' (Moore and Whelan, 2007: 88). Geographic determinism goes back at least to classical times, and was very much popularised by Montesquieu in his *De l'esprit des Lois* (1748). The English, he declared, are a moderate people because of their moderate climate, the Dutch are coarse because they eat coarse food, etc. But a popular theory need not be true. Geographic determinism is wrong because it fits the environment to a preconceived idea. With equal logicality, it could be argued that the English are extremists because they need to counter the dullness of their weather, and that living surrounded by mountains has not given the Swiss dignity and grandeur, but made them inward looking, limited, narrow-minded. The reasoning behind geographic determinism is always *a posteriori*. The real sources of perceived Anglo-European differentness are of course man-made. They are of political, social and cultural origin, springing not from natural but human history.

From the British perspective, there are good Europeans and bad Europeans. There is a positive image of Europeanness and a negative one. This is what one would expect, for every image of identity is bipolar. Alongside the militaristic German lives the romantic dreamer. Alongside Kaiser Wilhelm lives Werther Nieland. The positive British image of Europe is mainly connected with the arts. Renaissance ideals and the legacy of the Grand Tour have caused Europe to be seen as superior as far as the visual arts are concerned. To be sure, British artists are fine and special, but perhaps not as special as Rembrandt or Titian. George Orwell claims that the English 'lack artistic ability' and then states: 'This is perhaps another way of saying that the English are outside European culture' (Orwell, 1941: 29). The negative British image of Europe centres on the idea that the Europeans lack democracy, they are dogmatic, Cartesians, corrupt. They are, in a word, dishonest. In the 1993 BBC documentary *The Downing Street Years*, Margaret Thatcher famously claimed her demands for a rebate from Brussels were hampered by the fact that 'the Europeans', unlike the British, have no sense of 'probity and fairness'.

So where does this negative British image of Europeanness originate, if not from the fact that the British are islanders? The source can be found in the events of the English reformation in the sixteenth century. It was Henry VIII's break with Rome (in effect the first 'Brexit') that engendered the idea that England is different, not just from France, Spain or Germany, but from Europe. In short, the story runs as follows: The English Reformation commenced with two important acts. The Act in Restraint of Appeals of 1532 and the Act of Supremacy of 1534. The core of the first act is the claim that the English Church 'is at this hour sufficient and meet of itself, without the intermeddling of any exterior person or persons'. The second act adds that 'the king shall be accepted the only supreme head in earth of the Church of England', regardless of others from 'foreign land' or of 'foreign authority'. These Acts set the tone of things to come in Anglo-European perceptions. English religious practices began to be seen as native and markedly in contrast with 'foreign' practices from abroad.

Who were the 'exterior person or persons', 'intermeddling with English affairs'? The person was the Pope, and the persons were anybody who had an interest in undermining the English exit from the Holy Mother Church, in a word: Catholics. The most common adjective for Catholic was 'outlandish', states Linda Colley in her famous work *Britons: Forging the Nation* (Colley, 1992: 320), and the outland where they lived was, naturally, the continent of Europe. As these Catholics were often literally the enemy (notably the Spanish and French, who figured in countless wars), it did not take long for Catholicism to be firmly associated with European hostility, European immorality and European otherness. The religious schism of the English reformation developed over time into a cultural schism between Britain and Europe. In the words of David Armitage, 'A common Protestantism grew on a common anti-Europeanism' (Armitage, 2000: 66).

From the English point of view, it was both logical and legitimate to suppress Catholicism in their country. It began with the destruction of what was now a foreign culture under Henry VIII, who ordered monasteries to be sacked, followed by a string of laws to suppress Catholic practices. It became illegal to import crucifixes or rosary beads from the Continent, and Test Acts and Popery Acts made it impossible for non-Anglicans to enter public office. In practice, these acts were aimed mainly at Catholics, Protestant nonconformists often being excepted. In fact, nonconformists did much to boost the idea that the English were a special people outside the European domain. John Milton, serving under the Puritan dictator Oliver Cromwell, was convinced that only the English were God's Chosen People. When some of the restrictions against Catholics were lifted at the end of the eighteenth century, the government met with an extremely hostile reaction, which culminated in the 'Gordon Riots' of 1780. In June that year a huge crowd of about 50,000 people ran amok in London, destroying foreign embassies and plundering the houses of known Catholics. The leader of the mob was Lord George Gordon, a zealous Protestant Scot who founded the Protestant Association, claiming that he was defending the nation against 'the whole system of morality in Europe' (Watson, 1795: 122). These same perceptions arguably persist today. Though the religious context is largely gone (no banners in London against Popery), the fear of foreign intervention (and infection by an alien 'system of morality') is easily associated with Europe. One of the Brexit mottos was that Britain should not be 'ruled by Europe'. If Catholics have ceased to be 'outlandish', the same cannot be said of their outland: Europe.

By the nineteenth century, the English view of Europe as a cultural and religious outland was well-established. Europe was habitually portrayed as a dark, dangerous continent that was either to be avoided or evangelised.

After the defeat of Napoleon in 1815, it became possible again to tour Europe. This was a great opportunity for romantic adventurers like Lord Byron or Percy Bysshe Shelley, but the opening of borders was viewed with trepidation by many others. In 1819 'The Continental Society for the Diffusion of Religious Knowledge Over the Continent of Europe' was founded in London. Its aim was to spread the true protestant faith on the continent of Europe, or simply 'in Europe', for in 1836 the Society's name was changed to 'European Missionary Society'. A second nineteenth-century example of English religio-cultural exceptionalism is a remarkable booklet entitled *Cautions to Continental Travellers*, first published by the vicar of Harrow, John William Cunningham, in 1818 and reprinted, with corrections, in 1823.[4] Interestingly, in the context of present-day Euroscepticism, Cunningham opens his argument by warning not against Europeans moving to Britain, but Britons moving to Europe. The 'danger', Cunningham concludes, 'arising from the influx of foreigners into our own country, does not appear to be considerable'. But the influx of *English* travellers to *Europe* is another matter altogether. Here they are on foreign soil, laying themselves open to all sorts of moral risks (Cunningham, 1823: 2). Cunningham compares Europe to a hospital where irresponsible British travellers wander 'through the wards' and then return to spread infectious diseases in their home country. According to Cunningham, women are particularly at risk of catching European manners, because they are much 'more susceptible of impression than males'. If an Englishwoman cannot avoid entering Europe, she should first and foremost protect herself against infection. She should, as it were, only partake in safe cultural intercourse (Cunningham, 1823: 6). One is reminded of the Folkestone poster: 'Stop! Are you ready to enter Europe?'

If a hapless Englishwoman, or man, does find her- or himself on European soil, they should show mercy by teaching the natives proper morality.

If the inhabitant of a civilized country chance to travel among savages, he does not dream of degrading himself to their habits – he does not bore his nose, nor tear off his clothing, nor dine upon the companions of his expedition – but he strives to cherish in these barbarians a love of cleanliness, and refinement, and gentleness, and morality; and thus gently rears them up to the habits and tastes of cultivated men. In like manner, when ... *Europe* has sunk below our *own* country in the scale of morality, it is not just, nor humane, nor religious, nor common sense, to descend to *their* moral barbarisms. It is our wisdom and our duty to shew *them* a more excellent way. (Cunningham, 1823: 29)

Literature

Next to sermons and the like, works of literature can assist to illustrate and investigate the nature of the Anglo-European divide and English exceptionalism. There are good reasons to include literature as source material for ideas and cultural attitudes. Firstly, there is the 'mirror of society' argument, which was so convincingly put forward by Raymond Williams in his book *Culture and Society* in 1958. Much earlier, in 1914, H.G. Wells made a similar point when he stated: 'So far as I can see, it [the novel] is the only medium through which we can discuss the great majority of the problems which are being raised in such bristling multitude by our contemporary social development' (Wells, 1912: 8). The second and more fundamental reason why literature may serve as profitable source material lies in the potency of fictionalisation. Literature need not be true in a strict, historical sense. This liberates the author to focus on the message rather than the factual detail. Fiction can be stronger than truth, because it can dramatise and magnify the feelings, attitudes and emotions that drive human affairs. To understand the essential issues driving Anglo-European relations one could do worse than delve into the novel *Villette*, published by Charlotte Brontë in 1853. It is a story of a young Protestant Englishwoman called Lucy Snow, who moves to Brussels (which she prophetically calls 'the continental capital') to teach at a Catholic girls' school (Brontë, 1984: 51). There are some similarities with Cunningham's booklet *Cautions to Continental Travellers*, but the differences in depth and impact are massive. In *Villette* the themes of Protestantism, Catholicism, Britishness and Europeanness are truly explored, and presented in a memorable, effective manner that no treatise can match. In her fiction Brontë shows the struggles, the difficulties and uncertainties that the question of identity always entails. As she lands on the continent, Lucy recounts that 'the lights of the foreign sea-port town, glimmering round the foreign harbour, met me like unnumbered threatening eyes' (Brontë, 1984: 77). As the novel progresses, the continental satanic threat never quite abates, though Lucy is sometimes fascinated by the dark, mysterious practices of the Europeans. A clear case of 'fatal attraction'.

What *Villette* shows, and shows so forcefully, is that the perceived Anglo-European divide and its narrative of exceptionalism has two parallel storylines. The Other is continental or 'European', and the Other is Roman Catholic. Anti-Catholicism experienced a revival in the second half of the nineteenth century because of the so-called 'Papal Aggression' of 1850, when Pope Pius IX made England and Wales an ecclesiastical province of the Roman Catholic Church. But other events also stoked the fire. The Great Famine of the 1840s resulted in an enormous influx of Irish-Catholic immigrants in England, and around the same time, the Oxford or Tractarian Movement drew much attention. The movement, led by influential High Church Anglicans such as Cardinal Newman, was centred at the University of Oxford and aimed to converge Anglicanism with Catholicism. The Protestant reaction was not slow to emerge, with many anti-Catholic pamphlets, articles, but also novels, flooding the British market. The anti-Catholic novel became an established Gothic sub-genre in the nineteenth century, peddling gruesome stories of plotting Jesuits, abductions of Protestant maidens, sadistic torture and bloody murders by wicked priests taking orders from Rome.

Anti-Catholic discourse

Anti-Catholic discourse received a new impulse around the time of the Irish Home Rule Bills in the first decades of the twentieth century. Catholic Ireland was pressing for self-rule, but in England it was widely suspected that the Irish were actively encouraged by Catholics from Europe and even the Pope himself. In 1907 George Allen Upward published *The Fourth Conquest*. This novel describes how Britain, due to the visions of Cardinal Newman, slides back to Roman Catholicism and eventually loses its national independence to be ruled by a foreign court and foreign administrators. The Act of Settlement is abolished, forcing the British king and millions of his subjects who do not accept the new order, to flee to Australia where they regroup in the hope of making the United Kingdom independent again one day. A Stuart pretender, Mary III, ascends to the throne, but she rules solely by the consent of the Pope in Rome. Britain then enters into an economic and cultural recession, a new 'dark age', because it can no longer control its own destiny. Similar warnings are sounded in a novel simply entitled *Under Home Rule*, written by William Palmer in 1912. In this book the Irish are described as good at heart, but extremely gullible, making them susceptible to the teachings of the European Roman Catholic Church whose hordes of foreign priests have invaded the island as a first step to bringing England back to the fold. In Ireland, newly independent because of Home Rule, it does not take long before power is completely in foreign Catholic hands. Only at the eleventh hour is the situation saved thanks to the actions of a fearless Protestant maiden assisted by equally fearless Protestant English heroes.

Below follows a list of the narrative incidents and imagery which *The Fourth Conquest* (*TFC*) and *Under Home Rule* (*UHR*) share with each other, and with many of the other anti-Catholic novels:

The British enter into a union

The Anglican and Catholic church merge into a 'Church Union' (*TFC*: 24).

In the union Britain loses its national identity

'Protestantism and national greatness go hand in hand, and the Catholic Faith is a fungus fatal to the lip of nations' (*TFC*: 52).

Foreigners supplant the British

'The intolerable burden of a horde of spunging foreign interlopers' (*UHR*: 168).
    'A swarm of men of all nationalities came crashing like a flood to the gate' (*UHR*: 90).
    'Foreigners who were there for plunder and for the purpose of exploitation' (*UHR*: 145).

British law becomes secondary to foreign law

'A foreign priest above the native prince' (*TFC*: 8).

An increase in rules and regulations

'The list of forbidden subjects grew steadily' (*TFC*: 69).

Political correctness prevents the British from resistance

'Catholic "susceptibilities" became the bugbear of writers and speakers, and thus in the name of toleration Rome established a very real and effective censorship' (*TFC*: 10).

Parliament and democracy are abandoned

'The muzzling of the House of Commons' (*TFC*: 13).

Britain is enthralled by a foreign power

'Rivet the chains of Rome' (*TFC*: 23).

There is German collusion in the subjugation of Britain

'The following day the new Queen [Mary III] entered London in triumph, escorted by the Kaiser' (*TFC*: 54).

The people awake at the eleventh hour and rise to leave the union

'A crusade has been started in England' (*UHR*: 114).
'As the crowded congregation realised that their liberties and the secret of their national greatness, had fallen under the heel of Rome, a great wail burst from every throat, and each man turned and gazed into his neighbour's eyes, as though asking if all that had happened were an evil dream' (*TFC*: 66).

British Freedom parties arise

'You in England are a free people, and you have won your freedom through your ancestors' (*UHR*: 127).

The Union is ready to punish the British wish to break away

'"Oh, England!" exclaimed the Cardinal in a sudden burst of passion. If I had you in my grasp at this moment I would squeeze you until your blood dripped from a thousand hidden wounds, and you cried in your agony for mercy' (*UHR*: 115).

The anti-Catholic novels were answered by a number of English pro-Catholic novels. In spite of the grand national narrative, Britain is of course by no means a homogenised Protestant nation. But what is significant is that by and large these pro-Catholic novels accept the Self–Other discourse that claims England is unlike Europe, and that Europe is defined by Catholicism. So, while reversing the morality, the idea of an Anglo-European divide remains in place, only now the English are admonished to be more instead of less European. In the 1904 novel

Hadrian the Seventh, for instance, we read how an Englishman called George Arthur Rose (you cannot have a more English name than that) becomes Pope and then ushers the Catholic Church and Europe into an era of enlightened, English humanitarianism.

In the course of the twentieth century, the religious theme in the Britain-and-Europe narrative would steadily diminish, but never quite disappear. To mention a few: *While England Slept* (James, 1932) is a novel about an English priest (he has the 'admiration of the whole of the peoples of Europe'), who, aided by a mysterious gas that makes people forget, manages to re-unite his country to what he calls 'the church of the continent' (James, 1932: 168, 225). The novel *The End*, written by an English Benedictine monk in 1948, is about a Europe united under a dictator who is known by the Number of the Beast (666), but who is finally defeated when England decides no longer to appease him. In the 1966 novel *Pavane* the anti-Catholic theme makes a reappearance as it tells the what-if story of an England in which the Reformation never took place. The country is primitive and under the cosh of a cruel Inquisition. But there is hope as the English find courage to revolt and haul down the blue flag of Rome. The same idea is presented in Kingsley Amis' *The Alteration* (1976), which is also a novel about a dark, primitive and cruel England. Because there has never been a reformation the country is not independent, but part of a European Catholic empire. Similarly, the popular graphic novel *V for Vendetta* (published between 1982 and 1989) paints a bleak future in which England is ruled by a fascist regime, aided and abetted by a wicked national church. This church is no longer the Church of England as we know it, but clearly bears the Roman Catholic signature. Several of the drawings show how in future England rings of bishops must be kissed and transubstantiation must be taken as fact on pain of death. Apparently, only the Catholic Church will do to symbolise the rise of evil and corruption in Britain. At work is the mechanism of *vraisemblance*. British cultural conventions prescribe that evil and foreignness must be portrayed in a certain way. Not to link a dystopian vision with 'the church of the continent' would deprive the audience of an *Aha Erlebnis*.

The English narrative of exceptionalism received a fresh boost when continental Europe started seriously to explore institutional means of cooperation after the Second World War. As said before, the religious theme became less pronounced, but would occasionally resurface. In 1953, the year that saw the birth of the European Coal and Steel Community, Gilbert Frankau published *Unborn Tomorrow*, a story about an Englishman who wakes up in the fiftieth century to find himself in a European union ruled by the Pope. In 1957, when the EEC was established by treaty (binding the members to an 'ever closer union'), there were murmurs that it was no coincidence that this treaty was signed in Rome and would forever carry the name of this Catholic capital. Hugo Young writes that 'anti-Catholic prejudice was instinctive' to British politicians dealing with European plans of cooperation (Young, 1998: 50). A late literary echo of this image of the European Union as the Catholic Other appears in Tim Parks' novel *Europa* (1998) which tells the story of an Englishman who is troubled by EU corruption, but is instructed by his Catholic mistress to 'loosen up and become more European' (Parks, 1998: 47). In the media, links between Catholicism and the European Union are suggested with some regularity. For instance, when the Treaty of Maastricht was signed, the *Sunday Telegraph* declared: 'The Common Market started under the influence of Catholic politicians, and now the Pope may see the greatest possibility for an increase in Catholic political power since the fall of Napoleon' (25 August 1991).

Anti-European novels

The first anti-EU novel (or, actually, anti-EEC) novel was published by Angus Wilson in 1963, the year that the UK's initial application for EEC membership was vetoed by President de Gaulle. In *The Old Men at the Zoo*, Wilson describes how in 1973 England is invaded by uni-European troops after the country has refused to join the Europeans in their grand scheme of cooperation. There are no overt references to religion, but many of the anti-Catholic narrative incidents listed above make an appearance. There is European occupation, darkness, brutality and dictatorship. The two main 'Europeans' in Wilson's novel are the ironically named Dr Englander, who is the curator of reptiles at London Zoo, and an equally sinister Euro-enthusiast called Blanchard-White, who spent many years on the Continent and who aims to throw English nationalists to the lions during the celebrations of 'Europe Day' in London. Written by a mainstream author, *The Old Men at the Zoo* attracted enough attention to be made into a BBC TV series in the 1980s. Several changes were made to the original story, for instance an Arab-and-oil theme was introduced, no doubt to reflect one of the main political issues of the time. The changes made to the European theme are interesting as they highlight another fundamental issue in the contemporary Britain-and-Europe debate. Dr Englander is portrayed not just as a pro-European, but also quite obviously as a Nazi. He addresses the London crowd at events reminiscent of the Nuremberg rallies, and the big European E on his uniform and at the heart of the new Union Jack recalls the swastika. To this very day, the events of the Second World War play a big part in British attitudes to most things European. The Second World War was (and is) perceived as a war between Us and Them, and Them is of course the Nazis, the Germans, but in a vague and general way, Them is also the Europeans. This was particularly the case for 'the war babies': the young people who grew up during the war and then learned a simple lesson: To the west is America, where all the help and all the goodies come from. To the east is Europe, a place that brings destruction and where fathers are killed in action. Dr Englander's Nazi uniform is, in fact, another instance of *vraisemblance*. The producers of the BBC series apparently felt they could not ignore British cultural expectations.

It does not come as a surprise that the war played an important part in the Leave campaign. Boris Johnson claimed that Europe was in fact a Fourth Reich (*Sunday Telegraph*, 15 May 2016), thus echoing a view expressed by his father, Stanley Johnson, in his Eurosceptic thriller *The Commissioner*, which was published in 1987 and turned into a TV series in 1998. Something similar is suggested in the anti-EU novel *The Aachen Memorandum* (1995)[5] written by the historian Andrew Roberts, who now makes regular appearances as an 'expert' in BBC programmes. *The Commissioner* and *The Aachen Memorandum* are but two of a series of Eurosceptic novels which followed after Angus Wilson had founded the genre with his *The Old Men at the Zoo*. The novels vary in quality, many having spectacular plots and one-dimensional heroes and villains. In narrative technique, the Eurosceptic novels are closely linked to the British invasion stories that were popular in the late nineteenth and early twentieth centuries. The default was set by George Chesney in his tremendously successful *The Battle of Dorking*, published in 1871, shortly after the Prussian defeat of France had triggered speculation that Germany would now be tempted also to invade Britain. The novel is set in the future, with an old soldier narrating how Britain was overrun by cruel German troops and subsequently lost its independence, identity and national pride. The *Battle of Dorking* was followed by a host of similar future-fictions, some written by well-known literati such as Arthur Conan Doyle. The genre became so popular that P.G. Wodehouse published a spoof in 1909 called *The Swoop*. In this story, not one, but nine armies invade poor Britain, including the Germans, Russians, Chinese, Moroccans and the Swiss, who make full use of their excellent navy.

Like the Victorian and Edwardian invasion stories, Eurosceptic novels are almost always set in the future, while a narrator laments how the British people, at some point in the past, were swallowed up by a European superstate, usually as a result of being misled by a treacherous political elite. *The Aachen Memorandum*, for instance, is set in 2045 and describes life in an impoverished Britain, which is now an insignificant province of a European Union ruled from Berlin. How did this come to pass? Well, the British voted away their independence in a referendum. As the plot develops, we discover that the referendum was actually rigged by the Euro-enthusiasts using a simple algorithm. Every No vote was automatically transformed into a Yes vote, and thus the United Kingdom voted Remain, rather than Leave.

Owing their narrative structure to invasion novels, Eurosceptic novels are clearly successors to the anti-Catholic novels as regards the portrayal of Europeans and their machinations to force the British into submission. Both genres show a high degree of overlap of plot points and imagery. To mention but three: the influx of foreigners; the threat of foreign law taking precedence over national law; the image of being shackled to a foreign entity, like a slave to a galley. The idea of a nation chained by a foreign European power is quite obviously central to a Eurosceptic novel called *Euroslavia* (1997), which sports on its cover a picture of handcuffs. Similar images were favoured by the Leave campaign. Two days after the referendum of 23 June the *Sun* cried Hallelujah, showing a bright picture of Britain breaking the chains with Europe, propelling itself to a better future. Significantly, according to the headline, Britain was not shackled to the European Union, but to 'Germany, France, and the rest'. The Europeans are the Other. The Europeans had been keeping Britain in thrall.

Cultural exceptionalism

The reasons for the Leave vote are complex. Key factors are populism, dissatisfaction, a disconnect between the voters and their rulers. During the aftershock quite a few 'Leavers' argued that the British were merely doing what others in the EU actually also want to do, given the chance. Are the Dutch not keen to go Nexit, and what about a French Frexit, Italian Italeave, Portugese Departugal and Czech Czechout? Obviously, there are important overlaps between Euroscepticism in Britain and elsewhere. Still, it is no overstatement to say that British Euroscepticism is special, as it taps into deep roots of a sense of national identity that identifies 'Europe' and 'the Europeans' as the Other. To a large extent the referendum was not about the EU, but about Europe. The British are literally Euro-sceptic. Not realising his microphone was still on, Prime Minister Gordon Brown called Gillian Duffy 'bigoted' after she had challenged him on immigration during his campaign trail in 2010. Since then, Duffy has been quizzed as 'the member of the public' by the media on various occasions. Asked by the BBC what she would vote in the EU referendum, she declared that she definitely wanted the UK to leave. Her reason was simple and was headlined on the BBC news site: 'I DON'T WANT TO BE A EUROPEAN' (Duffy, 2016).

Underneath contemporary issues like EU immigration, more permanent and stronger tectonic forces are at work. One of these, as mentioned above, is the impact of the Second World War. Another is the loss of empire, which for many decades has prompted feelings of uncertainty and a need to reinvent British, and especially English, national identity. Apparently, in Whitehall the concept of 'Empire 2.0' is pondered as the destiny for post-Brexit Britain (*Guardian*, 17 March 2017). But by far the strongest, diachronic force is the force of culture. Originating in the English reformation, foreign Catholicism and, by extension, foreign Europeanness became the most significant Other. In Britain, 'Europe' is by no means a neutral term, and has not been so for a long time. It is not just 'abroad', but 'the Other', which over the centuries has acquired many connotations, some good but many bad, as is usual in matters of contrastive self-definition. Suppose the EEC had originally been called the G6 and the European Union (at its inception) the G12. It is an interesting thought experiment. It is just possible that the British might have found it easier to embrace such a de-Europeanised set of organisations. To ask Britain to join a *European* Union is a bit like asking Italy to join the Nordic Council. Cultural forces are as hard and enduring as diamonds, and as such much more significant than the transient economic and political forces that are so often the focus of studies of Britain and Europe. More than three hundred years of United Kingdom have done nothing to weaken Scottish exceptionalism. It would be foolish to think that a few decades of European co-operation would wipe out British exceptionalism.

Notes

1   A few lines in the first section of this article first appeared in my *A Cultural History of British Euroscepticism* (Spiering, 2015).

2   E.g. the *Daily Mail* headline: WE'RE FROM EUROPE LET US IN! (15 June 2016).

3   I am aware that Britain is a composite nation, and that the Scots in particular claim their own identity and their own relation with 'the Europeans'. The intricacies of Anglo-Scottish, Anglo-European and Scottish-European relations are not the concern of this chapter; for this see chapter 4 of this volume. The present chapter will, by and large, focus on the dominant nation in Great Britain, the English. In 1940 J.B. Priestley declared: 'when I say English I really mean British' (Gardiner, 2012: 40). The manual for this article reads 'when I say British I often really mean English'.

4   Significantly, in the current context, the book was reprinted various times in recent years, in 2010 by Nabu Press, an imprint of the historical reprints publisher BiblioLife based in Charleston, South Carolina, in 2012 by HardPress Publishing (hardpress.net), in 2018 by Forgotten Books, London, and by Wentworth Press in March 2019.

5   For an extended discussion of this influential novel see chapter 7 of this volume.

References

Armitage, David (2000), *Ideological Origins of the British Empire* (Cambridge: Cambridge University Press).

Auden, W.H. (1963), 'Going into Europe II', *Encounter*, January, pp. 53–64.

Black, Jeremy (1994), *Convergence or Divergence? Britain and the Continent* (Basingstoke: Macmillan).

Blake, Robert (1982), *The English World: History, Character, and People* (New York: Abrams).

Brontë, Charlotte (1984), *Villette* (Oxford: Clarendon Press).

Cameron, David (2013), 'Britain and Europe'. www.bbc.com/news/uk-politics (last accessed December 2017).

Colley, Linda (1992), *Britons: Forging the Nation 1707–1837* (New Haven and London: Yale University Press).

Cunningham, John W. (1823), *Cautions to Continental Travellers* (London).

Duffy, Gillian (2016), 'I don't want to be a European', 25 May. www.bbc.com/news/av/uk-36378870/gillian-duffy-i-don-t-want-to-be-a-european (last accessed December 2017).

Gardiner, Michael (2012), *The Return of England in English Literature* (Basingstoke: Palgrave Macmillan).

James, Rowland (1932), *While England Slept* (London: John Bale).

Ludlow, N. Piers (2002), 'Us or Them? The Meanings of "Europe" in British Political Discourse' in Mikael Malmborg and Bo Strath (eds), *The Meaning of Europe* (Oxford: Berg), pp. 101–24.

Macfarlane, Alan (1991), *The Origins of English Individualism* (London: Blackwell).

Moore, Niamh and Yvonne Whelan (2007), *Heritage, Memory and the Politics of Identity* (Aldershot: Ashgate).

Orwell, George (1941), *The Lion and the Unicorn* (London: Secker & Warburg).

Palmer, William (1912), *Under Home Rule* (London: Baines and Scarsbrook).

Parks, Tim (1998), *Europa* (London: Vintage).

Paxman, Jeremy (2007), *The English* (London: Penguin).

Spiering, Menno (2015), *A Cultural History of British Euroscepticism* (Basingstoke: Palgrave Macmillan).

Tice, Richard (2015), www.leave.eu/bloomberg-business-brexit-city/ (last accessed December 2017).

Upward, Allen (1907), *The Fourth Conquest* (London: The Tyndale Press).

Watson, Robert (1795), *The Life of Lord George Gordon* (London: H.D. Symonds).

Wells, H.G. (1912), 'The contemporary novel', *The Atlantic Monthly*, January, pp. 1–11.

Young, Hugo (1998), *This Blessed Plot* (London: Macmillan).

7

The dystopian nightmare of a European superstate: British fiction and the EU

Lisa Bischoff

Introduction

Britain's vote to leave the European Union (EU) provoked an outburst of responses and publications that reverberated far beyond the fields of politics or the media, but the rifts and tensions that surfaced during and after the referendum have always been discernible in British fiction about the EU. Between Britain's entry into the European Community (EC) in 1973 and the momentous in/out referendum in 2016, around a dozen novels about the EU with telling titles such as *Euroslavia* (1997) or *Super-State* (2002) were published in Britain. Most of them count as political thrillers, are set in the near future, and can be situated in the British Eurosceptic tradition. They range from slight criticism to outright hostility, thus reflecting the broad spectrum of opposing attitudes towards European integration as defined by the vast academic literature on (British) Euroscepticism.[1]

The Aachen Memorandum (*AM*) (1995) by historian Andrew Roberts is representative of one important branch of Eurosceptic novels. A bestselling novel, it received mixed reviews: on the one hand, it was lauded as 'a gripping novel about the European superstate' and 'required reading for all those who like their facts served up as fiction' (Cash, 1995), as a 'cracking thriller' and a 'rattling good yarn' (Littlejohn, 1995); on the other hand, it was exposed as a 'Euro-phobic thriller' (Buruma, 1995). *AM* seems to have been particularly popular among (Conservative) politicians (e.g. David Cameron, Michael Gove, Neil Hamilton).[2] The novel was even cited in a debate in the House of Commons as a cautionary tale about 'civil unrest' resulting from 'people f[inding] they were unable to change the laws of this country in their own interests' (*Hansard*, vol. 274, col. 551). Later, in the context of the referendum and having been re-issued by Biteback Publishing, *AM* was widely discussed, as it clearly anticipated Brexit. This chapter explores the novel as a paradigmatic example of how questions of British national identity and sovereignty are negotiated in popular literature.

Set in the near future of 2045, the plot of *AM* revolves around a manipulated referendum that legitimised the merger of Britain into Europe: Britain has been fully absorbed into a German-dominated European Union, a federal surveillance state, in which European directives govern everyday life and markers of British national identity have been extinguished. Having discovered that the turnout of the referendum was forged, the protagonist, Horatio Lestoq,[3] begins to question the rightfulness of the union. As events unfold, he aligns with the conspirators of the underground resistance and ultimately helps to overcome the European state and restore an independent United Kingdom. In *AM*, the cultural tensions of the relationship between Britain and the EU take centre stage, and the European integration project is advanced through a national lens or 'prism' (Lacroix and Nicolaïdis, 2010: 339). As will be argued, the novel clearly displays what Oliver Daddow calls 'the brand of nationalist-based Eurosceptic discourse' that is expressed in terms of nationalism and pertains to national history and national identity (Daddow, 2006: 315–17). Advocating a withdrawal from the union, *AM* qualifies as the 'hard/principled' type of Euroscepticism (Szczerbiak and Taggart, 2008: 7). With regard to its futuristic setting, resistance plot and thematic features (e.g. propaganda, history re-writing, surveillance), it can be further categorised as a dystopian novel, as a dys-EUtopia.

This chapter is divided into two main parts, the first focusing on the representation of the EU as a threat to the British nation. The novel is discussed as a dystopian narrative which features tendencies of the EU in exaggerated form while staying within the bounds of possibility (Claeys, 2010: 109). The second part elaborates on how Eurosceptic points of view are reflected and articulated in the novel.

Denying the nation

In *AM*, the EU is represented as a challenge to the long-established idea of a strong and independent British nation. Not only has the EU passed a directive to suppress nationalism (Roberts, 1995: 138), it also resorts to different, intertwined strategies of denationalisation and Europeanisation to cut the bond between the citizens and their former nation state, thus specifically targeting the 'narrative of the nation', i.e. stories, images and memories that are commonly associated with Britain (Hall, 1995: 613).

Above all, the EU in the novel encroaches on the terrain of national history, the country's 'continuity with the past' (Hobsbawm and Ranger, 1983: 1). In this attempt, the EU clearly aligns with the governments depicted in dystopian fiction, where the denial (Aldous Huxley's *Brave New World*), destruction (Ray Bradbury's *Fahrenheit 451*) and distortion of the records of the past (George Orwell's *Nineteen Eighty-Four*) is taken to extremes. Like the Inner Party in *Nineteen Eighty-Four* or the ten World Controllers in *Brave New World*, the EU takes control of information about the past to secure the stability and future of the integration project (Baccolini, 2003: 115; Ferns 1999: 119–20; Gottlieb, 2001: 12).

The EU in *AM* mainly interferes with national history as it is taught in school, (re-)told in textbooks and disseminated in public. Historical events, personages and institutions, which are considered important for the construction of nationhood and have sustained Britishness until today, are attacked. In particular, Britain's military history is targeted, as 'the prosecution of warfare undoubtedly played a role in forging a common sense of British identity' (Wellings, 2015: 42). Some war episodes are omitted – 'Nelson is taken off the syllabus' (Roberts, 1995: 27–8) – and other historical encounters (especially conflicts with other European countries) are framed differently to serve a different (anti-nationalist) purpose: 'The only times wars are mentioned is in order to admonish the kids about the horrors of nationhood' (Roberts, 1995: 162). Meanwhile, the Second World War is framed as 'a tragically unnecessary civil war between morally equivalent groups of competing *nationalists*. Hitler the National Socialist, Churchill the Tory Nationalist, Roosevelt the American Nationalist and Stalin the Communist-Nationalist' (Roberts, 1995: 298, italics mine). Besides tampering with historical junctures that give meaning to the nation, the EU in the novel tries to make people forget about the mythical age of the British nation and its alleged 'origins, continuity, tradition and timelessness' (Hall, 1995: 614). In *AM*, 'teaching dates has been completely phased out' as it is said to 'over-contextualise' history (Roberts, 1995: 162). Later, the EU regime fabricates and imposes a European reading of a common political past onto its citizens. In line with classic dystopian fiction (e.g. *Nineteen Eighty-Four*), '[h]istory [is] being written to emphasise the European dimension of everything'. (Roberts, 1995: 162). The Europeanised version of history justifies the present EU as a continuance of the past, giving particular weight to the idea of a European empire tradition as well as to the legacy of two world wars.

First, by building upon the medieval concept of *translatio imperii* (lat. transference of empire) (Goez, 1958: 104),[4] the novel renders European history as a sequence of empires, with the EU as heir to this tradition. '[T]he Roman, Charlemagne, Holy Roman and Austro-Hungarian empires' are explicitly listed as 'forerunners of the Union' (Roberts, 1995: 162). The EU thus becomes part of a 'historical chain' linking all efforts at unifying Europe under a single government (Foster, 2015: 3). Moreover, by claiming to be an empire, the EU deliberately evokes a specific and long-established discourse of 'civilisation, sovereignty, legitimacy, and superiority' (Foster, 2015: 46), justifying its policies with regard to deepening and widening processes of cultural homogenisation. In accordance with *translatio imperii*, the idea of a unified, prosperous Europe is then traced back to the Roman Empire, with Caesar as the first of Europe's 'Great Unifiers' (Roberts, 1995: 139). Like in the imperial discourse evolved over centuries, with many claiming to be descendants of Rome, the novel nostalgically evokes Rome's myth to legitimise Europe's newest empire.

Proclaimed successor of Caesar by Pope Leo in 800 (Foster, 2015: 16), Charlemagne is dubbed 'Second Great Unifier of Europe' (Roberts, 1995: 116). Until today the king of the Franks serves as an inspiration for European unification (Papiór, 2012: 45).[5] In the novel, the territory of the EU is said to cover almost exactly the same area as the Carolingian Empire (Roberts, 1995: 116). Moreover, the treaty that gave birth to the federal union was signed in Aachen, Charlemagne's permanent seat of residence and imperial administration: 'The shade of the Second Great Unifier of Europe was doubtless present when the Treaty was signed there by all the heads of European governments on 1 April 2015' (Roberts, 1995: 116). While Charlemagne's statue replaces Queen Victoria's in front of Buckingham Palace (Roberts, 1995: 269), the Carolingian Empire supplants the remembrance of the British Empire. Moreover, Napoleon's ghost pervades the novel (Roberts, 1995: 162), and Hitler is attributed a unifying role (Roberts, 1995: 127). The imperial tradition is then handed down over the centuries to today's EU, with politicians such as 'Jacques Delors' and 'Helmut Kohl' (Roberts, 1995: 162) among the most recent 'Great Unifiers'.

Second, besides building on *translatio imperii*, the EU regime in the novel has recourse to twentieth-century history – the loss of lives in two world wars and the post-1945 integrationist efforts – to create the EU's 'foundational myth' (Hall, 1995: 614). *AM* thus imitates and recontextualises the official EU discourse, as 'linking peace and European integration is a key component of the EU's legitimacy and forms the bedrock of its foundational mythology' (Wellings, 2015: 44). In the fictitious world of *AM*, the EU government retells and propagates the official founding story of the EU enthusiastically,[6] the union being fervently celebrated as 'the first superpower in history ever to be brought into being at the stroke of a pen rather than by bloodshed' (Roberts, 1995: 116). The two world wars are referred to as 'horrors of nationhood' (Roberts,

1995: 162) and contrasted with the EU project, which is described as 'a force for peace' (Roberts, 1995: 238). As in official EU discourse, the Second World War is framed as a 'temporal Other' (Diez, 2004: 325; Wæver, 1998: 90) 'against which Europeans are encouraged to identify as the foundation of their collective polity' (Wellings, 2015: 43). The shared legacy of the Second World War results in a shared future mandate, as the fictitious European anthem illustrates:

Peoples of Europe, arise as one!
From Centuries of mistrust and hate.
Let us march forward towards the sun,
Partners embracing one common fate!
Our Founding Fathers led the way,
And we arose at such a rate
That thirty-six peoples now can say,
'Europe is here! Not one moment too late!'
We're forging together a common land,
Protected, equal, unified, free,
Unbreakable bonds by which we stand,
An Eden on earth for you and for me!
                                    (Roberts, 1995: 142)

The anthem emphasises how the new Europe was constructed, forged by the 'Founding fathers' as a response to history. It emerged 'from Centuries of mistrust and hate' and has evolved into a paradisiacal, peaceful 'common land'. The novel thus both reflects and extrapolates the official EU discourse, embedding it in the framework of a dystopian narrative. In line with Eurosceptic thinking, it ridicules the EU government or Europhiles as 'utopian pie-in-the-sky dreamer[s]' (Daddow, 2013: 220) and represents their passionate integration plans as too grand, idealistic and unrealistic (Mautner, 2000: 192, 195).

Furthermore, not only the written records, but also the material and more tangible manifestations of British national history and national culture (e.g. the anthem) become the target of the EU regimes as they attack icons, symbols and traditions that tend to be associated with the British nation and play a central role in establishing, asserting and maintaining British national identity. The EU government has, for example, gone so far as to re-name national sites of remembrance (Nora, 1989) – such as Trafalgar Square into Delors Square (Roberts, 1995: 28) or Waterloo Station into Maastricht Terminus (Roberts, 1995: 33) – and replace statues of national war heroes (e.g. Nelson is substituted by Schuman) (Roberts, 1995: 28). This way the regime makes sure that popular gathering places neither stir memories of past hostilities between European partners (Britain v. France), nor encourage sentiments of nostalgia and superiority that could reawaken feelings of national attachment.[7]

As anticipated earlier, the EU's encroachment on British national soil becomes particularly discernible with regard to national emblems such as the Union Jack (Roberts, 1995: 238–40) or the British pound (Roberts, 1995: 33). Above all, the institution of the monarchy is challenged. According to the novel, the Mountbatten-Windsors left as a consequence of the Democratisation directive in 2017, accepted New Zealand's offer of sanctuary, and settled in Auckland (Roberts, 1995: 122). Meanwhile, the monarchy's 'public ceremonial manifestations' (Hobsbawm and Ranger, 1983: 1), the coins and banknotes, nursery rhymes and carols, school books, forms of address and site names, are also targeted: the statue of Charles at Madame Tussaud's has been removed (Roberts, 1995: 278), the 'Royal Albert Hall' is now 'Albert Hall' (Roberts, 1995: 202) and Buckingham Palace is called 'Attali House', housing 'the headquarters of the European Bank for Reconstruction and Development' (Roberts, 1995: 28). Every year, the EU Commission is said to jam the institution of the royal Christmas broadcast (Roberts, 1995: 278). In a similar vein as other dystopian regimes, the EU in *AM* deprives the British of their symbolic figurehead (monarch) as well as other manifestations of their former nation state. By regulating daily life, i.e. enforcing cultural homogeneity and imposing uniformity on its citizens, the EU tries to secure stability, which is the utmost aim of any dystopian society (Tripp, 2015: 39–40).

On top of that, the fictitious EU propagates the European idea (that relies on a shared past and culture) throughout the union. For example, the Union anthem (see above) is 'piped into the dormitories at … school[s] in an attempt to foster euro-patriotism' (Roberts, 1995: 187), recalling the sleep teaching in *Brave New World* that also serves to condition children's behaviour (with regard to consumerism and promiscuity) (Tripp, 2015: 37). As in Huxley's novel, hypnopaedia is used in *AM* to promote and guarantee the political order. Moreover, the pupils are expected to know the anthem by heart and sing it at the beginning of each class to the tune of Beethoven's Ninth (Roberts, 1995: 142). In addition, they have to memorise speeches by Schuman or Monnet (Roberts, 1995: 239), repeat nursery rhymes such as 'Citizen-Commissioner Cole was a very merry soul' (Roberts, 1995: 137), and most importantly, pass the weekly Union civics and lifestyle studies test (Roberts, 1995: 135) consisting of questions about the Union and its regions, and above all, the Europeanised version of the past. This way, the EU takes control over education (and curricula), safeguarding the future of the integration project.

Besides school, the EU in the novel disseminates state propaganda via the media. In line with regimes from other dystopian works,[8] it possesses advanced communication and entertainment technology to mass-medially manipulate its citizens (Heinze, 2015: 79). By way of so-called 'Subliminal Suggestion Advertising', it constantly spreads propagandistic slogans on TV such as 'Euro-Great', 'Anglo-Guilty' and 'Union is home' (Roberts, 1995: 256). While watching TV, people are subtly exposed to Euro-nationalism: '[T]he brain took in the message without any critical faculties being activated to question the crude political and social propaganda' (Roberts, 1995: 257). These means of state propaganda are further supplemented by visible and invisible surveillance technologies such as spy cameras, satellite tracking systems and surveillance bugs, mirroring the dystopian panoptic surveillance state, similar to the telescreens in *Nineteen Eighty-Four*.

A more concealed form of surveillance happens by means of the ID card, which Union citizens are obliged to carry with them at all times. It secures surveillance via invisible omnipresence: 'For the first time Horatio started to think of his ID as a potential enemy, rather than, as the Commission ads put it, "your empowering friend". With his photo, thumbprint, citizen number, identifying marks, D.N.A "fingerprint", biorhythm chart, blood type and signature printed on it, the card was believed to be impossible to forge' (Roberts, 1995: 113). The ID card moreover includes bank account details, medical records, health insurance, auto key and library card, and, above all, is able to betray its owner's whereabouts to the much-feared Europol. The issue of the ID card, however, not only visualises how the EU is depicted as a dystopian, totalitarian threat; it also demonstrates how the novel draws from the web of discourses organised around the central idea of the nation and how it extrapolates them. In the UK, citizens have no ID cards, which are widely perceived as a constraint and infringement on individual freedom and rights (Daddow, 2013: 212–16). By imposing them on the British, as done by the EU in the novel, the EU clearly adopts the role of the threatening Other.

Defending the nation

Despite the EU's tampering efforts, i.e. their anti-nationalism directives, the identification of British people with the British nation proves stronger. The novel thus reflects and voices long-held views in the UK about Britain's status as being apart from the Continent (Eurobarometer, 1996–2017).[9] This allegiance surfaces as the people still resort to their national symbols, remain attached to their monarchy, their currency, their flag, their hymns and literary heroes: 'The Union Jack was everywhere. People were singing the tribal songs; they knew the words to "White Cliffs of Dover" and "We'll Meet Again"' (Roberts, 1995: 244). With regard to sports, football games especially are used as a 'possible outlet for patriotic, partisan sentiments' (Roberts, 1995: 158). Moreover, they continue to read and quote from 'discouraged' national literature by Dickens or Shakespeare (Roberts, 1995: 62). Likewise, by posting pictures of (ex-monarch) William Windsor (Roberts, 1995: 159), or following his annual Christmas address (Roberts, 1995: 278), the British demonstrate their national attachment while defending their nation.

These incidences express a strong concern for British culture and identity. As Leconte argues, protecting the nation against the threat of a 'shapeless and fake European identity or culture underlies many Eurosceptic discourses' (Leconte, 2010: 52). References to nationhood, to the royal family, to 'typically British' symbols and traditions – all of which also figure in the British Citizenship Test (uktest.com, 2018), in the YouGov-Cambridge survey on national identity (YouGov Cambridge, 2011) and on the posters of the 'Britain is Great' campaign (greatbritaincampaign.com, 2011) – are frequently associated with British Euroscepticism (Daddow, 2006: 318; Lacroix and Nicolaïdis, 2010: 339; Mautner, 2000: 173; Medrano, 2003: 49–51, 227). Moreover, the underlying narrative of resistance clearly aligns with the typical plot structure of dystopian fiction (Baccolini, 2013: 38). By clinging privately to traditions and icons of nationhood, holding on to values of the past and evoking nostalgic moments, the British (the protagonist in front) develop an inner distance to the EU regime. Besides this soft (symbolic, defensive) resistance, *AM* also displays hard Eurosceptic attitudes. Opposition against the EU confines is most strongly voiced by the so-called English Resistance Movement (ERM), whose members do not accept the Aachen treaty and whose ultimate aim is an independent United Kingdom (thus echoing the manifesto of the UKIP). The ERM works underground and its military wing commits terrorist acts such as blowing up Commission buildings and statues, attacking the Channel Bridge, kidnapping, blackmailing or taking out people they term 'Euroquislings' (Roberts, 1995: 229).

Hard Eurosceptics (e.g. ERM) in the novel resort to two intertwined strategies: first, they present a different version of the past that largely draws from the components of a specific nationalist historiography to counter the Europeanised variant. Thus, as in other works of dystopian fiction, also in *AM* memory, historical knowledge, and storytelling become indispensable for the formation of collective resistance (Baccolini, 2003: 127). Second, hard Eurosceptics rely on techniques of othering and stereotyping to construct the Europeans *en masse*, and the Germans in particular, as culturally different, hostile, continental Others. The strong allegiance with and defence of the glorious nation is above all rooted in a particular understanding of British national history, as the frequent references to the 'thousand-year-old' nation state (Roberts, 1995: 197), 'Our Island Story' (Roberts, 1995: 298) and key historic junctures, like the victory against the Armada (Roberts, 1995: 300), suggest. This reading is in line with the grand nationalist narrative of British liberty, progress and exceptionalism (Daddow, 2006: 322) that Eurosceptics (regularly but not exclusively) evoke. It relies on historical, mainly military, encounters with Europe, the notion of continuity, and a set of recurrent sub-narratives (Ash, 2001: 6; Daddow, 2006: 320; Leconte, 2010: 86). In the novel the story is told by ex-king William Windsor himself. He understands his country's past, as 'one rooted in the foundations of our island story and our ancient, honourable policy of always preventing any one country from dominating the continent. It is the story of decent patriotism and of responsible, respectable nationalism. It is the story of British liberty' (Roberts, 1995: 298).

A number of scholars have pointed to a direct link between this reading – the British historiographical tradition – and Eurosceptic thinking (Bell, 1996: 5–19; Daddow, 2006: 322; Deighton, 2002: 103). They argue that the story of exceptionalism, uniqueness and separateness which originated in the nineteenth century ('Whig interpretation of history') and was then taken up by the famous twentieth-century historians George Macaulay Trevelyan, Herbert Fisher and Arthur Bryant, ultimately came to stand for 'the British national story' that still informs 'contemporary discussions on Europe and the EU' (Daddow, 2006: 321). In fact, the sub-narratives 'The Island Story', the 'Story of British Liberty' and the 'Europe as Other-Story' as they are alluded to by Windsor in the novel also figure in former prime minister David Cameron's speech. In the advent of the in/out referendum (2016), he stated:

> We are the product of our long history – of the decision of our forebears, of the heroism of our parents and grandparents … We are special, different, unique. We have the character of an island nation which has not been invaded for almost a thousand years, and which has built institutions which have endured for centuries … And the moments of which we are rightly most proud in our national story include pivotal moments in European history. Blenheim. Trafalgar. Waterloo. Our country's heroism in the Great War. And most of all our lone stand in 1940, when Britain stood as a bulwark against a new dark age of tyranny and oppression. (gov.uk, 2016)

As this extract illustrates, both literary and political discourse draw from the same repertoire of images, stories and memories to assert Britain's differentness from EUrope. For a start, Britain's 'foundational myth' (Hall, 1995: 614), Britain's age, timelessness and antiquity as well as its status as unconquerable nation is exaggerated. Phrases like the 'thousand-year-old nation state' (Roberts, 1995: 197) or 'nine hundred years of British sovereign independence' (Roberts, 1995: 292) evoke the foundation of the English kingdom by Alfred the Great in the ninth century and likewise the memory of the Norman Conquest. EU membership is represented as the end of 'a millennium of tribal allegiance' (Roberts, 1995: 160). This clearly echoes Labour leader Hugh Gaitskell who famously claimed at the Labour Party Conference in 1962 that entering the EC would mean 'the end of a thousand years of history' (UK Office of the European Parliament, 2010: 6). Prime Minister John Major (1992) used the same nationalist rhetoric thirty years later in a speech about the Maastricht Treaty (British Political Speech.org, 2018) and also former prime minister Cameron (2016) referred to Britain's 'thousand years' of independence (gov.uk, 2016). 'A thousand' as a mythical figure has been applied by politicians, journalists, and historians alike to signify timelessness, eternity, time immemorial (e.g. the Third Reich was propagated to last for a thousand years). Contrasting the old uninvaded nation with the new European project emerges as one of the most popular tropes of anti-EU discourse.

Historical continuity in the literary EU discourse is above all maintained by recalling specific dates and encounters from the country's past. The focus is on Britain's military history, the 'story of progress through conflict' (Tombs, 2014: 885). The popular 'island story' – i.e. 'the story of separateness' (Ash, 2001: 5), with its roots in nineteenth-century historiography (Bell, 1996: 16) – forms the backdrop to this narrative (Roberts, 1995: 298). It 'tells of irredeemable differences between Britain and the Continent; one that adapts Shakespeare's tale of a "sceptr'd isle set in a silver sea" fighting off the pernicious effects of continental intrusions into British affairs' (Daddow, 2006: 319–20). In AM, this discourse is evoked by Windsor who recounts how their ancestors saved 'their isles from the incursion of foreign institutions and systems of government' (Roberts, 1995: 292). To mark Britain's 'insular otherness', the novel employs Eurosceptic keywords (Teubert, 2001: 62), such as 'continental' and 'continent' (Roberts, 1995: 195, 241, 298). Conversely, the novel largely ignores the continental influence on the German ancestors of William Windsor, deliberately concealing or denying that Britain's history is connected and interwoven with Europe's history, especially with regard to the royal dynasties.

Among the continental invasions successfully warded off figure 'Armada, Trafalgar and the Battle of Britain' (Roberts, 1995: 300), presenting British history as a story of military successes over foreign (European) threats. The Second World War experience and Britain's particular role predominates this narrative in both political and literary discourse. In 2045 (alluding to the defeat of Germany in 1945), ex-monarch Windsor commemorates and celebrates the centenary of the end of the Second World War, i.e. 'Allied victory over Nazi Germany' (Roberts, 1995: 291) and thus 'over the most evil tyranny ever to have besmirched this planet' (Roberts, 1995: 300). The British heroically 'stood against Nazi Germany', which 'ravaged the continent' (Roberts, 1995: 293). According to Windsor, Britain's role was to guarantee liberty on the isles, in Europe and the wider world: to 'liberate all the many and various nations and peoples of Europe' (Roberts, 1995: 293), and to 'preserve world liberty' (Roberts, 1995: 292).

His speech aligns in content and style with the dominant form of viewing and representing the Second World War in Britain: 'Apart from a few blunders and blemishes, the war is understood almost universally as honourable and noble[,] fought with right and justice exclusively on the Allied side' (Cesarani, 1997: 28). Britain is celebrated for its victory against all odds and its 'special role in withstanding Nazi Germany' (Spiering, 2015: 10). The victory is seen as proof of Britain's superiority and distinctiveness from the European Continent. The 'mythologized vision' (Tombs, 2014: 877) of the Second World War is said to explain Britain's reluctance in joining the EU in the first place (and its eventual departure). As Anne Deighton argues: '[T]he "founding myths" of integration on the Continent were not necessary for the British, given their different experience of empire and war' (2002: 105–6). Framing the Europeans as Others and reassuring the British in their sense of superiority, uniqueness, exceptionalism and difference from the European Continent, continues to incite Eurosceptic attitudes (Lenz, 2002: 51; Spiering, 2015: 30).

The role of the threatening Other in *AM* is most particularly taken by the Germans, usually equated with Nazis. As in political or media discourses, in the literary discourse the 'link between Europe and German evil proves remarkably resilient' (Spiering, 2015: 11). Throughout the novel, the European Union is specifically depicted as a German-dominated project or as 'fourth Reich in disguise' (Spiering, 2015: 12). Roberts contrasts the '[o]ne hundred and ten million hard-working' with 'committed Germans bang in the centre of the Union – or Reich as I've heard them call it among themselves when they don't think anyone's listening' (Roberts, 1995: 161). By using the German term *Reich*, a parallel is drawn between the alleged German-dominated EU and National Socialism. According to *AM*, the

Germans not only have the 'motive' but also the 'opportunity and method' to gain predominance in Europe (Roberts, 1995: 119). They are said to have 'succeeded by hard work and stealth in doing what [the] British twice stopped them doing by force' (Roberts, 1995: 160). As the Union's 'primus inter pares' (Roberts, 1995: 300), the Germans are alleged to be 'de facto running the United States of Europe' (Roberts, 1995: 119). Exclamations like '[T]hey've won … They're in control' mirror the underlying fear of a powerful Germany (Roberts, 1995: 161). The novel thus activates and amalgamates long-established Germanophobic and Eurosceptic discourses. References to Germany's supposed hegemonic role in the EU have remained popular among Eurosceptics to this day, where politicians such as Nigel Farage and Boris Johnson still openly accuse Germany of wanting to take over Europe.[10]

Conclusion

The relationship between Britain and the EU is vividly debated in popular fiction. In *AM*, the European political project is pictured as (another) threatening intrusion from the Continent. Opting for a setting in the near future, it depicts the EU as a dys-EUtopia, where Britain is projected as an undesirable and unpleasant place that shares features with the dys-topian societies of *Nineteen Eighty-Four* or *Brave New World*. As this chapter has shown, *AM* demonstrates a Europhobic view that vilifies the EU's integration efforts and policies, turning them into a totalitarian means of control through constant surveillance, propaganda, or the re-writing of history.

This hypothetical extrapolation offers worthwhile insights into how the British feel and think about EU politics, especially in light of the results of the 2016 referendum, revealing the dystopian fears that underlie a Eurosceptic perspective. Drawing upon a storehouse of Eurosceptic images, the novel can be seen as a precursor to the simplified and hostile in/out discourse that pervaded the referendum debate. *AM* is 'embedded in a specific understanding of the British nation' (Leconte, 2010: 85), repeating a certain nationalist version of British history that sets Britain against a specifically German European Other: pride in Britain's long history of being unconquered and its stalwart opposition to Germano-European oppression stands in stark contrast to Britain's fictional fate at the hands of the EU 'Reich' (Roberts, 1995: 161), and Britain's failure to withstand that which they had managed to stop twice before (Roberts, 1995: 160).

Furthermore, British identity is conflated with English identity, the terms being used interchangeably in the novel, which increasingly becomes a marker of later Eurosceptic fiction. According to a number of writers today, the strengthening of English nationalism is among the central factors that explain Euroscepticism in Britain and the Brexit vote in particular (e.g. Barnett, 2017; O'Toole, 2017; Tombs, 2016). British fiction on EU matters highlights the cultural pathologies of British Euroscepticism, showing the huge impact of political narratives. As Maureen Whitebrook argues, fiction 'allows for the fullest representation of the world of politics: not political facts as such, but "reality" presented by way of different kinds of evidence and thereby offering a different, fuller, realism' (Whitebrook, 1991: 5). Within this context, Roberts' novel not only expresses widespread Eurosceptic fears and attitudes, it also anticipates Brexit, in fact predicting the in/out referendum and its outcome to one decimal place. While the referendum triggered a new wave of novels (e.g. Board, 2016; Cartwright, 2017; Smith, 2016) that paint a picture of a torn nation and offer more complex, profound answers to the question: Why Brexit?, there is a notable absence of pro-EU novels, telling stories in favour of (British membership in) the EU, that would challenge the dominant Eurosceptic literary discourse.

Notes

1   Early classification schemes of Euroscepticism can be found in Forster (2002), Kopecký and Mudde (2002), Harmsen and Spiering (2005), Flood and Usherwood (2007), Szczerbiak and Taggart (2008), Sørensen (2008), Hooghe and Marks (2007, 2009) and Mudde (2012). The soft-hard-typology by Szczerbiak and Taggart held the field for many years; its shortcomings were acknowledged only recently in view of most recent political developments in Britain and other European countries (Szczerbiak and Taggart, 2016). Especially in view of British Euroscepticism, the soft-hard dichotomy is not sufficient to include all 'the many varieties of Euroscepticism that can currently be mapped onto British political discourse' (Baker and Schnapper, 2015: 62). On British Euroscepticism in particular see Baker and Seawright (1998), Forster (2002), Spiering (2004), Leconte (2010), Wellings (2012), Usherwood and Startin (2013), Gifford (2014), Gifford and Tournier-Sol (2015), Spiering (2015), Baker and Schnapper (2015), Grob-Fitzgibbon (2016) and Simms (2016). For new, more nuanced approaches see Caiani and Guerra (2017) or DeVries (2018).

2   Environment Secretary Michael Gove, former prime minister David Cameron and MP Bill Cash went to London to celebrate the publication of *AM* on 5 October 1995 at the invitation of Lord Weidenfeld.

3   Horatio Lestoq is a telling name: 'Horatio' alludes to Admiral Nelson, thus evoking memories of a national war hero while drawing a symbolic parallel: like Nelson, Horatio will defend Britain against European threats.

4   For the scholars of late antiquity and the early Middle Ages, Rome was the 'natural successor to a sequence consisting of Alexander the Great, Persia, and Babylonia' and thus the 'fourth and final realm of civilisation outlined in the Book of Daniel whose existence was necessary for defence against the forces of the apparently imminent Apocalypse' (Foster, 2015: 45). In the course of the centuries, several other countries came to see themselves as the subsequent new, fifth empire (Foster, 2015: 45). On Roman Empire and European Unification see also Erskine (2010), Smith (2007) and Stein-Hölkeskamp and Hölkeskamp (2006).

5   He is commemorated as the founder of the idea of a united Europe and, most tellingly, gives his name to the renowned Charlemagne Prize. The prize honours public figures or bodies 'distinguished by their outstanding work toward European unity or cooperation between its states' (Stiftung Internationaler Karlspreis zu Aachen, 2018). On the Charlemagne Prize as European Memory Site, see Hefty (2012).

6   The European Coal and Steel Community (ECSC) was in fact built upon the idea of preventing further war. It was officially 'set up with the aim of ending the frequent and bloody wars between neighbours, which culminated in the Second World War. As of 1950, the European Coal and Steel Community begins to unite European countries economically and politically in order to secure lasting peace' (European Commission, 2018). The aim as such was embedded in the EU law. Art 3 (1) of the EU treaty reads: 'The Union's aim is to promote peace, its values and the well-being of its peoples' (European Union, 2012). In 2012, the EU was awarded the Nobel Peace Prize, because 'for over six decades [it] contributed to the advancement of peace and reconciliation, democracy and human rights in Europe' (Nobelprize.org, 2012).

7   Both battles – Trafalgar (1805) and Waterloo (1815) – have been decisive for shaping British national identity (e.g. Colley, 2009 [1992]). Even today, the battle-myths linger in the minds of the British, as the 200-year anniversary festivities (see BBC, 2007) and corresponding publications (e.g. Clayton, 2015; Forrest, 2015) demonstrate. Trafalgar Square with 'its proximity to sites of power and leisure, accessibility, its history as a site of public comment and popular identification' is still considered vital for constructing national identity (Sumatojo, 2009: 414); re-imagining the battle of Waterloo (as in 2015) is said to have shaped British attitudes towards the EU (Brown, 2015).

8   For example, '*Fahrenheit 451* portrays a world in which television and entertainment have outruled independent thinking and learning; books are forbidden and the fire brigades' only responsibility is to burn books' (Voigts and Boller, 2015: 420).

9   According to the Eurobarometer opinion polls, the UK claims undivided allegiance from its people. The polls (before the referendum) show 60 per cent

(1996) / 64 per cent (2015) of the respondents to regard themselves as 'only British', whereas 26 per cent (1996) / 33 per cent (2015) feel 'both British and European' and 5 per cent (1996) / 1 per cent (2015) see themselves as 'only European'. These results imply a clear rank order; Europeanness is relegated to the last position (European Commission, 2018b).

10   In the weeks before the in/out referendum, Johnson stated: 'Napoleon, Hitler, various people tried it ... The EU is an attempt to do this by different methods' (Mason, 2016). In the European Parliament, Farage commented: 'It is an irony, is it not, that a project that was designed to contain German power has now given us a totally German-dominated Europe' (European Parliament, 2015).

References

Aldiss, Brian (2002), *Super-State* (London: Orbit).

Ash, Timothy Garton (2001), 'Is Britain European?', *International Affairs* 77, pp. 1–14.

Baccolini, Raffaella (2003), '"A useful knowledge of the present is rooted in the past": Memory and Historical Reconciliation in Ursula K. Le Guin's The Telling' in Raffaella Baccolini and Tom Moylan (eds), *Dark Horizons: Science Fiction and the Dystopian Imagination* (London: Routledge), pp. 113–34.

(2013), 'Ursula K. LeGuin's Critical Dystopias' in M. Keith Booker (ed.), *Critical Insights: Dystopia* (Ipswich: Salem Press), pp. 37–53.

Baker, David and Pauline Schnapper (2015), *Britain and the Crisis of the European Union* (Basingstoke: Palgrave Macmillan).

Baker, David and David Seawright (eds) (1998), *Britain For and Against Europe: British Politics and the Question of European Integration* (Oxford: Clarendon Press).

Barnett, Anthony (2017), *The Lure of Greatness* (London: Unbound).

BBC (2007), 'Trafalgar 200'. http://news.bbc.co.uk/2/hi/in_depth/uk/2005/trafalgar_200/default.stm (last accessed 26 May 2018).

Bell, Philip (1996), 'A historical cast of mind: some eminent English historians and attitudes to continental Europe in the middle of the twentieth century', *Journal of European Integration History*, 2, pp. 5–19.

Board, Douglas (2016), *Time of Lies* (Hertfordshire: Lightning Books).

British Political Speech.org (2018), *Major, John*. www.britishpoliticalspeech.org/speech-archive.htm?speech=138 (last accessed 30 January 2018).

Brown, Colin (2015), *The Scum of the Earth: What Happened to the Real British Heroes of Waterloo?* (Stroud: The History Press).

Buruma, Ian (1995), 'Hun parliament', *Observer*.

Caiani, Manuela and Simona Guerra (eds) (2017), *Euroscepticism, Democracy and the Media: Communication Europe, Contesting Europe* (Basingstoke: Palgrave Macmillan).

Cartwright, Anthony (2017), *The Cut* (London: Peirene Press Ltd).

Cash, Bill (1995), 'The Aachen Memorandum', *The Mail on Sunday*, 15 October.

Cesarani, David (1997), 'British War Crimes Policy and National Memory of the Second World War' in K. Lunn and M. Evans (eds), *War and Memory in the Twentieth Century* (Oxford: Berg), pp. 27–42.

Claeys, Gregory (2010), *The Cambridge Companion to Utopian Literature* (Cambridge: Cambridge University Press).

Clayton, Tim (2015), *Waterloo: Four Days that Changed Europe's Destiny* (London: Abacus).

Colley, Linda (2009 [1992]), *Britons: Forging the Nation 1707–1837* (New Haven: Yale University Press).

Daddow, Oliver J. (2006), 'Euroscepticism and the culture of the discipline of history', *Review of International Studies* 32, pp. 309–28.

——— (2013), 'Margaret Thatcher, Tony Blair and the Eurosceptic tradition in Britain', *BJPIR* 15, pp. 210–27.

Deighton, Anne (2002), 'The Past in the Present: British Imperial Memories and the European Question' in Jan-Werner Mueller (ed.), *Memory and Power in Postwar Europe* (Cambridge: Cambridge University Press), pp. 100–20.

DeVries, Catherine E. (2018), *A Divided Union: Public Opinion and The Future of European Integration* (Oxford: Oxford University Press).

Diez, Thomas (2004), 'Europe's others and the return of geopolitics', *Cambridge Review of International Affairs* 17, pp. 319–35.

Erskine, Andrew (2010), *Roman Imperialism* (Edinburgh: Edinburgh University Press).

European Commission (2018), *The History of the European Union*. https://europa.eu/european-union/about-eu/history_en (last accessed 30 January 2018).

European Parliament (2015), 7 October. www.europarl.europa.eu/sides/getDoc.do? pubRef=//EP//TEXT+CRE+20151007+ITEM013+DOC+XML+V0//EN (last accessed 30 January 2018).

European Union (2012), *Treaty on European Union*. http://eur-lex.europa.eu/legal-content/EN/ALL/?uri=celex%3A12012M%2FTXT (last accessed 30 January 2018).

Ferns, Chris (1999), *Narrating Utopia: Ideology, Genre, Form in Utopian Literature* (Liverpool: Liverpool University Press).

Flood, C. and S. Usherwood (2007), 'Ideological Factors in Party Alignments on the EU: A Comparison of Three Cases', paper presented at the European Union Studies Association 10th Biennial International Conference, Montreal.

Forrest, Alan (2015), *Waterloo: Great Battles* (Oxford: Oxford University Press).

Forster, Anthony (2002), *Euroscepticism in Contemporary British Politics: Opposition to Europe in the Conservative and Labour Parties Since 1945* (London: Routledge).

Foster, Russell (2015), *Mapping European Empire: Tabulae Imperii Europaei* (Abingdon: Routledge).

Gifford, Chris (2014), *The Making of Eurosceptic Britain*, 2nd edition (Hampshire: Ashgate).

Gifford, Chris and Karine Tournier-Sol (2015), *The UK Challenge to Europeanization: The Persistence of British Euroscepticism* (Basingstoke: Palgrave Macmillan).

Goez, Werner (1958), *Translatio Imperii. Ein Beitrag zur Geschichte des Geschichtsdenkens und der politischen Theorien im Mittelalter und in der frühen Neuzeit* (Tübingen: Mohr Siebeck).

Gottlieb, Erika (2001), *Dystopian Fiction East and West: Universe of Terror and Trial* (Montreal, Kingston, London and Ithaca: McGill-Queen's University Press).

gov.uk (2016), *Cameron, David: Speech on the UK's strength and security in the EU*, 9 May. www.gov.uk/government/speeches/pm-speech-on-the-uks-strength-and-security-in-the-eu-9-may-2016 (last accessed 30 January 2018).

Greatbritaincampaign.com (2011), GREAT Britain Campaign. www. greatbritaincampaign.com (last accessed 30 January 2018).

Grob-Fitzgibbon, Benjamin (2016), *Continental Drift: Britain and Europe from the End of Empire to the Rise of Euroscepticism* (Cambridge: Cambridge University Press).

Hall, Stuart (1995), 'The Question of Cultural Identity' in Stuart Hall, David Hell, Don Hubert and Kenneth Thompson (eds), *Modernity: An Introduction to Modern Societies* (Malden, MA: Wiley-Blackwell), pp. 596–632.

Hansard (1996), HC Deb., vol. 274, col. 551, 21 March.

Harmsen, Robert and Menno Spiering (2005), *Euroscepticism: Party Politics, National Identity and European Integration* (New York: Rodopi).

Hefty, Georg Paul (2012), 'Der internationale Karlspreis zu Aachen' in Pim den Boer, Heinz Duchhardt, Georg Kreis and Wolfgang Schmale (eds), *Europäische Erinnerungsorte 2: Das Haus Europa* (Munich: Oldenbourg Verlag), pp. 83–8.

Heinze, Rüdiger (2015), 'Anti-Humanist Dystopia: Ray Bradbury, *Fahrenheit 451* (1953)' in Eckart Voigts and Alessandra Boller (eds), *Dystopia, Science Fiction, Post-Apocalypse: Classics – New Tendencies – Model Interpretations* (Trier: Wissenschaftlicher Verlag), pp. 67–84.

Hobsbawm, Eric J. and Terence Ranger (1983), *The Invention of Tradition* (Cambridge: Cambridge University Press).

Hooghe, L. and G. Marks (2007), 'Sources of Euroscepticism', *Acta Politica* 42, pp. 119–27.

――― (2009), 'A postfunctionalist theory of European integration: from permissive consensus to constraining dissensus', *British Journal of Political Science* 39, pp. 1–23.

Kopecký, P. and Mudde, C. (2002), 'The two sides of Euroscepticism: party positions on European integration in east central Europe', *European Union Politics* 3, pp. 297–326.

Lacroix, Justine and Kalypso Nicolaïdis (2010), *European Stories: Intellectual Debates on Europe in National Contexts* (Oxford: Oxford University Press).

Leconte, Cécile (2010), *The European Union Series: Understanding Euroscepticism* (Basingstoke: Palgrave Macmillan).

Lenz, Bernd (2002), ' "This Scept'red Isle": Britain's insular mentality, interculture and the Channel Tunnel', *Journal for the Study of British Cultures* 9, pp. 51–67.

Littlejohn, Richard (1995), 'A future imperfect', *Daily Mail*, 4 November.

Mason, Rowena (2016), 'Tories divided by Boris Johnson's EU-Hitler comparison', *Guardian*, 16 May. www.theguardian.com/politics/2016/may/16/tories-divided-by-boris-johnsons-eu-hitler-comparison (last accessed 30 January 2018).

Mautner, Gerlinde (2000), *Der Britische Europa-Diskurs: Methodenreflexion und Fallstudien zur Berichterstattung in der Tagespresse* (Wien: Passagen Verlag).

Medrano, Juan Díez (2003), *Framing Europe: Attitudes to European Integration in Germany, Spain, and the United Kingdom* (Princeton: Princeton University Press).

Mudde, C. (2012), 'The comparative study of party-based Euroscepticism: the Sussex versus the North Carolina school', *East European Politics* 28, pp. 193–202.

Nobelprize.org. (2012), *The Nobel Peace Prize 2012*. www.nobelprize.org/ nobel_prizes/peace/laureates/2012/ (last accessed 24 January 2018).

Nora, Pierre (1989), 'Between memory and history: Les Lieux de Memoire', *Representations*, 26, pp. 7–24.

O'Toole, Fintan (2017), 'George Orwell's idea of a better England is stirring again today', *Guardian*, 18 June. www.theguardian.com/commentisfree/2017/jun/17/george-orwell-idea-of-better-britain-stirring-again (last accessed 30 January 2018).

Palmer, Terry (1997), *Euroslavia* (London: Pallas Publishing).

Papiór, Jan (2012), 'Der Mythos "Europa" in der europäischen Literatur', *Europäische Erinnerungsorte 1: Mythen und Grundbegriffe des europäischen Selbstverständnisses* (Munich: Oldenbourg Verlag), pp. 41–55.

Roberts, Andrew (1995), *The Aachen Memorandum* (London: Weidenfeld & Nicolson).

Simms, Brendan (2016), *Britain's Europe: A Thousand Years of Conflict and Cooperation* (London: Allen Lane).

Smith, Ali (2016), *Autumn* (London: Hamish Hamilton).

Smith, Julia (2007), *Europe after Rome: A New Cultural History 500–1000* (Oxford: Oxford University Press).

Spiering, Menno (2004), 'British Euroscepticism', *European Studies* 20, pp. 127–49.
(2015), *A Cultural History of British Euroscepticism* (Basingstoke and New York: Palgrave Macmillan).

Stein-Hölkeskamp, Elke and Karl-Joachim Hölkeskamp (eds) (2006), *Erinnerungsorte der Antike: die Römische Welt* (Munich: C.H. Beck).

Stiftung Internationaler Karlspreis zu Aachen (2018), 'Who is awarded the prize'. www.karlspreis.de/en/the-charlemagne-prize/who-is-awarded-the-prize (last accessed 30 January 2018).

Sumatojo, S. (2009), 'Britishness in Trafalgar Square: urban place and the construction of national identity', *Studies in Ethnicity and Nationalism* 9, pp. 410–28.

Szczerbiak, Aleks and Paul Taggart (2008), *Opposing Europe? The Comparative Party Politics of Euroscepticism* (Oxford: Oxford University Press).

(2016), 'Brexit will boost "hard Euroscepticism" elsewhere in Europe', *LSE Blog*, Ed. LSE. http://blogs.lse.ac.uk/brexit/2016/08/25/hard-euroscepticism-to-become-a-more-viable-political-project/ (last accessed 30 January 2018).

Teubert, Wolfgang (2001), 'A Province of a Federal Superstate Ruled by an Unelected Bureaucracy: Keywords of the Euro-Sceptic Discourse in Britain' in Andreas Musolff, Colin Good, Petra Points and Ruth Wittlinger (eds), *Attitudes Towards Europe: Language in the Unification Process* (Burlington: Ashgate), pp. 45–88.

Tombs, Robert (2014), *The English and Their History* (London: Allen Lane).

(2016), 'Make England great again', *ForeignPolicy.com*, 22 February. http://foreignpolicy.com/2016/02/22/make-england-great-again-brexit-eu-david-cameron/ (last accessed 30 January 2018).

Tripp, Ronja (2015), 'Biopolitical Dystopia: Aldous Huxley, *Brave New World* (1932)', in Eckart Voigts and Alessandra Boller (eds), *Dystopia, Science Fiction, Post-Apocalypse: Classics – New Tendencies – Model Interpretations* (Trier: Wissenschaftlicher Verlag), pp. 29–46.

UK Office of the European Parliament (2010), 'Gaitskell, Hugh', *Britain and Europe in 10 Speeches* (London). www.europarl.europa.eu/unitedkingdom/resource/static/files/public-ations_ressources/ep_speeches_dps_final.pdf (last accessed 30 January 2018).

uktest.com (2018), www.theuktest.com/facts/ (last accessed 30 January 2018).

Usherwood, S. and N. Startin (2013), 'Euroscepticism as a persistent problem', *Journal of Common Market Studies*, 51, pp. 1–16.

Voigts, Eckart and Alessandra Boller (eds) (2015), *Dystopia, Science Fiction, Post-Apocalypse: Classics – New Tendencies – Model Interpretations* (Trier: Wissenschaftlicher Verlag).

Wæver, O. (1998), 'Insecurity, Security and Asecurity in the West European Non-War Community' in E. Adler and M. Barnett (eds), *Security Communities* (Cambridge: Cambridge University Press), pp. 69–118.

Wellings, Ben (2012), *English Nationalism and Euroscepticism: Losing the Peace* (Bern: Peter Lang).

(2015), 'Beyond Awkwardness: England, the European Union and the End of Integration' in Chris Gifford and Karine Tournier-Sol (eds), *The UK Challenge to Europeanization: The Persistence of British Euroscepticism* (Basingstoke: Palgrave Macmillan), pp. 33–50.

Whitebrook, Maureen (1991), *Reading Political Stories: Representations of Politics in Novels and Pictures* (New York: Rowman & Littlefield).

YouGov Cambridge (2011), *Census 2011 National Identity*, 12 April 2011. https://d25d2506sfb94s.cloudfront.net/cumulus_uploads/document/rs9i46duyy/National%20Identity.pdf (last accessed 30 January 2018).

8

A case for a Green Brexit? Paul Kingsnorth, John Berger and the pros and cons of a sense of place

Christian Schmitt-Kilb

Introduction

'sum there is who mofs and sum who stays it now seems to me and i was one who stayed' (Kingsnorth, 2014: 233). There are people who move and people who stay, and buccmaster of holland [*sic*], the not altogether likable narrator-protagonist of Paul Kingsnorth's post-apocalyptic historical novel *The Wake* (2014), is a stayer. Kingsnorth, former editor of the *Ecologist*, once green activist and radical environmentalist, co-founder and by now ex-editor of the online platform *The Dark Mountain Project*, poet and novelist (*The Wake, Beast*), has set *The Wake* in the three years after the Norman invasion. The novel highlights the resistance of a group of native guerrilla fighters led by buccmaster, a Lincolnshire farmer, against the Norman invaders. For buccmaster, 'a world ends' with the arrival of the French (Kingsnorth, 2014: 2). Unwilling to accept the new regime and after having lost home and family, what is at stake for buccmaster is his whole world, being and identity – putting it in the balance is less a choice than the only thing he can do if he wants to live. In the context of this narrative, being a stayer means to resist and fight the foreigners (*ingengas*), but it also means to keep the memory of the native culture alive and to defy the violence with which the French, after having successfully invaded and conquered the land, impose their rules, laws and language upon *angland* and its inhabitants in an act which, according to Kingsnorth, was 'probably the most catastrophic single event in this nation's history' (Kingsnorth, 2014: 357). Kingsnorth shows a dislike of compromise similar to his protagonist by inventing a difficult language for his tale, a language he calls 'shadow tongue' (Kingsnorth, 2014: 353). It is based on contemporary (twenty-first-century) English in combination with syntactical and lexicological elements of Old English, an artificial

Anglo-Saxon English stripped of (most of) its Latinate influences. This imagined language has a literary historical and a political side to it: it is a means of forced alienation, a stylistic resistance against a misleadingly easy access to a distant and strange past; and it is meant to render the Anglo-Saxon world of around 1066 in a language untainted by French influence.[1]

The author is largely successful in keeping the narrative within the discursive and intellectual boundaries of the medieval world it depicts. However, Adam Thorpe noticed, in his *Guardian* review of the novel, 'a subdued sense that [it] intends a modern parallel with our own dispossessed times' (Thorpe, 2014).[2] I propose a reading of *The Wake* in the context of the imminent Brexit; indeed, I want to read it as a Brexit-novel.[3] Usually, apocalyptic or post-apocalyptic novels are set in the near or not so near future.[4] *The Wake*, on the other hand, imagines the Norman Conquest from the point of view of the conquered as a template for all kinds of historical situations, past, present and future, in which the apparently stable and fixed parameters of life change dramatically to the point that they lose the self-evidence on which the old world was built. Kingsnorth suggests a parallel to our own time concerning the dimension of the change which is beyond symbolism. He looks back to the eleventh century from the point of view of a historian who supports the theory of the Norman Yoke as a singular catastrophe in the history of England, the negative repercussions of which are tangible until today: in land ownership, in the attitude to place, region and local culture, in notions of freedom, in the various forms of alienation in a world characterised by globalised capitalism and equally globalised environmental catastrophe, ultimately in an identity crisis of the English.

The sentiments underlying Brexit have been turned into fiction long before the actual Brexit was on the agenda of daily politics, as Fintan O'Toole has convincingly shown. In *Heroic Failure: Brexit and the Politics of Pain* (2018), O'Toole investigates the 'strange sense of imaginary oppression that underlies Brexit' as a deep-rooted 'structure of feeling' in Raymond Williams' sense (O'Toole, 2018: xvii). The overall argument of O'Toole's book is based on the claim that a peculiar combination of self-pity and superiority complex has shaped the attitude of post-Second World War England to Europe in general, Germany in particular, and to itself. In this context, a chapter entitled 'SS-GB: Life in Occupied England' traces the rhetoric of Brexit in the anti-European and anti-German sentiments fuelling a number of best-selling alternative history thrillers such as Len Deighton's *SS-GB*, published in 1978 and turned into a five-part TV series screened in 2017(!), and Robert Harris's *Fatherland* (1992). Both novels, O'Toole shows, turn the moment of

Britain's greatest triumph into the moment of greatest humiliation and defeat, both imagine the occupation of England by Nazi Germany and the subsequent decline 'from being at the heart of Empire to being an outpost of an occupied colony' (O'Toole, 2018: 29), and both voice 'profound national anxieties' about how English (or British, for that matter, though O'Toole considers Brexit as an altogether English affair) national identity could be defined (O'Toole, 2018: 31). Robert Harris himself is a convinced European, but the novel, written shortly after the fall of the Berlin Wall, presents an only slightly veiled characterisation of the European Union as a site of German power politics and a colonial project in which England features as an unimportant outpost about which there is nothing significant to say.

> In the West, twelve nations – Portugal, Spain, France, Ireland, Great Britain, Belgium, Holland, Italy, Denmark, Norway, Sweden and Finland – had been corralled by Germany, under the Treaty of Rome, into a European trading bloc. German was the official second language in all schools. People drove German cars, listened to German radios, watched German televisions, worked in German-owned factories, moaned about the behaviour of German tourists in German-dominated holiday resorts, while German teams won every international sporting competition except cricket, which only the English played. (Harris; qtd. in O'Toole, 2018: 33)

In O'Toole's account, the 'desire to *have actually been invaded* so that one could – gloriously – resist' (O'Toole, 2018: 44; italics in the original) is the ultimate national imaginary of a country which follows, at least in these fictional accounts, the binary logic of coloniser and colonised to the point at which it imagines itself occupied and colonised by Europe. This is exactly the scenario of *The Wake*, and O'Toole's short history of pre-Brexit literature thus the literary prehistory to Kingsnorth's *The Wake* as a Brexit-novel. Without being openly engaged with the political developments of today, it inscribes itself, in various ways, into this logic – via symbolism, analogy and *longue durée*-history. On a more pragmatic level, this logic finds expression in Kingsnorth's essay 'Rescuing the English', where the author remarks and complains that English history as it is taught in schools often begins with 1066, 'the date at which England was colonized', so that the history of England is taught as a history of dispossession with the 'English as the first victims of the British Empire' (Kingsnorth, 2017b: 207). *The Wake* itself rewrites this beginning as an end, marking the potential point of departure for English national identity as the apocalyptic point of no return.[5]

The context for this reading of the novel is provided by a selection of the political-environmental texts that Kingsnorth published in the past decade: the book-length *Real England: The Battle Against the Bland* (2008), the apocalyptic *Dark Mountain Manifesto* (2009), as well as two essays which directly deal with Brexit. The problematic issue of whether there is a green case for Brexit, and how this question informs *The Wake*, can only emerge in this context. Drawing these texts into the discussion of the novel shall provide a sense of the metaphorical-symbolical network of cross-references underlying the fictional text which makes plausible its reading as a Brexit-novel. The fundamental opposition which emerges from these readings as a structure of thought makes use of terms such as place, authenticity, belonging and the particular in the context of an imagined apocalyptic scenario. These terms lie at the hub of a rather nebulous semantic field organised between the poles of cosmopolitan globalism and capitalist liberalism on the one hand, and communitarian ideas of home, cultural and national identity and the unity of folk and land, dangerously close to blood-and-soil ('this ground is in our bodigs deop' [Kingsnorth, 2014: 18]) on the other.

On 3 November 2016, five months after the surprising Brexit referendum and five days before the by then a little less surprising triumph of Donald Trump in the US presidential elections, Kingsnorth published an article headed 'Small is Still Beautiful' (later re-issued on the author's homepage as 'Brexit and the Culture of Progress', Kingsnorth, 2016b) in which he defends Brexit. Setting out to think about Britain's decision to leave the European Union from an environmentalist's perspective as a controversial event rather than as a priori worthy of condemnation, his defence is based on a self-declared green idealism and a fundamental criticism of what he considers the destructive forces of a globalised neo-liberal consumer capitalism supposedly embodied by the EU and its institutions. Four months later, he picks up on these issues in a *Guardian* essay entitled 'The Lie of the Land'. While the November 2016 essay made a strong personal case for Brexit but avoided the question as to his own vote in the referendum, the *Guardian* article opens with the declaration that he 'voted to leave the European Union' (Kingsnorth, 2017a).[6] A biography of radical green activism and a widely recognised promotion of environmentalism: these were once trustworthy indicators comfortably to pigeonhole a person in the camp of the political left. However, Kingsnorth voted leave on the basis of sentiments, convictions and terms which used to be the stock in trade of the right: dreaming of 'a new era of genuine democracy' in England which ought to be accompanied by the establishment of an English Parliament in 'the old Viking capital' of York (Kingsnorth, 2008: 280), by 'debates about Englishness' and by a 'new type of patriotism, benign and positive, based on place not race, geography not biology … A national mission to reclaim the land and the landscapes for the people who live in them and care about them' (Kingsnorth, 2008: 285). That stance poses several questions at once, not the least interesting of which is: what has happened to the descriptive validity of the great political binary 'left' and 'right'?[7]

After Kingsnorth's coming out as a Leave-voter, he has voiced astonishment that his position on Brexit was almost uniformly attacked by green activists, public intellectuals and NGOs who, like he himself, came 'from a tradition founded on localisation, degrowth, bioregionalism and a fierce critique of industrial capitalism' (Kingsnorth, 2017a). His former allies, the author claims, fail to see Britain's withdrawal from the EU as an opportunity; instead, they consider it a national disaster even though the EU 'violates just about every green principle going' by being 'the opposite of local', 'destructive to the natural world' and 'anti-democratic' (Kingsnorth, 2016b).[8] In 'The Lie of the Land', Kingsnorth predicts the end of globalism ('the rootless ideology of the fossil fuel age') and hopes for a future 'benevolent green nationalism' in which human beings – 'animals in a place' – merge their ecological identity with their cultural identity and rediscover in themselves the necessity to belong and a sense of place (Kingsnorth, 2017a).

The contested ground in this context is structured by the apparent binary oppositions of the global and the local, the universal and the particular, metropolitan cosmopolitanism and rural communitarianism, knowledge of place and world-citizenship. On this field, the familiar political categories of right and left no longer work, or they are at least temporarily suspended. Why have they lost the differential sharpness they once had? Andreas Reckwitz, German sociologist and author of *The Society of Singularities*, has provided a template which helps to explain the reconfigurations of left and right between the poles of what he calls a universalist and differential liberalism ('der apertistisch-differenzielle Liberalismus' [Reckwitz, 2017: 375]) and a form of particularism including cultural essentialism and communitarianism. According to Reckwitz, this opposition has created, in the course of the structural transformation of modernity, a new political frontline which cuts through the binary of left and right which governed industrial societies: the frontline between a globalist, cosmopolitan, urban, mobile elite on the one hand and national(ist) rural communitarians who follow the logic of nativism, tribal allegiance and stability on the other. Both have their share of left and right. (Neo) liberal 'citizens of nowhere' are to be found on the spectrum from a politically right economic neoliberalism to a left liberalism focusing on issues of diversity, individual fulfilment, the importance of education, cultural heterogeneity, LGBTQ-rights etc. Their mirror image are the communitarians on *The Road to Somewhere*[9] who are sceptical about globalisation and who perceive the openness of the first as threatening and destructive. Economically, this group often demands stronger public regulations of the free market, a rather left position, while their sense of collective identity and the construction of identity via history and place is traditionally associated with the right of the political spectrum. Questions of culture have turned out to be a contested field on both sides.[10]

Long before the actual Brexit debate, Kingsnorth's *Real England* has inscribed itself into, and contributed to, this very logic. The book, ranging from the first chapter, 'Citizens of Nowhere', to the last, 'Know Your Place', entails the political poetics of *The Wake*. In *Real England*, the critique of the modern homogenisation and 'destruction of place, meaning and culture' (Kingsnorth, 2008: 263) is linked to a critique of language ('The old words don't work' [Kingsnorth, 2008: 269]) in the context of the assumption that the old political ascriptions no longer work either. 'This is not about Left versus Right' because both sides subscribe to the ideology of progress which crushes 'the life out of people and places' (Kingsnorth, 2008: 269). In Kingsnorth's account, a sense of place is under pressure, and as a result, many people suffer from rootlessness rebranded as freedom, and placelessness packaged as cosmopolitanism. In order to recover the *genius loci*, we (that is the people, *the folc* in *The Wake*) have to know our place and be prepared to stand up for it – as buccmaster does in *The Wake* 'in our land that is no longer our land' (Kingsnorth, 2014: 16).

One year later, in 2009, Kingsnorth, together with fellow activist Dougald Hine, wrote a pamphlet entitled *Uncivilisation: The Dark Mountain Manifesto* as a foundational text for their website *The Dark Mountain Project*. The latter is a network of writers, artists and thinkers who share the belief that 'the world is entering an age of ecological collapse, material contraction and social and political unravelling, and [who] want our cultural responses to reflect this reality',[11] preferably in forms of writing grounded in a sense of concrete place and time. The manifesto picks up some of the issues of *Real England* and, in combination with ecocritical, environmentalist concerns, presents them in the context of a pending apocalypse. Even though we know that we are doomed, says Kingsnorth, the 'idea of history in which the future will be an upgraded version of the present' (Kingsnorth and Hine, 2014: 15) is still strong.

The Wake

A sense of place under threat in the context of imminent apocalypse provides the coordinates of *The Wake*. Buccmaster knows his place in the beginning ('i had my land i cnawan my ham and my folcs i was a great man there' [Kingsnorth, 2014: 233]) until the arrival of the French, only to become a dispossessed migrant in his own country who leaves his dead wife and destroyed home behind. He turns into a 'green man' and notoriously unreliable chronicler of a development represented as a cultural genocide. Land is seized, political and cultural institutions are overturned, languages banned, leaders persecuted and families disrupted in a transformation which pervades all realms of life. However, in his self-centred and deluded way, buccmaster seems to come into his own only when the breakdown of the social order forces him to take sides and define for himself what exactly is *anglisc*. Katrin Thier has convincingly claimed that the 'fall of the old order presents him with the opportunity of opposing the invaders not with attempts to restore the previous regime, but with what he holds to be the true values of England' (Thier, 2016).[12] In this sense, buccmaster is a perfect personification of the structure of feeling underlying Brexit according to Fintan O'Toole, namely the above quoted 'desire to *have actually been invaded* so that one could – gloriously – resist' (O'Toole, 2018: 44; italics in the original).

The personal and national-tribal breakdown is, according to the protagonist and the chorus- and dream-like passages set in italics, as much a result of the French invasion as of the sin to which the people of England had succumbed even before the arrival of the *frenc*. The *enemi*[13] within is as important for the construction of the imagined community of the nation as the invading foreigners: 'there is deop synn all through this land and thu will be strac down o angland for what thu has done' (Kingsnorth, 2014: 15). The combination of apostrophe and personification makes of England an organic unity of land, plants, trees, human beings, language and religion – and *stayan* (staying) in one's place is the imperative which this unity demands: 'i had growan from that eorth lic a treow and then lic a treow i was tacan up by the roots and cast on hard ground ... i had seen what mofan was and mofan is sorness mofan is fear. stayan is right stayan where the gods has put thu if all folcs wolde stay then all things wolde be in their right place i telt this to my father' (Kingsnorth, 2014: 233–4). Repeatedly insisting that he does not want to talk about his father, he idealises his grandfather who represents the 'eald daegs' of freedom when 'our fathers fathers stalcced the wilde fens' (Kingsnorth, 2014: 4).

The continuity of a family tradition is symbolised in buccmaster's home by a sword made by weland, the legendary blacksmith who made Beowulf's mail shirt, which is handed down from father to son. With the sword in hand, he believes himself well-equipped to beat the hated *ingengas* (foreigners). Weland's sword signifies a continuity both of family tradition and historical tradition from the beginnings of Anglo-Saxon England until 1066. Now, the magic no longer works, which is also a result of buccmaster's egocentrism. His own son dunstan, after being called by the king to fight the French, is not worthy in buccmaster's eyes to carry this sword into battle. Dunstan argues that it was made to fight for England, but buccmaster insists that 'this sweord is for when this hus moste be feoht for' and that 'it is not to be tacan from my land' (Kingsnorth, 2014: 46). Pretending to throw his life in the balance for the protection of an idea of England, it is the much pettier cause of his own house and land which actually drives him. But owning the rune-covered sword does not prevent buccmaster from losing his land and following his illusions until he is completely isolated and defeated. Later on, when weland begins to talk to buccmaster, challenges him and gives him confusing advice, this marks the beginning of the personal breakdown of buccmaster which goes hand in hand with the breakdown of Anglo-Saxon England.

It is not the only instance in the novel where the unity of signifier, signified and referent, itself a form of magic, fails to produce the desired effect. The topic is evoked in the context of buccmaster's imagined *angland* which is marked by a natural bond between signifier (language) and referent (nature, things). This bond is destroyed by the linguistic imperialism of the conquerors and colonisers, and there is much more than language at stake. Words belong to the things they signify in a specific place only so that 'the names of the folcs of angland was part of anglisc ground', and wherever one language is superseded by another, when the ground 'can not spece its tunge … then sum thing deop and eald' had been made wrong (Kingsnorth, 2014: 146). Linguistic and cultural nativism govern buccmaster's reflections on language. Even if the people will forget, hope resides in the long-term resistance and stubbornness of the 'eald places'. Their second coming may one day restore the broken unity and all will be made right again (Kingsnorth, 2014: 146).

Contrary to buccmaster, other inhabitants of the region have arranged themselves with the new lords. They emphasise as positive developments an increased security ('before the frenc cum this was a wilde place there was out laws in these wuds now there is mor laws from abuf and there is no out laws' [Kingsnorth, 2014: 197]) and unmask the tale of ancient freedom as what it is: a myth without immediate meaning in the face of material needs, everyday concerns and an ongoing history of exploitation of servants by masters. 'we is all thralls all the time and has always been in angland … we worcs for thegns and is these thegns anglisc or frenc well these is names only. thralls for harald thralls for geeyome if we can bring in our baerlic and sing for the gift of it we does not asc why' (Kingsnorth, 2014: 198).[14] Buccmaster wishes to find allies in the name of an ideology of blood-and-soil and overlooks that the first priority for the people he meets lies in the banal continuity of life as they know it.

Ultimately, it is the broken voice and character of buccmaster which turns the novel into a literary success and rescues it from endorsing a simplistic black and white scheme. His character is reflected by people around him showing the reader that he was never fully integrated in society in the first place, that he was always a difficult case, an outsider even in his own place whose violence and arrogance was equalled only by his feelings of insecurity and inferiority. (Towards the end, he confesses to a terrible crime which he committed long before the French invaders arrived, which deprives him of all authority he might have claimed for himself.) Therefore, buccmaster's straightforward sermons on the authenticity of place and life which demand immediate action are deconstructed by his own discourse. Reading *The Wake* as a tragic tale about a man who is losing his grip on reality because his greatest strengths – persistence, toughness, idealism – are also his greatest flaws, the novel may be compared with Chinua Achebe's postcolonial classic *Things Fall Apart*. This 1958 novel introduces a very similar protagonist (Okonkwo) in a situation which is historically far apart but symbolically comparable: the arrival of the English in Nigeria. Okonkwo shares many character traits with buccmaster. Both fail to realise that their worldviews are built upon fundamental misconceptions and structural self-deceit, but while Achebe's tale manages to counterbalance the historical atrocities of colonisation and the individual strengths and flaws of its hero, *The Wake* is too much a novel of ideas for the personal tragedy of buccmaster to emerge as convincingly as Okonkwo's.

If *The Wake* is indeed Kingsnorth's attempt to respond in literary form to the realities of today's 'uncivilisation' (the title of the *Dark Mountain Project*'s manifesto), the response is challenging and problematic. The novel's post-apocalyptic outlook, as fascinating in its radicalness as it is disturbing, does not steer clear of narrow-minded forms of localism and exclusionary discourses of nationhood. *The Wake* posits an unalienated Englishness threatened and ultimately destroyed by the continental Other. The Norman invasion thus serves as the vehicle for a tenor which may be summarised as the homogenising effect of globalisation on English culture which Kingsnorth targeted in the books and essays discussed before. Facing the dissociation of human being and nature, myth of progress run amok, the hubris of anthropocentrism and a seemingly unstoppable environmental catastrophe, the 'tiger's leap into the past' (Benjamin, 1977: 259) staged in *The Wake* uneasily suggests that the origins of our contemporary globalised crisis lie in the destruction of a more authentic national and/or tribal past. Bold and simple, the threat which the foreigners of buccmaster's *angland* pose to English identity is a template to the threat which globalisation and the 'myth of progress' (Kingsnorth and Hine, 2014) – the main principles of which, for Kingsnorth, are an integral part of British EU-membership – pose to contemporary English identity. The surplus which is added by the text's literariness, the complexities resulting from a discourse which demands to be read against the grain, does not alleviate the uneasiness the reader may well feel in the face of supposedly existential and unalterable truths determined by a metaphysical reshaping of terms such as place, tribe or nation. Or, as Joe Kennedy puts it, in *The Wake*, 'particularism is knowing where you come *from*, not attempting to conceive of new ways in which where you *are* might assert its right to shape the terms of the universal' (Kennedy, 2017; emphasis in original).

Conclusion: John Berger's perspective

The initial urge to write this chapter, if this personal statement be allowed, was an uneasy fascination with Paul Kingsnorth's essays and fiction. This uneasiness was a result of the fact that I share many of his positions about the nature of the current crisis, but am convinced at the same time that his inferences are misguided. I consider myself both an environmentalist and a pro-European, anti-Brexit, anti-nationalist, anti-xenophobic citizen of the EU, and there are aspects of the kind of environmental thinking that I support which are at odds with my EU-citizen self. At the heart of this conflict is an understanding of place and belonging as important categories of life and identity formation. In this field, I consider Kingsnorth one of the most challenging, sometimes overly didactic but always productively polarising contemporary writers; his writings touch a chord by exposing the aporias and contradictions in my own thinking. It disturbs me that his experiences as an environmental activist and his radical criticism of liberalist globalism have made him a supporter of Brexit and a spokesperson for a new English identity and nationalism (albeit a 'green benevolent' one). The question with which I set out has remained as yet unanswered: is it possible to embrace a notion of identity which is based upon the specificity, particularity and character of place and local identity under the sign of an anti-globalisation environmentalism without getting dangerously close to the navel-gazing of nativist thinking and nationalism and a rhetoric of exclusion endorsed by right-wing Brexit supporters and populists all over Europe and beyond?

One way to throw this problem into sharper relief is to contrast Kingsnorth's positions with those of the late John Berger who has been equally straightforward in emphasising the importance for human beings

of a sense of place, belonging and location and in identifying as the antagonist to these parameters the levelling, homogenising and totalitarian
forces of globalised capitalism, neo-liberalism and consumerism. For
both writers, these issues have gained urgency and political currency in
the context of the environmental crisis, but also in the context of the rise
of new nationalisms all across Europe and of the Brexit debate. Berger's
countless publications (novels, essays, poetry, art criticism, plays etc.)
are driven by an unorthodox version of the Marxism of the 1960s and
1970s and, later in his life, by a Spinoza-oriented spiritual materialism.
This is the background against which his invectives on place, home and
belonging need to be measured.

'The key term of the present global chaos is de- or re-localization',
writes Berger, and the dream of the ruling powers is 'to undermine the
status of and confidence in all previous fixed places' (Berger, 2007: 115–
16). Berger's and Kingsnorth's diagnoses of the contemporary economic,
political and environmental crises correspond to a large extent. Making
allowance for the temporal distance of almost forty years, their positions
overlap especially concerning the critique of then EEC, now EU agrarian
politics, the necessity to defend cultural difference and the importance
of defending place and local identity at a time when they are threatened
by the stratifying and homogenising forces of neo-liberal capitalism.
However, they respond to these diagnoses in fundamentally different
ways. While Kingsnorth supports Brexit in the name of a new English
identity and nationalism as forces of resistance against global consumer capitalism in the name of people's identity, Berger, deep-rooted
in a Marxist-humanist tradition which always kept the upper hand over
notions of nationalism in all shades and colours, remained a convinced
European all his life. And while the line between Kingsnorth's nationalism and the xenophobic blood-and-soil nationalism embraced by many
right-wing Brexit supporters is dangerously narrow, tribal allegiances do
not have positive reference value anywhere in Berger's work.

Kingsnorth directly references Berger in some of his texts. The phrase
'culture of progress' in the essay 'Brexit and the Culture of Progress' is
a direct reference to John Berger's 'Historical Afterword' published
together with the fictional prose volume *Pig Earth* (1979). *Pig Earth*, the
first volume of the *Into Their Labours*-trilogy (Berger, 1979, 1983, 1990),
chronicles the transformation of rural life and the disappearance of the
peasant in Europe in the second half of the twentieth century. Berger
understood the destroying of the peasantries as a concerted attack by
'corporate capitalism in all its brutalism' (Berger, 1979: 212) on historical
understanding, a perspective which Kingsnorth subscribes to, I gather.
'The forces which in most parts of the world are today eliminating or

destroying the peasantry, represent the contradiction of most of the hopes once contained in the principle of historical progress … Destroying the peasantries of the world could be a final act of historical elimination' (Berger, 1979: 212–13). Berger juxtaposes the peasant's 'culture of survival' to a notion of 'culture of progress' embraced by consumer capitalism and socialism in equal measure.

Kingsnorth's essay opens with a review of some of Berger's positions to which he (Kingsnorth) claims like-mindedness. Indeed, central for both writers are reflections on the complex triangular relationship of a) the individual human being's identity with b) a sense of place-bound, physical belonging in the context of an antagonistic c) 'ongoing power' which dreams of 'undermining the status and confidence of all previous fixed places so that the entire world becomes a single fluid market' (Berger, 2007: 116). Both address these themes in fictional, poetic and essayistic form with an apparently similar agenda and by using the same political-philosophical frames of reference, ask urgent questions about the role of the environmental crisis in this context and even answer them, at first glance, in a comparable fashion. However, the apparent proximity of positions is misleading, which shows in their oppositional conclusions.

Kingsnorth speaks in favour of a new English nationalism where Berger feels universal rather than particular, European rather than English or French. Consequentially, Kingsnorth voted 'Leave', maintaining that 'there's a green radical case to be made for leaving Europe' (Wagner, 2016). Berger, when asked about Brexit in one of the last interviews he gave in October 2016, replied that he had 'voted with his feet long ago' when he moved from London to the French Alps in the early 1970s, a statement which testifies to his European identity as much as to his dislike and mistrust of life in the modern metropolis. The landscape of the Haute-Savoie, he explains, 'was part of my energy, my body, my satisfaction and discomfort. I loved it not because it was a view – but because I participated in it' (Kellaway, 2016).

Kingsnorth looks at the notion of place and placelessness, somewhere and nowhere, from the point of view of 'us' in the still affluent West, of those, that is, who can or could still claim to own a place ('Here I am in a place with some people around me. What does that relationship look like? How can I deepen it? How can I be here?' [Wagner, 2016; emphasis in original]). Berger, on the other hand, always confronts his own search for a sense of self-sufficient identity (e.g. by sitting on a field with four donkeys – the ninth dispatch about place) by taking the side and perspective of 'them', the dispossessed, be they peasants, labouring poor, homeless people or the millions who are forced, month by month, to leave their homelands, 'once rural places … turned into zones' where people 'lose all sense of residence' (Berger, 2007: 114).

The political differences are striking. It is doubtful if the 'Citizens of Nowhere' that Kingsnorth addresses[15] are in fact much different from the ones which Theresa May targeted with what Fintan O'Toole has called '*völkisch* rhetoric' (O'Toole, 2018: 148) in her first speech as leader of the Tory Party conference: 'If you believe you are a citizen of the world, you are a citizen of nowhere' (May, 2016). When Berger talks about citizens of nowhere, he has in mind, first and foremost, the dehumanising experience of migration under the sign of globalised capitalism.[16] Migration, forced or chosen, across national borders or from village to metropolis, marks a constant presence throughout his writings as the quintessential experience of our time, and its treatment a touchstone for the validity of any meaningful statement about contemporary politics. 'The way to resist globalization', Berger quotes Edouard Glissant in 'Ten Dispatches About Place', 'is not to deny globality, but to imagine what is the finite sum of all possible particularities and to get used to the idea that, as long as a single particularity is missing, globality will not be what it should be for us' (Glissant; qtd. in Berger, 2007: 117–18). In comparison with Kingsnorth, Berger is concerned with social perspective in the Here and Now rather than with reflections about the end of time; with individual fates rather than with anxieties about lost national identities. In the face of the complex and diverse catastrophes (to which Britain has contributed significantly, as all major European nations have, in the past and the present) which are responsible for today's mass migration, Kingsnorth asks: 'What does it mean to be "us" in England? It's such a big question at the moment because the level of migration is so high' (Wagner, 2016). The suggestive causal nexus between the two elements, ' "us" in England' and 'high migration', leaves little doubt as to its underlying essentialist and exclusionary nationalism. English identity is under stress because of the migrants, as *anglisc* identity because of the *ingengas*. The nationalism resulting from the green case for England may not be so benevolent after all.

Berger stands the argument on its feet, highlighting who is really under stress: 'Month by month millions leave their homelands. They leave because there is nothing there, except their everything, which does not offer enough to feed their children.' Berger's 'Dispatches About Place' are accompanied by photos taken by Anabell Guerrero in the Red Cross shelter for refugees and emigrants at Sangatte near Calais and the Channel Tunnel.[17] The story of the person on the photos, representative for many million stories which could be told in its stead, is woven into the theses. An image which helps us to 'take account of how a man's fingers are all that remain of a plot of tilled earth' provides a dimension of political empathy for the place- and homeless in the context of a 'Portrait of an emigrant continent'. On many levels, Berger shows the way to thinking about place and local identity without becoming infatuated with new right rhetoric: in his writings, place remains an open and potentially liberating concept which demands to be realised universally in order to be valid at all. This may be because he considered himself, as he points out at the end of the 'Dispatches', 'still amongst other things a Marxist' (Berger, 2007).

Notes

1   German speakers have an advantage as they do not need to consult the glossary quite as often as English readers. *Petersilie* (parsley), *esol* (ass), *fogul* (bird), *geld* (tax), *sige* (victory) or *melu* (flour) are easily understandable.

2   In a *New York Times* review, Hari Kunzru also underlines that the tale 'feels strangely contemporary in its concern for what is lost when a social order perishes', and 'all is broc ... all is gan' (2015).

3   It is much more than that, of course. Leaving aside the political agenda emphasised in this chapter, *The Wake* is a brilliant psychological novel about the lies buccmaster tells himself, a novel about a father problem, an impressive historical novel also about war trauma, and a great success, through its language, in convincing historical alienation, but these aspects must be treated elsewhere.

4   John Lanchester's *The Wall* (2018) is a good example of a post-apocalyptic novel, which, in our historical moment, must also be read as a Brexit-novel.

5   In an essay for *New Socialist*, Joe Kennedy has pointed out that it is 'unclear how ironic Kingsnorth is being when he allows Buccmaster to claim Saxon indigeneity' (2017). Moreover, the presence of the Anglo-Saxons in Britain is of course the result of an earlier invasion, which turns buccmaster's and the novel's struggle for authenticity, truth and point of origin of an unalterable Englishness into a choice of favoured conqueror.

6   For an engagement with similar themes, see also the essays in *Confessions of a Recovering Environmentalist* (Kingsnorth, 2017b).

7   It would be fascinating, but not manageable here, to trace the genealogy of Kingsnorth's politics, a kind of conservative green radicalism which is difficult to tag according to contemporary notions of left and right, back through the various politically shady 'ruralisms' of the twentieth (e.g. the Kinship in Husbandry-movement) and nineteenth (e.g. Thomas Hardy, Edward Carpenter) centuries to the contradictory figure of William Cobbett and his times. In 'Beyond Left and Right: A Cobbett for Our Times', Craig Calhoun has convincingly argued that there are ideological and material parallels between the early nineteenth and the early twenty-first centuries which deserve to be taken seriously. Cobbett, he argues, wrote at a time

'when long-term economic growth came with job destruction for many ordinary workers, when opportunities for the lower classes lagged dramatically behind opportunities for those able to own financial capital, when government protected the banking system but not poor relief, when ordinary people felt parliament did not represent them, when international entanglements sparked major upheaval in politics at home', all this in the context of a 'debate over whether traditional English (or British) values are under attack'. Cobbett was, in the words of Karl Marx (as quoted by Calhoun), 'an anticipated modern Chartist ... and an inveterate John Bull. He was at once the most conservative and the most destructive man of Great Britain – the purest incarnation of Old England and the most audacious initiator of Young England ... With him, therefore, revolution was not innovation, but restoration; not the creation of a new age, but the rehabilitation of the "good old times"' (Calhoun, 2015: 157–8). Looking at the ways in which the categories of left and right lose their explanatory potential in the context of the global–local dichotomy in the twenty-first century through the lens of Cobbett as seen by Marx and Calhoun, today's blurring of the line between right and left gains historical contours which may help to throw into relief and explain the current ideological predicament. The structure of feeling underlying Brexit is informed by a similar mix of nostalgia for good old times and a politically radical critique of the forces and institutions which are (made) responsible for their (i.e. the good old times's) demise.

8   George Monbiot, environmental and political activist and self-declared Remainer, sees as one of only a few potentially positive results of Brexit an end of EU agricultural policy (Monbiot, 2018).

9   Joe Kennedy, in 'The Brexit Novel?', has shown how David Goodhart, 'advocate of Brownite nativism and now an anti-immigration ideologue, offers terminology for this account in his 2017 work *The Road to Somewhere* ... "Anywheres", he claims, are uprooted, footloose metropolitans surfeited with cultural capital, while "somewhere" are salty provincials, struggling with admirable courage for their particular identities' (Kennedy, 2017).

10   See Reckwitz (2017), ch. VI: 'Differenzieller Liberalismus und Kulturessenzialismus: Der Wandel des Politischen' (Differential Liberalism and Cultural Essentialism: The Transformation of the Political).

11   http://dark-mountain.net/about/the-dark-mountain-project/ (accessed 10 September 2016; no longer available).

12   Thier's essay is the most thorough linguistic examination of Kingsnorth's 'shadow tongue' from the point of view of a medievalist.

13   'enemi' is one of the rare occasions in *The Wake* where Kingsnorth uses a non-Anglo-Saxon term. According to the *OED*, it is an Old French word with a truly European heritage: it corresponds to Provençal, Catalan, Spanish, Italian and, of course, Latin. The *inimicus* is the non-friend; *enemi* has found its way into English only in the fourteenth century.

14   'names only' is a provocation for a protagonist for whom words signify, as has been shown, much more than what they denote, a conviction leading

to a meaningless murder which throws into relief buccmaster's real issue, a personal and psychological one rather than *angland*.

15 'Citizens of Nowhere' is the title of the first chapter of his non-fiction volume *Real England* (Kingsnorth, 2008).

16 This is a theme which is at the heart of Berger's thinking. It has preoccupied him since he co-published *A Seventh Man* (together with the photographer Jean Mohr), a book about European migrant workers, in 1975. Already there, he envisages it as a transnational, truly global problem. 'The subject is European, its meaning is global. Its theme is unfreedom' (Berger and Mohr, 1975: 11).

17 This refers to the *Orion Magazine* version, which has a few text passages on these photos which are left out, as are the photos, in the Verso-edition.

References

Achebe, Chinua (1958), *Things Fall Apart* (London: Penguin).

Benjamin, Walter (1977), 'Über den Begriff der Geschichte' in *Illuminationen: Ausgewählte Schriften I* (Frankfurt/M.: Suhrkamp), pp. 251–61.

Berger, John (1979), *Pig Earth* (London: Writers and Readers Publishing Cooperative).

(1983), *Once in Europa* (London: Bloomsbury).

(1990), *Lilac and Flag* (London: Bloomsbury).

(2007), 'Ten Dispatches About Place' in John Berger, *Hold Everything Dear: Dispatches on Survival and Resistance* (London and New York: Verso), pp. 113–21.

Berger, John and Jean Mohr (1975), *A Seventh Man* (London: Penguin).

Calhoun, Craig (2015), 'Beyond Left and Right: A Cobbett for Our Times' in James Grande and John Stevenson (eds), *William Cobbett, Romanticism and the Enlightenment: Contexts and Legacy* (London and New York: Routledge), pp. 157–72.

The Dark Mountain Project, http://dark-mountain.net/about/the-dark-mountain-project/ (last accessed 10 September 2016; no longer available).

Kellaway, Kate (2016), 'John Berger: if I'm a storyteller, it's because I listen', *Guardian*, 30 October. www.theguardian.com/books/2016/oct/30/john-berger-at-90-interview-storyteller (last accessed 1 March 2019).

Kennedy, Joe (2017), 'The Brexit novel?', *New Socialist*, 29 October. https://newsocialist.org.uk/the-brexit-novel/ (last accessed 1 March 2019).

Kingsnorth, Paul (2008), *Real England: The Battle Against the Bland* (London: Portobello Books).

(2014), *The Wake* (London: unbound).

(2016a), *Beast* (London: Faber & Faber).

(2016b), 'Brexit and the culture of progress', *Resurgence & Ecologist*, 299. http://paulkingsnorth.net/2016/11/03/brexit-and-the-culture-of-progress/ (last accessed 1 March 2019).

(2017a), 'The lie of the land: does environmentalism have a future in the age of Trump?', *Guardian*, 18 March. www.theguardian.com/books/2017/mar/18/the-new-lie-of-the-land-what-future-for-environmentalism-in-the-age-of-trump (last accessed 1 March 2019).

(2017b), 'Rescuing the English' in Paul Kingsnorth, *Confessions of a Recovering Environmentalist* (London: Faber & Faber), pp. 197–212.

Kingsnorth, Paul and Dougald Hine (2014), *Uncivilisation: The Dark Mountain Manifesto* (Croydon: The Dark Mountain Project).

Kunzru, Hari (2015), ' "The Wake" by Paul Kingsnorth', *New York Times*, 4 September. www.nytimes.com/2015/09/06/books/review/the-wake-by-paul-kingsnorth.html (last accessed 1 March 2019).

Lanchester, John (2018), *The Wall* (London: Faber & Faber).

May, Theresa (2016), 'Theresa May's conference speech in full', *Telegraph*, 5 October. www.telegraph.co.uk/news/2016/10/05/theresa-mays-conference-speech-in-full/ (last accessed 1 March 2019).

Monbiot, George (2018), 'The one good thing about Brexit? Leaving the EU's disgraceful farming system', *Guardian*, 10 October. www.theguardian.com/commentisfree/2018/oct/10/brexit-leaving-eu-farming-agriculture   (last accessed 1 March 2019).

O'Toole, Fintan (2018), *Heroic Failure: Brexit and the Politics of Pain* (London: Head of Zeus).

Reckwitz, Andreas (2017), *Die Gesellschaft der Singularitäten: Zum Strukturwandel der Moderne* (Berlin: Suhrkamp).

Thier, Katrin (2016), 'Paul Kingsnorth: *The Wake*', in *Perspicuitas: Internet-Periodicum für mediävistische Sprach-, Literatur- und Kulturwissenschaft*. www.uni-due.de/imperia/md/content/perspicuitas/rez_thier_ 0616.pdf (last accessed 1 March 2019).

Thorpe, Adam (2014), 'The Wake by Paul Kingsnorth review – "A Literary Triumph" ', *Guardian*, 2 April. www.theguardian.com/books/2014/apr/02/the-wake-paul-kingsnorth-review-literary-triumph (last accessed 1 March 2019).

Wagner, Erica (2016), 'The constant gardener: the novelist Paul Kingsnorth on Anglophobia, voting Leave and teaching his children to live off the land', *New Statesman*, 30 June. www.newstatesman.com/politics/uk/2016/06/constant-gardener (last accessed 1 March 2019).

9

Brexit and the Tudor turn: Philippa Gregory's narratives of national grievance

Siobhan O'Connor

As Benedict Anderson established, the construction of the 'imagined community' of a nation rests upon a mutual understanding of a shared past (Anderson, 1983: 196). And as Patrick Parrinder remarks, 'novels have been influential sources of ideas of nationhood and national belonging' and 'numerous English novelists from Defoe to Peter Ackroyd have doubled as commentators on England's history and national identity' (Parrinder, 2006: 14). The historical novelist therefore, writes the nation at a particular time through a re-visioning of its collective past, and in fictionalising real-life events and people, helps to shape the contemporary moment by offering continuities between past and present, which contributes to the nation's view of itself.

The Brexit era (by which I mean the ten years or so preceding the 2016 referendum) has seen the rise of a new discourse of Englishness that is distinct from the rest of the UK and from the European mainland. It is marked by resentment of the proximate other and aggrieved yearning for a feudal, pre-industrial past. England's relationship with the continent has often been presented as one of encroachment, servility and cultural loss. Vocalisation of this discontent has accelerated since the referendum and is sometimes expressed in the language of synthetic medievalism as exemplified by Jacob Rees-Mogg's coinage 'vassal state' as well as the oft-repeated noun 'sovereignty' which has connotations of courtly antiquity (Poole, 2018). The ascendancy of pseudo-aristocrats like Rees-Mogg and Boris Johnson is itself symptomatic of a national vision widely advocated by nostalgic voices on the right (for example Roger Scruton and Simon Heffer), allied with self-styled environmentalists such as Paul Kingsnorth whose 2008 'elegiac' polemic *Real England: The Battle Against the Bland* is the source of Theresa May's phrase 'citizens of nowhere' (Kingsnorth, 2011; see also chapter 8). These writers and politicians call for an England defined by pre-modern, rural resources and a reversal of leftist discourse. According to Simon Featherstone, their imaginary consists of 'an alternative feudal nation' and an English tradition that lies beyond the origin of contemporary patriots (Featherstone, 2008: 13).

This nostalgic vision apparently rejects pluralism and values ancestry and inheritance. A number of scholars have drawn attention to the English preference for cultural integrity over progressive politics. For Paul Gilroy, post-imperial Englishness is melancholic, marked by a 'habitual resort to culture as unbridgeable division' which he regards as a 'defensive gesture' centred upon ideas of racial hierarchy and employed by those who feel threatened by 'postmodern assaults on the coherence and integrity of the self' (Gilroy, 2005: 5–6). In a world where 'we are now condemned to work upon ourselves in conformity with the iron laws of mechanical culture just to hold our imperiled [sic] and perennially unstable identities together', an understanding that 'race, nationality, and ethnicity are invariant, relieves the anxieties that arise with a loss of certainty as to who one is and where one fits' (Gilroy, 2005: 6). Michael Kenny suggests that in 'the New Labour years, Englishness offered a language of inheritance and tradition that expressed a deep opposition to the metropolitan hubris and state-led managerialism with which those governments were often associated' (Kenny, 2012). For Kingsnorth, 'England is a nation; Britain is a political convenience'. Kingsnorth is preoccupied with a 'cultural landscape' that is being 'eroded'. Crucially in relation to this chapter's concerns, he claims to 'know its landscapes and its history, and feel connected to both' (Kingsnorth, 2011: 12–13).

Perhaps unsurprisingly, Brexit-era Englishness has been accompanied by a hunger for the historical in popular culture (de Groot, 2009: 2), and the Tudors have been particularly prominent. A month before the referendum, Charlotte Higgins noted in the *Guardian* that, 'Right now, the Tudors hold the nation in an especially fearsome grip' (Higgins, 2016). A year before that, the *Bookseller* of 29 May 2015 reported that 'Tudor-themed' titles were earning '36% of the top 100's value – far more than any other historical era' ('Top 10', 2015). The two best-selling authors of Tudor fiction in that year were Philippa Gregory and Hilary Mantel with Gregory's *The King's Curse* (a focus of this chapter), topping the historical fiction best-seller list ('Top 10', 2015). Since 2000, more than three hundred books about Henry VIII's court have been published, and to date, Gregory herself has published a Tudor novel annually since 2013. This fixation on the Tudors typifies a more general and marked fascination in historical fiction with the dynastic family saga and a return to kings and queens history which is indicated by the concurrent best-selling status of Bernard Cornwell's *Last Kingdom* series and Winston Graham's *Poldark*. It suggests that the fascination with the English past is entwined with a revived reverence for the aristocracy. This in turn reflects a renewed obsession with the celebrity royal that has followed the Thatcherite assault on working-class identity. Originating in the cult of Princess Diana, it now centres on her sons and daughters-in-law, reinforcing Englishness as what Tom Nairn terms 'the metaphorical family unity of a Shakespearian (or pre-modern) nationalism' (Nairn, 1988: 90). Furthermore, repeated re-imagining of the Tudor accession and subsequent Henrician Reformation, suggests that these events are perceived as pivotal in England's story.

This chapter explores the two Tudor novels, published by Gregory in the years immediately preceding the 2016 EU referendum: *The King's Curse* (2014a) and *The Taming of the Queen* (2015a). The first centres upon Margaret Pole, matriarch of the Plantagenet family who lost the crown in 1485 to Henry VII at Bosworth Field at the end of the Wars of the Roses. A representative of the old feudal order which was increasingly alienated by the Henrician Reformation, Pole, along with her family, moved in and out of royal favour throughout her life. She was eventually executed in 1541 at the age of sixty-seven. The protagonist of the second novel is 'Kateryn' [*sic*] Parr, Henry VIII's sixth wife, and the plot spans the period of her royal marriage. For much of this period, Parr was at risk. She was a committed religious reformer, which made her unpopular with the more conservative factions of Henry VIII's court, and at times her creed was at odds with the king's own beliefs. Furthermore, evidence suggests an attachment to the king's brother-in-law, Thomas Seymour.

Both novels are read in the context of the Brexit vote and in relation to Gilroy's prescient notion of postcolonial melancholia. I argue that they emerge as narratives of national grievance, permeated by yearning for a lost hegemony and a desire to return to a bygone age, whose protagonists resent the diminishing of their power and the meritocratic success of outsiders like Henry VIII's advisors, to whom they attribute a perceived national decline. I contend that the language of social class codifies a wider yearning for cultural and ethnic homogeneity. Through empathic engagement with the texts' exclusionary discourses of resistance and loss, which is engendered by an immersive first-person narrative, the reader is made complicit with the rehabilitation of feudalism as integral to Englishness.

Prior to *The Other Boleyn Girl* (2001), Gregory's historical fiction had consisted of family sagas: the *Wideacre* trilogy (1987, 1989 and 1990) and the *Tradescant* series (1998 and 1999). Her transition to royal narratives followed the death of Princess Diana and the unleashing of what Jonathan Freedland has referred to as 'anti-establishment rage', which he regards as having been 'a foretaste of something' which would eventually lead to the Brexit vote: an end to deference, a willingness to express emotion and 'vent their fury with the head of state, waving aside protocol and tradition'. For Freedland 'there is a line that can be traced that connects the EU referendum and the late summer of 1997' (Freedland, 2017).

It is, in fact, unlikely that the public rage felt on Diana's behalf was ever 'anti-establishment'. As Simon Featherstone and Tom Nairn have both pointed out, the function of the British royalty is to maintain 'oligarchic caste rule' and quell the democratic instincts of nationhood (Featherstone, 2008: 172; Nairn, 1988: 136). This demands 'a monarchy replete with the signs of tradition and continuity but also endlessly adaptable to the changing circumstances of the modernity it apparently denied' (Featherstone, 2008: 172). To some extent, this finely tuned blend of mystery and relatability had eluded the Windsors in the increasingly egalitarian 1960s and 1970s, and whilst the vocal Diana exposed their dysfunctionality, it was she who would rehabilitate their allure, thus averting threats to the political power they existed to front.

The narrative of Diana is one of romance. Featherstone points out that her 'courtship by the heir to the throne was cast as a fairy-tale romance' while the 'crowded' marriage that followed 'became in multiple retellings a royal *Rebecca*'. The emotional narrative following her divorce positioned her 'as a royal at odds with the stodgy compromises of royal pageantry and bourgeois family life visible elsewhere' so that she appeared to challenge the status quo (Featherstone, 2008: 174). Diana's death provided a focus for populist passion and collective national mourning that was, according to Hilary Mantel, 'a "natural and necessary" act of communion' (Mantel, 2017). Diana's death facilitated a form of national solidarity, of Benedict Anderson's simultaneity, but its articulation was retrospective: it took the form of yearning for something that had been taken away (Anderson, 1983: 23). The feeling engendered was grievance.

Popular disaffection with the rest of the royal family, though temporary, would have important long-term implications. The nationalism that emerged from it left the underlying principles of monarchy unquestioned. The object of royal maltreatment, rather than being an ordinary subject, was instead the figure to whom Tony Blair attached the paradoxical epithet 'People's Princess' (*BBC News*, 1997). Identity lay in shared emotion prompted by an imagined communion with an affronted faction of the aristocracy. This maintained the sense of an Orwellian England – as 'a family with the wrong members in charge' – and it left open the possibility of redemption for the monarchy's image (Orwell, 1941: 8). That rehabilitation was duly achieved when, as Freedland notes, 'the royals deflected that anti-establishment rage away from themselves' and 'the anger was directed instead at the political class' and at what became known as the metropolitan elite (Freedland, 2017). Despite her real-life cosmopolitanism (she was an international celebrity and embraced global causes), the posthumous Diana became an icon of melancholy Englishness. At her funeral, Elton John sang of her as 'England's rose' and 'our nation's golden child'. Evoking the sense of a nation in pain, his lyrics proclaim Diana to have 'called out to our country' and 'whispered to those in pain' while her 'footsteps will always fall here / Along England's greenest hills'. England itself is 'a country lost without your soul' (John and Taupin, 1997).

The coinciding turns to history and the Tudors, alongside a continuing preoccupation with royal women, indicate a national consciousness that has increasingly incorporated notions of hierarchy, heredity and birthright. Elements of Diana's narrative are reiterated in the Tudor novels that Gregory has subsequently published. As Diana re-presented contemporary royal personhood as transgressive and tragic, Gregory has done the same for the feudal figures of the past, emphasising their suffering at the hands of Tudor kings. For Gregory in particular, the Tudor story is entwined with that of the Plantagenets they defeated, as she re-casts the end of the Wars of the Roses as a national tragedy. This revisionism can be seen as part of a wider cultural context: the year in which *The King's Curse* was published also saw the exhumation, funeral and cultural rehabilitation of Richard III. The Tudors were, arguably, early architects of the modern British state and were also the last ethnically native monarchs, but Gregory's narrative evokes an oppressed country by drawing on the fact that Henry VII grew up mainly in Brittany and landed in England with soldiers from the Continent. She accordingly associates them with the tropes of invader and usurper despite their kinship with the family they displaced. There is, of course, a certain irony in the position this implies, as it requires a degree of historical forgetfulness: Pole's own family origins are easily traced to the Continent and thus to past mainland intrusions. As with Brexit itself, however, engagement with the world of these novels centres upon cultural imagination rather than factual accuracy. In its transition to early modernity, Reformation England is portrayed as a country 'in pain': for example, following the arrest of her son, Pole thinks of 'the abbey doors banging open in the moonlight of the English summer night, of the sacred chests and holy goods tumbled onto shining cobbles in darkened squares as Cromwell's men pull down the shrines and throw out the relics' and 'that England, His [God's] own special country, has gone all wrong' (Gregory, 2014a: 536). Pole and Parr (along with Katherine of Aragon in *The King's Curse*) are transmuted into versions of the 'People's Princess'. By adopting the perspectives of royal women, displaced from power or ill at ease with Tudor governance, Gregory's narrative links contemporary figures with their historical counterparts, aligning past grievances and affinities with those of the present.

Tony Blair's famous appellation for Diana implies a blend of populism and deference as does her self-ascription, 'queen of people's hearts' (Bashir, 1995). Both are infused with condescension, suggesting the emotional power of populist icons and diminishing those who succumb to it through implying that some people are more valuable than others. Gregory's treatment of England's past populace is similarly reductive. In *The Taming of the Queen*, Parr simultaneously champions and infantilises them. For example, when the king wants to deny them access to the Bible, she declares that 'the piety of simple people is beautiful' and asserts that they 'were brought up in your England, they know you make the laws that keep them safe', 'protect their country' and 'love you as their holy father' (Gregory, 2015a: 325–6). Pole revels in the popular acclaim she receives. Travelling to Katherine's funeral in Peterborough, for example, she finds 'men pulling off their hats and one or two men even kneeling down in the freezing mud as I go by, and they call out blessings on the late queen, on her daughter, and on me and my house' (Gregory, 2014a: 402). In self-congratulatory fashion, she concludes that 'they cheer for me as one of the old royal family who would never have led them so badly astray' (Gregory, 2014a: 403). This is a remark that epitomises notions of class hierarchy, elite paternalism and resentment of the upwardly mobile who threaten to undermine her eminence.

The first-person narrative voice is correlated with Englishness. The words 'England' and 'English' occur at points when the protagonists are expressing opposition to the Tudor monarchy. For example, in recounting the execution of her brother for being 'the true heir to the throne of England', Pole claims that 'half of England would turn out just for that haunting flicker of white embroidery, the white rose' and that at the point of death he would have heard 'the shouts and laughter of free men, free Englishmen, his subjects' (Gregory, 2014a: 3). When condemning Henry's retreat from the threat of plague, she is troubled by the 'thought of the court of England, my family's court, hiding like outlaws from the natural lords and advisors, living near a port so they can buy food from foreigners rather than honest fare in the English markets', asserting loyalty to 'my own lands' and 'my own people' which she 'would never willingly leave'. She describes herself as 'a Plantagenet born and bred in the heart of my country' for which she feels a 'deep, loving connection' (Gregory, 2014a: 181). Pole's continental affiliations – her Catholicism, and her son 'Reginald Pole's openly treasonous behaviour abroad' – are effectively de-centred in order to position her as the voice of English loss (Pierce, 2003: loc. 3647).

A substantial element of national grievance in *The Taming of the Queen* centres on the supposed fight for the English language and freedom from the encroachment of other tongues: a theme that aligns with the reported hardening of monolingual attitudes surrounding the Brexit vote (Cain, 2018). Parr's promotion of vernacular religious texts is framed as the enlightenment of ordinary people misled and beguiled by foreign tongues. In exchanges between Parr and the King that resonate with contemporary English 'linguaphobia' (Cain, 2018), Latin is dismissed as 'yammer yammer yammer' whilst prayers in the 'simple language' of English are described as 'both true and beautiful' (Gregory, 2015a: 122). Repeatedly Parr's narrative conflates the English language with truth and extols its simplicity. She declares it to be composed of 'beautiful but simple words that anyone can read' (Gregory, 2015a: 160), an unlikely claim given that less than 20 per cent of the adult population are estimated to have been literate in sixteenth-century England (Ortiz-Ospina and Roser, 2016). Possession of this 'simple language' promises liberty, self-determination and equality: the 'more that I study, the more certain I am that men – and equally women – can take charge of their own souls, can work for their own salvation, and can pray directly to God' (Gregory, 2015a: 160). Her vernacular texts promise to foster the simultaneity that Anderson identifies as key to the imagined community of nation as she predicts that 'all of England will read them a thousand times, they will be read every day in church' (Gregory, 2015a: 200). Indeed, for Gregory, one of the most important aspects of Parr's legacy is the fact that 'she was the first woman to publish in English as we speak it today' therefore making her 'an extraordinary contributor to the culture of the country' (Gregory, 2015b). Parr's narrative, with its persistent exaltation of the English language as a totemic and almost magical force with transformative power reflects a more general, popular preoccupation with England's supposed linguistic greatness.

Pole calls herself a member of the 'old royal family', the adjective associating her immediately with stability and tradition. The current king, Henry VII at this point, is conversely termed 'a usurper' who 'came in with an invading army, followed by disease'. Whilst the Plantagenets 'rode through the highways and byways of England, unarmed' because they 'never feared the people', the Tudors 'are still like invaders' (Gregory, 2014a: 11). This establishes, early on, a link between Pole's melancholic account of the transition to early modernity and a sense of encroachment from abroad. Historical events are described through a series of emotive metaphors that ascribe malignant motives to the Tudors and link them to the eradication of established identities. In answer to the questions she imagines them asking – 'what should be done with the York princesses?', she claims to have been 'married into obscurity', 'wedded to shadows', 'cut down by degrees, until I am small enough to conceal under a poor knight's name' and 'stuffed into obscurity like an embroidered emblem into a forgotten clothes chest' (Gregory, 2014a: 2). The reader is further alienated from the Tudors through the third-person plural pronoun – 'they took his fortune and his lands. Then they took his liberty' (Gregory, 2014a: 3). This pronoun, an inevitable component of first-person narrative, works as a device to other Plantagenet opponents.

Pole's third-person ascription indicates her bias in favour of political and economic self-interest and this is demonstrated by her account of her brother's fate. The Tudors are said to pack 'him away like a forgotten banner, among other worthless things' and Edward Plantagenet is described as a 'living constant reproach to the Tudors who captured that throne and now call it their own' (Gregory, 2014a: 3). In their presentation as simultaneously occlusive and foreign, Gregory's Tudors resemble Kingsnorth's metaphorical 'beast which crushes all before it and calls that crushing progress' which he regards as 'the real enemy now' (Kingsnorth, 2011: 269).

An element of flattery further aligns the reader with these representatives of an older social order. Like all speech, the inner voice, both real and fictional, is dialogic. As Alan Palmer notes, 'the word is always oriented toward an addressee. In the absence of a real addressee, as in the internal world of inner speech, the presupposed addressee is a normal representative of the speaker's social group' (Palmer, 2004: 153). The reader is both internal and external to Pole and Parr. When they are external, they are being addressed and the assumption is that they are socially equivalent. In effect, they collude in an ideology of class. In *Imagined Communities*, Anderson identifies class-consciousness, with its language of breeding, as the origin of racial thinking that is fixated on notions of contamination and does not derive from nationalism (Anderson, 1983: 149). The assumption that the reader participates in hierarchical ideology is demonstrated in *The King's Curse* by Pole's imperviousness to the significance of her servants and tenants and dismissiveness of their suffering. For example, during a plague epidemic from which she and her family are 'hiding behind the high walls of my great estate' (Gregory, 2014a: 262), she reflects 'that we will get through this summer with nothing worse than a few deaths in the village and a kitchen boy who was probably sick but ran away to his own home and died there' (Gregory, 2014a: 263).

According to Gregory, *The King's Curse* is a novel that 'lies in the personal' which suggests that, though clearly concerned with political issues, its focus is on the emotional aspects of politics – the way politics makes people feel (Gregory, 2014b). Gregory's historiographical concerns, her avowed disruption of the notion of 'Merrie Englande' and characterisation of Henry VIII as a tyrant forcing unwanted change on his people for his own 'selfish needs', evoke emotions such as loss, melancholia, powerlessness and anger (Gregory, 2014b). Her revised view of the Reformation resonates with what David Goodhart in his analysis of Brexit, *The Road to Somewhere* (2017), refers to as 'the constrained vision'. This is an outlook that sees external constraints such as institutions and traditions, as essential to civilised behaviour. Such constraints are built slowly and organically over time 'but can be destroyed quickly by radical reformers who don't understand their value' (Goodhart, 2017: 30). In effect, Gregory presents Henrician reform as a battle between the binaries of conservative and liberal; tradition and progress, the local and the global. The concerns of her historical figures resonate with the contemporary English 'anxiety of absence' (Aughey, 2010: 508) articulated in the pre-Brexit rhetoric of those such as Kingsnorth who claim to hear 'the sound of people who care about the place they live in – who feel they belong to it, who understand why it matters and who are prepared to fight for it' (Kingsnorth, 2011: 15). Whilst some have hailed the Reformation as a precedent for Brexit (see chapter 6 of this volume), Gregory's narratives frame this, along with the defeat of the House of York at the Battle of Bosworth, as an assault on English traditions and an older way of life, thus codifying conservative instincts. For example, in an address to an American audience, she accounts for the Pilgrimage of Grace as 'a massive uprising by the north, by the poor men of the north'. Utilising a discourse of loss and return that recalls Brexit fixations with sovereignty and control, she defines their cause as one of 'respecting the old religion and restoring the lords to the King's Council'. These 'passionate rebels', she claims, 'didn't want the middle class, what they regarded as upstarts coming in advising the king. They wanted the traditional lords to rule England and advise him' (Gregory, 2014b). This language of invasion, of the restoration of tradition and the old ways, manifests Svetlana Boym's notion of 'restorative nostalgia': an outlook 'at the core of recent national and religious revivals', whose 'conspiratorial worldview reflects a nostalgia for a transcendental cosmology and a simple premodern conception of good and evil' (Boym, 2007: 14). The connection is reinforced by Gregory's claims to awaken previously untold histories. In relation to the Pilgrimage of Grace, she asserts that 'the English haven't heard of it very much'. As far as Pole is concerned, she insists that there is 'no biography about her at all' (Gregory, 2014b).

The decline of feudal power is shown to parallel the ascendancy of the new man. For Anderson, the formation of nations was tied to the development of absolute monarchies, and this political system in turn was dependent on talented functionaries like Thomas Cromwell (Anderson, 1983: 55). Using the indefinite pronoun that has acquired considerable rhetorical power in the Brexit era, Gregory's narrators repeatedly dismiss these figures as men 'from nowhere'. In *The Taming of the Queen*, Parr is warned by her friend of 'men like William Paget and Richard Rich and Thomas Wriothesley, men who have risen from nowhere' (Gregory, 2015a: 53). When Henry VIII, promises to 'raise you from nothing', Parr indignantly reflects that he 'doesn't raise me from nothing, I don't come from nowhere: I was born a Parr of Kendal' (Gregory, 2015a: 2).

The growing absolutism of Henry VIII is portrayed as an entropy for which the men 'from nowhere' are responsible. For example, Pole reflects that the 'king has been seduced and entrapped by bad advisors' and that 'we have to win him back from them' (Gregory, 2014a: 332). Later, she tells the villagers who oppose a government visitation to her Warblington priory, that 'we must beg the king to dismiss his wrong-thinking advisors' which will 'put the country to rights again. As it was in the old days' (Gregory, 2014a: 417). In *The Taming of the Queen*, advisors are shown to be duplicitous and self-interested whilst having 'enormous power', which makes it 'easy for them to withhold information that he should have, or cast the law in a way that suits themselves' (Gregory, 2015a: 120). They are linguistically diminished: in *The King's Curse*, for example, Richard Layton and Thomas Legh, who inspect Warblington, are said to 'scuttle' and 'sidle'. Legh makes 'a funny little nodding gesture with his head'. Their untrustworthiness is implied by a 'quickly suppressed smile' (Gregory, 2014a: 412–20).

The conservative organicism of Pole, as imagined by Gregory, is evident in her preoccupation with the usurper figure, and her distaste is repeatedly articulated in ways that resonate with Theresa May's 'citizen of nowhere' speech attacking progressive cosmopolitanism. The leading architect of the Reformation, Thomas Cromwell, is referred to as 'another man from nowhere' (Gregory, 2014a: 260) linking modernisation to 'men without principle' (Gregory, 2014a: 332). For Pole, 'Thomas Cromwell, is neither of the Church nor of the nobility. He's a man from nowhere without education, like an animal. He seeks only to serve the king, like a dog' (Gregory, 2014a: 332). Gregory's portrayal of Cromwell and other meritocratic figures as rootless and abject, is also congruent with the current hostility towards immigrants who are charged with undermining national entitlements and culture.

In choosing an affronted, aristocratic perspective, Gregory's narratives privilege identity and emotion over progressiveness and rationalism. As such, they reflect the populist counter-narrative to neo-liberalism: in telling history through emotional experience and affinity with place, they contribute to what Matthew D'Ancona identifies as 'a cultural shift', partly generated by Diana's 'bequest' which 'was to help legitimise the role of feeling in the public space' (D'Ancona, 2017). Gregory's English history is experienced through kinship and land ties: social mobility is despised, and the porousness of boundaries that comes with the increasing opportunity of a globalising world is transmuted to a form of diaspora. Wolsey's strategic and managerial abilities are disparaged in ways that recall the populist backlash against experts seen at the time the texts were published and articulated by Michael Gove during the referendum campaign. Pole expresses contempt for a technocracy that would be beneath her peers. In describing the preparation for war with France, she observes that the 'detail, the constant orders about transport, supplies and timing – which no nobleman can be bothered to follow – is all that Wolsey thinks about, and he thinks about nothing else' (Gregory, 2014a: 128). He is portrayed here as limited, joyless and, like Cromwell, self-serving – somebody who, in the words of Katherine of Aragon, 'always seems to get what he wants' (Gregory, 2014a: 188). Similarly, Gregory's Duke of Norfolk, who keeps the 'old ways in his great hall' complains that 'the king is prey to any clever talker who can put an argument together' and laments the days 'when we knew where we were' (Gregory, 2014a: 138). These expressions of aristocratic distaste for managerialism and meritocracy resound strikingly with Boris Johnson's 'Fuck business' and the posturing proclamations of other pseudo-traditionalists such as Jacob Rees-Mogg (Shrimsley, 2018).

Pole in particular is the narrative vehicle for Gregory's reactionary historiography that presents England's past as the conflict between established families whose very names synonymise them with the land, and aspirational citizens of nowhere who threaten ancient birth-right. The social order is sacred to her. She disapproves when 'the bastard Henry Fitzroy, is honoured beyond belief' (Gregory, 2014a: 239) and finds it unimaginable that Anne Boleyn, 'the daughter of my steward' has 'walked before a princess born' (Gregory, 2014a: 293). Social mobility is repeatedly presented as threatening to an English idyll. As Pole reflects that it 'seems like a long time since I was pruning back the vine and hoping for English wine', she blames Boleyn's ambition for 'how much more danger we are all in' (Gregory, 2014a: 327). Pole's incredulity at the overthrowing of social convention is expressed through a series of outraged rhetorical questions that situate England as a victim of the aspirational usurpers: 'Who would have thought that the daughter of my steward should threaten the Queen of England? Who would ever have dreamed that a king of England would overthrow the laws of the land and the Church itself to get such a girl into his bed?' (Gregory, 2014a: 327).

This positioning of nation within the framework of class thinking, is in keeping with a reactionary, supremacist historiography that re-centres the nobility, emphasises monarchic power and reduces English history to the stories of a titled minority. It is symptomatic of English nationalism's peculiarity: its deference to hierarchy and enduring respect for a social structure in which all know their place and outsiders are excluded. The disruption of ancient precedent is therefore synonymous with a national decline brought about by the usurping of Plantagenet by Tudor, the miscegenation associated with their subsequent, 'cursed' union, and in turn, the individualised tyranny of Henry VIII. Though articulated through class and kin rather than race, this sense of lost hegemony codifies in contemporary terms, what Gilroy describes as 'the destructive impact of race thinking and racial hierarchy' upon 'ways of understanding history and society'. Adherence to 'the rules of a deep cultural biology' mitigates 'the anxieties that arise with a loss of certainty as to who one is and where one fits' (Gilroy, 2005: 5–6). Sympathy with Pole and her kin rests on this sense of 'cultural biology' which is perhaps most apparent in the narrative reverence for English land.

For Gilroy, the 'publishing bonanza dominated by books that either seek to diagnose or remedy the national pathology' is notable not just for its 'casual employment of the language of race in order to articulate the English particularity', but also for its 'geo-piety' – the expression of affinity with and reverence for England's natural landscape (Gilroy, 2005: 113–14). This geo-piety is also displayed by Gregory, who, in an author talk on *The King's Curse*, professed to 'love the English countryside' before going on to remark that in Shakespeare 'you get such a sense of this marvellous, unspoilt rural life'. 'In the view of the English', she remarks, 'there is nowhere more beautiful than the Thames Valley before we put Heathrow there' (Gregory, 2014b). By means of a network of organic and geographical motifs that intertwine Plantagenet identity with that of the land, the Tudors are further characterised as alien and destructive through emphasis of both their Breton connections and their apparent fastidiousness. Henry's avoidance of the sweating sickness epidemic is contrasted with the pious stoicism of the English people as he is shown to be extrinsic to the materiality of English land. 'While other people rest at home, try to avoid travel, discourage strangers, and, quietly, trustingly, put their faith in God, the king roams the countryside demanding safety in a dangerous world, trying to get a guarantee in an uncertain realm, as if he fears that the very air and streams of England are poison to the man whose father claimed them against their will' (Gregory, 2014a: 177).

The king's lack of patriotism is further signalled by the fact that he 'does not want English goods, fearing that they are contaminated'

(Gregory, 2014a: 181) and it is directly linked with the promotion of the new man, Wolsey. Noble families like the Poles, on the other hand, are seen as organically enmeshed with England and Englishness:

> The thought of the court of England, my family's court, hiding like outlaws from the natural lords and advisors, living near a port so they can buy food from foreigners rather than honest fare in the English markets, taking advice only from one man, and he not a Plantagenet, not even a duke, nor a lord, but a man dedicated to his own rise, troubles me very deeply as I celebrate the turn of the year at the heart of my newly built home, and ride around the fields where my people are walking behind the plough, and the ploughshare is turning over the rich earth. (Gregory, 2014a: 181)

Pole claims familial ownership of 'the court of England', uses the adjective 'natural' to describe those who inherit proximity to the king and locates herself on the fertile land in 'the fields' and amidst the 'rich earth'. Thus, she and her fellow aristocrats are shown to be integral to English materiality. Henry VIII, on the other hand, is placed on the margins of the land 'near a port' and is shown to prefer the food of foreigners, rejecting the 'honest fare' of England. His lack of Englishness is correlated with his dependence on one who is not a 'natural' advisor and who, in being 'dedicated to his own rise', displays an individualism which is the opposite to Pole's identity politics.

The motif of ploughing in this novel and in *The Taming of the Queen* further elides the identities of both Pole and Parr with an English land from which Henry is fatally disconnected. Parr's simile to describe her memories of love-making with Thomas Seymour – 'as if I were his field and he a plough' infers an affinity with nature which has been disrupted by marriage to the wrong man: the king (Gregory, 2015a: 131). This displacement is apparent in her reflection on the day of accepting Henry's marriage proposal that if 'I were at home we would start ploughing on a day like this and the sound of the curlews would ring out as loud as the ploughboy's whistle' (Gregory, 2015a: 9). When the king, uneasy in the middle of the night, asks her to perform the duties of a 'housewife' including making a fire and cooking his breakfast whilst insisting that she 'slam the window closed on the fresh cool air' (Gregory, 2015a: 46), Parr reminds him that, as the wife of a feudal lord, she commanded 'all our lands in the North when my husband was away from home' (Gregory, 2015a: 46). This associates her aristocratic heritage with an expansive landscape, with space and scope, and makes an unfavourable contrast with the claustrophobic atmosphere that surrounds the king who, as

Pole declares in *The King's Curse*, is 'usually travelling between his rich palaces, mostly by barge, always heavily guarded' (Gregory, 2014a: 462). Parr's reminiscences about her previous marriage 'when the desperately poor men in rags came against the castle and begged for a return to the good days, the old days when the churches were free with charity and the king was guided by the lords' echo Pole's nostalgia (Gregory, 2015a: 47). Correlation of the old ways and old families with the will and welfare of the people permeates both texts. As she watches the ploughing of her own 'rich earth', Pole declares that 'I would not choose to live anywhere but on my own lands, I would not eat anything that we have not grown. I would not be served by anyone but my own people. I am a Plantagenet born and bred in the heart of my country' (Gregory, 2014a: 181). Whilst the king eats imported food and locks himself away from 'the rumble of a thousand critical whispers' (Gregory, 2014a: 462), Pole chooses, whenever possible, to 'stay at my home while the court is on progress and walk in my fields, and watch the wheat turn golden' (Gregory, 2014a: 471). She is associated, not just with agricultural bounty but also with rural tradition: the generational continuity of the Plantagenets which is constantly attacked by the Tudors, is linked to social cohesion and welfare. This is exemplified by the passage below where dynamic verbs such as 'stride' and 'race' along with adjectives like 'brawny' suggest that, in contrast to the Tudor in-comers who bring plague and disease, Plantagenets empower the populace:

> I go out with the reaping gang on the first day of harvesting and watch them stride side by side across the field, their sickles slicing down the waving crop, the hares and the rabbits darting away before them so the boys race after them with yapping terriers.
>
> Behind the men come the women, embracing great armfuls of stooks and tying them with one practised movement, their gowns hitched up so that they can stride, their sleeves rolled up high over their brawny arms. Many of them have a baby strapped to their back, most of them have a couple of children trailing behind with the old people gleaning the fallen heads of wheat so that nothing is wasted. (Gregory, 2014a: 471)

In contrast with the wholesomeness of Plantagenet land, the usurping Tudors are linked to disease. The 'Tudor disease' (specifically the sweating sickness) is repeatedly referred to in both texts and is attributed to Henry VII's connection to the Continent – 'the curse that the king trailed behind him when he marched into his kingdom with his army of mercenaries who brought it from the gutters and prisons of Europe'

(Gregory, 2014a: 39). Through her repeated reminders that Tudor forces arrived from Brittany and speculations that they brought a foreign plague, Gregory associates migration with contamination. The origins of the sweating sickness, of which the last epidemic occurred in 1551, are unknown, but Gregory draws on one theory that it might have been brought to England by French mercenaries fighting for Henry VII at the Battle of Bosworth. For Gregory's Pole, the Tudor monarchy is synonymous with 'the new illness that we all fear, the disease that followed the Tudor army and nearly wiped out the City of London when they assembled to welcome him' (Gregory, 2014a: 25) and her response to her son's observation that for Henry, 'the Sweat is his particular dread', again evokes superstition: ' "No wonder, since it was his father who brought it in, and it killed his brother Arthur", I remark. "They called it the Tudor curse even then. They said that the reign had begun in sweat and would end in tears" ' (Gregory, 2014a: 174).

The association of Tudor rule with the Sweat can also be seen in *The Taming of the Queen*. Parr recounts that it 'is a Tudor plague; it came in with this king's father'. What is regarded as Henry's capriciousness and unpredictability as a ruler is correlated with the disease, which serves as a metaphor for the precariousness of life in his circle: Parr's ladies, for example, 'are all terrified of the Sweat. It can kill a man in four hours, and there is no easy way to tell if he will die' (Gregory, 2015a: 226). For Pole in *The King's Curse*, 'this tyranny is like the other Tudor disease, The Sweat. It comes quickly, it takes those you love without warning, and you cannot defend against it' (Gregory, 2014a: 543). Such organic motifs biologise the polarity of belonging and not belonging. The notion of a 'Tudor disease' consolidates Gregory's conservative sense of a blood and soil nation delineated by exclusive dynastic networks.

To conclude, Gregory re-imagines the Tudor accession and Henrician Reformation as fatal lapses in England's past. Her conservative depiction of a Reformation England held hostage by cosmopolitan usurpers trampling on rights and traditions decouples the notion of English exceptionalism from the anti-Catholicism that has previously informed it and codifies present-day national grievances. Her Tudor England is severed from its past, and the forces that have invaded it are degenerate, degraded and culturally bereft. Her Henry VIII, who embodies Kingsnorth's culture-sapping beast of progress, along with his agents, the men of nowhere, can be read in the contemporary context as the tyranny of Brussels, cosmopolitans, and the so-called metropolitan elite. By implication, a pure, prelapsarian England endures beneath the effacements of history. Gregory writes a nation rooted in class and ethnicity (ultimately the basis of racist thinking) that is hostile to change and to those deemed outsiders. Given the sales figures of her books, there is every reason to regard her historiography as influential and certainly as a barometer of English consciousness in the age of Brexit.

References

Anderson, Benedict (1983), *Imagined Communities: Reflections on the Origin and Spread of Nationalism* (London: Verso).

Aughey, Arthur (2010), 'Anxiety and injustice: the anatomy of contemporary English nationalism', *Nations and Nationalism, Journal of the Association for the Study of Ethnicity and Nationalism* 16:3, pp. 506–24.

Bashir, Martin (1995), Transcript of Martin Bashir's *Panorama* interview with Princess Diana, broadcast in November 1995, www.bbc.co.uk/news/special/politics97/diana/panorama.html (last accessed 6 January 2019).

BBC News (1997), 'Tony Blair comments on Princess Diana's Death' (last accessed on *YouTube*, 4 February 2018).

Boym, Svetlana (2007), 'Nostalgia and its discontents', *The Hedgehog Review* 9:2, pp. 7–18.

Cain, Sian (2018), 'British "linguaphobia" has deepened since Brexit vote, say experts', *Guardian*, 28 May.

D'Ancona, Matthew (2017), 'Diana showed that we need emotion, but it's had a downside', *Guardian*, 28 August.

de Groot, Jerome (2009), *Consuming History: Historians and Heritage in Contemporary Popular Culture* (Abingdon: Routledge).

Featherstone, Simon (2008), *Englishness: Twentieth Century Popular Culture and the Forming of English Identity* (Edinburgh: Edinburgh University Press).

Freedland, Jonathan (2017), 'Diana's life shaped Britain: but in death she's changed us too', *Guardian*, 5 August.

Gilroy, Paul (2005), *Postcolonial Melancholia* (New York: Columbia University Press).

Goodhart, David (2017), *The Road to Somewhere: The Populist Revolt and the Future of Politics* (London: Hurst & Company).

Gregory, Philippa (2014a), *The King's Curse* (London: Simon & Schuster).
    (2014b), Author Talk: 'Philippa Gregory at Wilton Library – *The King's Curse*'. https://vimeo.com/109057836 (last accessed 12 April 2018).
    (2015a), *The Taming of the Queen* (London: Simon & Schuster).
    (2015b), 'Philippa Gregory introduces *The Taming of the Queen*'. www.youtube.com/watch?v=_KwBIgYlQ3M (last accessed 30 May 2018).

Higgins, Charlotte (2016), 'Tudormania: why can't we get over it?', *Guardian*, 4 May.

John, Elton and Bernie Taupin (1997), *Candle in the Wind 1997*. www.bbc.co.uk/news/special/politics97/diana/lyrics.html (last accessed 31 May 2018).

Kenny, Michael (2012), 'The many faces of Englishness: identity, diversity and nationhood in England', *Public Policy Research* 19:3, pp. 152–9.

Kingsnorth, Paul (2011), *Real England: The Battle Against the Bland* (London: Portobello Books).

Mantel, Hilary (2017), 'The princess myth: Hilary Mantel on Diana', *Guardian*, 26 August.

Nairn, Tom (1988), *The Enchanted Glass: Britain and its Monarchy* (London: Radius).

Orwell, George (1941), *The Lion and the Unicorn: Socialism and the English Genius* (London: Secker & Warburg).

Ortiz-Ospina, Esteban and Max Roser (2016), 'Literacy'. https://ourworldindata.org/literacy/ (last accessed 11 August 2017).

Palmer, Alan (2004), *Fictional Minds* (London: University of Nebraska Press).

Parrinder, Patrick (2006), *Nation and Novel: The English Novel from its Origins to the Present Day* (Oxford: Oxford University Press).

Pierce, Hazel (2003), *Margaret Pole, Countess of Salisbury, 1473–1541: Loyalty, Lineage and Leadership* (Cardiff: University of Wales Press).

Poole, Steven (2018), 'What is a "vassal state"? Jacob Rees-Mogg's mid-Brexit vision explained', *Guardian*, 2 February.

Shrimsley, Robert (2018), 'Boris Johnson's Brexit explosion ruins Tory business credentials', *Financial Times*, Opinion section, 25 June.

'Top 10: historical fiction' (2015), *The Bookseller*, 29 May, p. 11 (last accessed 24 July 2018).

Part III

Negotiating borders in British travel writing and memoir

10

Guards of Brexit? Revisiting the cultural significance of the white cliffs of Dover

Melanie Küng

The land- and seascape around Dover is an area where one might say Britain's relationship with continental Europe has geographically crystallised, in both a real and a symbolic sense. The most notable recent example concerns the debates surrounding the United Kingdom's vote to leave the European Union. In a post-referendum *Guardian* supplement called 'Farewell to Europe', Timothy Garton Ash expressed his frustration with this geographical focal point:

> Many television programmes during the referendum campaign featured lingering aerial shots of the white cliffs of Dover (it must have been good for the local helicopter trade). Yes, being an island makes a difference, but geography is not destiny. For centuries after the Norman invasion, England's rulers saw it as part of a trans-Channel polity, together with their possessions in France. As in personal relationships, you can be together but apart – or apart, but still together. (Ash, 2016: 1)

Ash's comment reminds us that this natural boundary is less clear-cut than some would like to think. Rather, it marks a border zone, a liminal space which shows that, in Homi Bhabha's words, 'national culture is neither unified nor unitary in relation to itself, nor must it be seen simply as "other" in relation to what is outside or beyond it' (Bhabha, 1990: 4).

The shortest distance between Britain and mainland Europe is just over thirty-three kilometres at the Strait of Dover. Dover port has long served as a threshold, enabling a steady cross-Channel flow of goods, people and ideas. From the mid-fourteenth to the mid-sixteenth century Calais was even in British possession, turning the Strait of Dover, according to David Wallace, into 'an extension of the highway from London to Canterbury' that was used by traders, the clergy and the military in equal measure

(Wallace, 2004: 22). The arrival of steam-powered passenger boats in the early nineteenth century and the establishment of the first train connection to Dover not long after saw a sharp rise in people travelling to and from the continent. Today, Dover and Calais are the busiest ferry passenger ports in Europe. Over nine million passengers travelled the Dover–Calais route in 2016, while the number of people travelling the Strait of Dover subterraneously via the Channel Tunnel was more than twenty million.[1] The common descriptions of Dover as 'Gateway to Europe' or, reversely, as 'Gateway to England' reflect the town's role as a conduit and space of contact. While fortifications and the physical traces of war around Dover show that this contact has not always been of a friendly nature, conflicts have rarely put a halt to cross-Channel exchanges.[2]

On a symbolic level, the bridging of the gap has been a more complex matter, since insularity, with the white cliffs as its most prominent physical marker, has been crucial to British discourses of identity. The 2012 national appeal by the National Trust to secure a 0.8 mile of the white cliffs coastline is indicative of how inextricably these material and discursive dimensions are intertwined. In support of the campaign, the conservation organisation commissioned writer and philosopher Julian Baggini to spend a week exploring the cliffs' significance for the British nation. In an article for the *Guardian*, Baggini wrote of the cliffs' potential to serve as a *lieu de mémoire* recalling the many events that shaped the nation's history, such as the Roman conquest, the Battle of Britain, and the numerous sea journeys that started and ended at the cliffs. 'But perhaps most important', he argued, 'the coast is both a border and a porous point of entry, and so the cliffs remind us that we are a nation of immigrants. That is something the country still seems to be ambivalent about' (Baggini, 2012a). While multiculturalism is often celebrated, Baggini observed, so are low immigration numbers. Baggini's appeal to the British people to think of their island home less in terms of 'blood or genes' and more in terms of the many boats embarking and disembarking at the port of Dover is at the same time a bid to think of the white cliffs as harbouring – quite literally – diversity rather than uniformity (Baggini, 2012a). It took just over four months to reach the campaign's target amount of 1.2 million pounds. Baggini's proposal 'to link the cliffs and the port more firmly in the imagination' (Baggini, 2012b: 8) in order to 'build an open, inclusive, generous and hospitable patriotism' (Baggini, 2012b: 16), however, still seems to be a distant goal.

In the build-up to the vote on the EU referendum, the white cliffs were far from symbolising togetherness and openness, standing instead overwhelmingly for divisiveness and inhospitality, since the Brexit debate has been riddled throughout with the question of immigration and border control. Examples of the tangible dimension this took in Dover over the last few years still resonate: in 2015, then UKIP leader Nigel Farage stood at the bottom of the cliffs when he unveiled his party's new campaign poster. It showed three huge escalators, meant to represent the high number of immigrants, running up the cliffs. To many it threatened the unthinkable, the breaching of the symbolic bulwark of British insularity and, on a more subtle note, the loss of a clear boundary between Kent, the well-kept 'Garden of England', and Calais's 'Jungle', the squalid temporary home of refugees and migrants seeking to cross the Channel.[3] The British satirical website *The Poke* reacted to Farage's lingering presence in Dover with an article entitled 'White cliffs to take out restraining order against Nigel Farage'.[4] Several months before voting day, the cliffs were used as a canvas for the Vote Leave campaign, who projected 'Let's Take Back Control' onto the cliffs, but also for a campaign by an organisation called Global Justice Now, who in turn projected 'Refugees Welcome' onto the cliffs. The latter was a timely move aimed at counteracting the right-wing groups who came to Dover the next day to protest against the arrival of immigrants. Months after the vote, projections illuminated the chalk formation once again. When Prime Minister Theresa May triggered Article 50 at the end of March 2017, the *Sun* had its own messages for its European neighbours: 'Dover & Out', 'See EU Later' and 'Goodbye'.

The overwhelmingly nationalist and exclusionary ways in which the white cliffs have recently been instrumentalised chime with the still dominant perception of borders, centring round binary categories of Us and Them as well as protection and security issues (see Newman, 2007). Dover port may serve as a corridor, but the cliffs 'stand guard at the Gateway to England', as the Dover Museum's website rather aptly puts it (Dover Museum Website, n.d.). In order critically to reassess the cliffs' cultural significance, it is useful to think of the coastal landscape around Dover as a cultural palimpsest where meanings are multi-layered and overlapping. How have cultural evocations of the cliffs been informed by and constitutive of dominant ideas of Britishness, and even more so, of Englishness? What kind of alternative narratives of identity emerge if we shift our focus to the liminal, the hybrid and the in-between?

The cliffs' associations with Englishness are manifold. Apart from the fact that the white cliffs form part of England's southern border, the rock of which they are made has come to stand for England more specifically. As Shelley Trower has pointed out, chalk is very much connected with the South-East of England, as compared to, for example, granite, which lines the South-West of England and is more readily associated with a Cornish and Celtic identity (Trower, 2015). The South-East is often considered to epitomise the very idea of Englishness.[5] One of the most abiding literary links with Englishness has been secured through the cliffs' association with William Shakespeare. The promontory west of Dover Harbour is called 'Shakespeare Cliff' for its association with a scene in *King Lear*, in which Gloucester asks his son Edgar to lead him to the edge of a cliff in Dover 'whose high and bending head / Looks fearfully in the confined deep', so he can jump to his death (Shakespeare, 1998a: 943–74, 4.1.67–8). Inevitably, the location also brings to mind a speech from another Shakespeare play, which has become the iconic expression of the geo-cultural basis of English patriotism, although it in fact laments a loss of former greatness: in *Richard II*, John of Gaunt celebrates England as a 'sceptre'd isle' and 'fortress built by nature for herself' and the sea surrounding it as a protective 'wall' and 'moat' (Shakespeare, 1998b: 367–95, 2.1.42–52). Written at the end of the sixteenth century, the play in fact addresses England's geopolitical recalibration: the end of the Hundred Years War with France in the mid-fifteenth century had left the English monarchs bereft of their major landholdings on the continent, while the English Reformation had led to a split with the Church of Rome (see Spiering, 2015: 40–1, and chapter 6 of this volume). The recent defeat of the Spanish Armada in 1588 would additionally have added to the per-ception of the sea as a natural boundary that keeps the 'fortress' England safe from invasions from the Continent.

In any case, the cliffs matter to both English and British insularity, and the boundary between the two is often discursively blurred. In the course of the nineteenth century, the cliffs increasingly symbolised, according to Readman, 'an insular national identity, one shaped less by the expanding overseas empire than by Britain's place in Europe, particularly as affected by historical rivalries with continental powers' (Readman, 2014: 250). This rivalry was also noticeable in visual depictions of the cliffs, as in J.M.W. Turner's painting *Dover from Shakespeare Cliff* (1826), which shows soldiers taking aim at France on Dover's eastern cliffs and, further in the back, the castle on Dover's western cliffs. As Readman observes, 'artistic depictions often exaggerated their height, so emphasizing their status as bulwarks or battlements' (Readman, 2014: 252). The growing powers on the Continent, especially France and the German states of Prussia, which defeated France in the Franco-Prussian War (1870–71) and were unified as the German Empire thereafter, increased fears of an invasion from across the Channel. These were further inflamed by the numerous turn-of-the-century invasion stories and novels, which have become known as invasion literature.[6] A considerable number of these works centred around an invasion by a tunnel and thus played into the hands of the opposition against the construction of a subterranean link with France, plans for which had been circulating since the beginning of the nineteenth century. Lord Randolph Churchill is said to have underscored his argument against a tunnel by insisting that '"the reputation of England has hitherto depended upon her being, as it were, *virgo intacta*"' (qtd. in Pick, 1993: 131; emphasis in original).

The cliffs were thus not only perceived as ramparts, but also as the soft and pervious boundaries of a national body that has long been associated with a female figure, most notably that of Britannia.[7] A tunnel would have made for a strong symbol of penetration.[8] As Daniel Pick explains, '[t]he Tunnel evoked the dread not only of war and conquest, but also more subtly of miscegenation, degeneration, sexual violation and the loss of cultural identity' (Pick, 1993: 121). The reverberations of framing the threat from across the Channel in terms of an invasion of a female body can be felt in today's Eurosceptic political discourses. UKIP has expressed its stance against immigration and the European Union by lamenting that '"Britain no longer has control over her borders. This is driving unemployment up and wages down ... Britain's borders are now effectively North Africa, Russia and Turkey; not the White Cliffs of Dover"' (qtd. in Trower, 2015: 2). It is not just the use of feminised borders that makes this statement interesting. The suggestion that borders beyond the white cliffs would be no British concern, were it not for the European Union, denies the legacy of British imperial expansion and rule over vast territories in other parts of the world. Even without looking back, questions of sovereignty can hardly be reduced to the white cliffs, especially if one takes into account Northern Ireland, and Gibraltar, which, as a British overseas territory, makes North Africa a British border issue anyway.

If the cliffs represented the vulnerable boundaries of a female national body that needed protection, they similarly came to demarcate the boundaries of the 'motherland', 'home' and the 'domestic'. Travel accounts played a vital role in establishing the cliffs as markers of an insular home- and motherland, and it is these that the remainder of the chapter will focus on. Considering that the cliffs can only be seen properly when viewed from a boat, it is not surprising that there is a strong link between the growing number of people travelling through Dover in the nineteenth century and the increasing importance of the cliffs in evoking a nostalgic sense of leaving, as in Ford Madox Brown's iconic painting *The Last of England* (1852–55), or of 'homecoming' (Readman, 2014: 256–7). The more the image became entrenched in the cultural memory of the nation through travel accounts and visual representations, the better it could be exported abroad to the far edges of empire.[9] The white cliffs of the mind helped create a sense of home and familiarity in the British colonies, even to the extent that, as Readman demonstrates, similar geological features were named after them, a process that no doubt also served the purpose of territorial appropriation (Readman, 2014: 258).

At the same time, the cliffs continued to stand for an England that, in Ian Baucom's words, was 'unique, local, differentiated' (Baucom, 1999: 10). The opening of H.V. Morton's *In Search of England*, published in 1927, illustrates this particularly well: the author-narrator relates how, taken seriously ill and fearing he will have to die in Palestine, he climbed a mountain and tried to face in the direction of England: 'As I looked out over the inhospitable mountains I remembered home in a way which, given any other frame of mind, would have astonished me. I solemnly cursed every moment I had spent wandering foolishly about the world, and I swore that if ever I saw Dover Cliffs again I would never leave them' (Morton, 1984: 1). The cliffs are the entry point to an imaginative chain reaction, which marks the transition from an inhospitable outside to a hospitable inside, from unknown to known territory, and from foreign lands to home- and motherland. The mental map of England that unfolds consists of 'a village street at dusk', thatched cottages and the sound of church bells (Morton, 1984: 1; see also Habermann, 2010). The perception of England is based on an already existing trope: 'I have learnt since that this vision of mine is a common one to exiles all over the world: we think of home, we long for home, but we see something greater – *we see England*' (Morton, 1984: 2; emphasis in original). The use of the plural personal pronoun suggests the existence of a collective identity that is defined by a specifically English space. As 'the germs of all we are', rural sites constitute the motherland that guarantees continuity (Morton, 1984: 2). The subsequent use of the gendered pronoun reinforces the association with the motherland: 'I was shamed to think that I had wandered so far and so often over the world neglecting those lovely things near at home, feeling that England would always be there whenever I wanted to see her; and at that moment how far away she seemed, how unattainable!' (Morton, 1984: 2). Morton fashions himself as the lost son and solemnly promises, should he recover, to 'go home in search of England' (Morton, 1984: 2).

According to Michael Bartholomew's study of Morton's unpublished memoir and diaries, Morton did fall ill in Palestine after completing a newspaper assignment for the *Daily Express* in Egypt in 1923, but it was not until three years later that he set out on his journey to discover England (Bartholomew, 2006: 68–70). Morton's notes for his memoir hint at an illness-induced 'vision of England' he had in Palestine, although, as expected and as Bartholomew emphasises, it is not the embellished and vivid version that found its way into the travelogue (Bartholomew, 2006: 70). Overall, the opening scene offers a generic presentation of rural Englishness. It is the reference to the cliffs which delineates and localises England, and, furthermore, directs the gaze inwards. The England described in *In Search of England* is an insular cosmos, where aristocrat and tramp alike appear to merge with the land. The people are seemingly autochthonous, which makes this England, at least implicitly, racially exclusive. The cliffs evoke a sense of belonging, of familiarity and, essentially, of a clearly bounded insular homeland. In any case, it is travel accounts like these that testify to and further consolidate the strong connection between the white cliffs and Englishness. While *In Search of England* was already popular at the time, the fact that it is still in print shows that Morton's vision of England and Englishness still has currency today.

There are other travellers of the interwar years, however, who move into focus the history of transgression and subversion surrounding this national boundary. As Paul Fussell argued in *Abroad: British Literary Travelling between the Wars*, Dover's liminal position at the edge of Britain and its closeness to the continent made it 'a prominent jump-off stage' for writers in 1930s Britain (Fussell, 1980: 23). W.H. Auden, Christopher Isherwood and other homosexual writers of the era in particular took a liking to the town, which according to Auden's poem 'Dover' teemed with pleasure-seeking soldiers and travellers alike and thus offered an exciting atmosphere of sexual promise and chance meetings. As an English border town in close proximity to France, Dover was a place where the stifling rules of home did not necessarily apply and where, Fussell emphasises, the influence of the Napoleonic Code was tangible. Under the French civil code, homosexual acts were not considered a criminal offence, whereas in England, they were not decriminalised until 1967. To some travellers, then, Dover opened up to a sea of opportunities and liberties, offering an escape route. Conversely, it could epitomise the narrowing down of this sense of freedom when glimpsed on the return journey, subverting the common trope of homecoming associated with this stretch of coast.

In Christopher Isherwood's semi-autobiographical novel *Down There on a Visit*, published in 1962, the cliffs are portrayed in considerably less welcoming tones than in Morton's *In Search of England*. In the section called 'Waldemar', the narrator describes his arrival on a cross-Channel steamer into Dover Harbour in 1938 as follows:

How tiny it always seems! No more than a cranny in the old cheese cliffs; a drab doll town with the stubborn little castle standing guard above it, in a light summer drizzle. Oh, the staring, unblinking, uncompromising familiarity of it all! The loud, rude squawking of the gulls! How compactly the English sit, confronting their visitors: here we are, take us or leave us – this is where you'll do things our way, not yours. Byron saw the last of them here. So did Wilde. You say goodbye to them forever and go away to fame and death among the dagoes, and they couldn't care less. Oh, yes, when your name has been a household word everywhere else for the past two generations, they'll concede that they used to know you – slightly. But they'll never really admit that they were wrong about you or about anything. They are indomitable, incorrigible, and so utterly self-satisfied that they no longer have to raise their voices or wave their arms when they address the lesser breeds. If you have any criticisms, they have one unanswerable answer: you can stay off our island. (Isherwood, 2012: 145)

As in Morton's travelogue, the cliffs are described as a familiar sight, but in this case, they do not evoke a sense of home and certainly not the warm feeling of a motherland. Whereas in Morton's vision, the cliffs give way to an expanding England, this traveller's England is contracting. Rather than an imposing sight, the gateway to England is rendered small and insignificant. Dover is described in derogatory terms, and the portrayal of the cliffs neither calls to mind Turner's imposing heights nor Shakespeare's natural fortress. Instead, they resemble crumbling old cheese. The presentation of the island's inhabitants is equally unflattering. The height of the cliffs, on top of which they sit, becomes an expression of their sense of cultural superiority and insular complacency. They provide the vantage point from which to look down on the 'lesser breeds'[10] across the Channel, but also on 'others within'. These included the likes of Byron and Wilde, who did not conform with the sexually repressive and homophobic attitudes within English society, as well as the English volunteers who went to fight in the Spanish Civil War, thus going against Britain's non-interventionist policy. For the narrator, who cannot identify with an English society defined by parochial views and restrictive values, the cliffs' familiarity thus comes with a sense of alienation.

The Second World War did little to reduce the sense of superiority associated with the cliffs, as alluded to by Isherwood. Quite the opposite: the cliffs became an important military frontline and were home to a complex tunnel system, which served as a military command centre. Crucially, they also became a symbol of British steadfastness and heroism in the face of adversity. While the strategic usefulness of this natural boundary space is not to be denied, the continued cultural reproduction of the notion that 'Britain stands alone' demands scrutiny. It is a theme critically explored in Jonathan Raban's sailing travelogue *Coasting: A Private Voyage*, published in 1986. The author's circumnavigation of the British Isles over a period of several years, too, is a search for England, including its place in the greater context of Britain and Europe. Unlike Morton, however, Raban deliberately positions himself in the boundary zone, the liminal space between land and water. He describes himself as a 'coaster', as someone who 'doesn't quite belong either to the land or to the ocean. He is a betwixt-and-between man, neither exactly a citizen nor exactly a foreigner' (Raban, 2003: 25). Raban hopes for his trip to be some sort of 'homecoming' and imagines that by circumnavigating, his home-land can be clearly delineated, or as he puts it, *'encompassed'* (Raban, 2003: 26; emphasis in original). A 'shifting frontier' or 'open frontier', as he also calls it, the sea allows him an outsider perspective on the British, which he increasingly comes to perceive as 'third persons and not first' (Raban, 2003: 25, 39, 221–2).

Shortly after he sets out on his journey from Fowey on the Cornish coast in 1982, Britain starts preparing itself for a war with Argentina over the ownership of the Falkland Islands. Whether in the form of the media or personal encounters, Raban suddenly finds himself surrounded by a jingoist assertiveness over 'Sovereign territory' and 'British soil' (Raban, 2003: 101). '[T]he phantasmal imperial exercise in the Falklands' is heavily informed by the memory of the Second World War (Raban, 2003: 121). Raban relates that even Vera Lynn, whose interpretation of the song 'The White Cliffs of Dover' (1941) was meant to maintain the nation's morale and hope, takes a break from retirement to help the war effort in the Falklands. Known as 'the forces' sweetheart', she also revives the already existing association of the female body with the homeland and thus serves to remind soldiers of what they are fighting for:

A lot of dust had gathered on Miss Lynn's voice since I'd last heard it, warbling sweetly about bluebirds o*ho*ver the white cliffs of *Do*hover, but its dustiness was like the scratchy burr of a 78 played on a horn gramo-phone; it made it more evocative, not less; it brought back memories of the gallant little ships, the blackout, whale-meat steaks and London-can-take-it. The song was called 'I love This Land', and it hinged on the refrain: It will stay this way for e-e-ver / Which is why I love this land! On each reprise, the couplet sounded slightly more driveling than it had the last time round. You had only to look at Vera Lynn at sixty-five to see that it enshrined a wonderful, vainglorious untruth. But there was a dotty kind of truth in it too. It stated – more nakedly than anyone had dared to do so far – the terms of the daydream in which England was living in 1982. (Raban, 2003: 190)

The national self-perception associated with the cliffs is one in denial of England's, and, for that matter, Britain's increasing irrelevance on a global stage. Throughout his travel account, Raban emphasises his alienation with a nation that is obsessed with continuity, ancestry and the 'heroic solitude of their geography' and that seems to thrive on 'international disapproval' (Raban, 2003: 221). The British insistence on their geographical and cultural separateness – their 'aggressive assertions of their differences from the continental giant across the water' – becomes even more questionable when Raban is sailing in the Strait of Dover and experiences the proximity of the French coast first-hand (Raban, 2003: 105). He wonders for a moment whether he should leave Britain behind for good. After a rough night at anchor in Dover Harbour Raban remarks: 'In the early sun, Vera Lynn's white cliffs were maculated with grime; drained of color under a ragged fringe of green, they looked much as I felt – not in good shape at all' (Raban, 2003: 222). His observation on the faltering resilience of the cliffs is a fitting image for the crumbling narrative of British exceptionalism and superiority. The penultimate chapter of the travelogue, which addresses the miners' strike in the North and draws attention to the mass unemployment and social unrest in early 1980s Britain is a stark reminder of this.

The need for a new narrative of identity in post-war Britain also pervades Caryl Phillips's essay 'The Pioneers: Fifty Years of Caribbean Migration to Britain' (1998), in which he retraces the experiences of West Indian immigrants and the changing attitudes to race and multiculturalism in British society since the arrival of the *Empire Windrush* at the port of Tilbury outside London in 1948. Phillips pictures the passengers on board the *Windrush* or those who followed in their wake on their way to London, wondering about their emotional reactions as they would set eyes on the white cliffs for the first time. He imagines their feelings to have been a combination of sadness about the home they left behind and cautious anticipation of a new start in Britain.[11] Within the context of their socialisation they would have come to know Britain as 'the "mother country"', which leads him to assume that 'their first glimpse of the white cliffs of Dover suggested a homecoming of sorts' (Phillips, 2002: 264–5). It quickly becomes clear, however, that the process of making Britain their home was not a straightforward task and was accompanied by racist abuse and the struggle for equality and public recognition. As Phillips criticises, the public was hardly made aware that the British Nationality Act 1948, under which people living in the colonies received British citizenship and the right to settle in Britain, was in fact beneficial to many British companies, which 'were in desperate need of labour' after the war and therefore had an interest in facilitating migration to Britain (Phillips, 2002: 268).[12]

As a child of West Indian immigrants himself, Phillips's tribute to the *Windrush* generation is closely connected to his own search for identity growing up as a black person in 1960s and 1970s Britain. His experiences demonstrate Britain's failure to confront the racism underlying its imperial project. He gives the example of Margaret Thatcher, who, not long before she became prime minister, expressed her sympathy for a nation that was 'fearful of being "swamped by alien cultures"' (Phillips, 2002: 277). Phillips also quotes part of Thatcher's victory speech after the Falklands War, in which she refuted those who had thought 'that Britain was no longer the nation that had built an Empire and ruled a quarter of the world. Well, they were wrong' (Phillips, 2002: 277). Like Raban, he strongly disapproves of the imperial nostalgia that surfaced during the Falklands conflict, but due to his ancestry, he is more intimately affected by it: 'This was not a comfortable speech for many Britons to listen to. For Britons, such as I, whose heritage was blighted by the inequities and cruelties of Empire, this was a disgraceful speech, and one which served only to remind us of our tenuous position in British society' (Phillips, 2002: 277). Despite this display of an 'imperial mindset', Phillips continues by noting that Thatcher's focus on economic growth and social mobility rather than hereditary privilege equally created opportunities for black people in Britain (Phillips, 2002: 277). He ends by reminding the reader that it was the pioneers who paved the way, 'for as they stood on the deck of the ship and stared out at the white cliffs of Dover, they carried within their hearts a dream' (Phillips, 2002: 282). The essay thus suggests that the cliffs might serve as a more inclusive image of home, although it never quite loses sight of their role as an emblem of a narrowly defined island race, which has revolved around exclusionary narratives of '"Keep Britain White"' (Phillips, 2002: 273, 280).

The pain of exclusion and feelings of racial inferiority that Phillips alludes to is brought to life vividly by writer Jamaica Kincaid, who grew up in colonised Antigua. Her autobiographical essay 'On Seeing England for the First Time', published in 1991, is a scathing criticism of British colonial rule and the racial exclusivity of Englishness that constituted its cultural dimension. Kincaid relates the difficulties of growing up in a British colony, where the 'right' tastes in food and clothes, as well as manners and customs were 'made in England', despite their remoteness from the islanders' everyday life and environment. The first time she sees England is on a map at school. She describes it as a place where she does not belong, an exclusive place: 'England was a special jewel all right, and only special people got to wear it. The people who got to wear England were English people' (Kincaid, 1991: 32). In comparison with the 'source of myth' that is England, their own way of life and their sense of self continually falls short (Kincaid, 1991: 32). Kincaid begins to wonder what England, the country she had never seen with her own eyes and 'had never set foot, [her] own foot, in', is really like (Kincaid, 1991: 37). In order to come to terms with the colonisation of the mind she has experienced, she realises that she will eventually have to address '[t]he space between the idea of something and its reality [which] is always wide and deep and dark' (Kincaid, 1991: 37). This same in-between space allows for the necessary revision, 'so when they meet and find that they are not compatible, the weaker of the two, idea or reality, dies' (Kincaid, 1991: 37).

As a grown-up woman, no longer living in Antigua and feeling more powerful and secure in her social status, Kincaid finally travels to England to see it for the first time. Her trip becomes an angry retaliation, during which she denounces everything from the bad weather and food, to people's looks and behaviour, their obsession with royalty, and above all their glorification of their imperial past, which happened at the expense of people like herself. The abyss between idea and reality is nowhere more apparent than when she sees the white cliffs of Dover:

> The moment I wished every sentence, everything I knew, that began with England would end with 'and then it all died, we don't know how, it just all died' was when I saw the white cliffs of Dover. I had sung hymns and recited poems that were about a longing to see the white cliffs of Dover again ... And so there they were, the white cliffs, but they were not that pearly majestic thing I used to sing about ... The white cliffs of Dover, when finally I saw them, were cliffs, but they were not white; you would only call them that if the word 'white' meant something special to you; they were dirty and they were steep; they were so steep, the correct height from which all my views of England, starting with the map before me in my classroom and ending with the trip I had just taken, should jump and die and disappear forever. (Kincaid, 1991: 40)

Kincaid's perception of the cliffs is heavily influenced by her experience as a colonised subject, whose own culture was always considered inferior. She deconstructs the cliffs' associations with the warm and nostalgic feelings of home that she has come across time and again during her colonial education by adding a different set of associations that takes into view the perspective of the colonised: cultural oppression, exclusion and white supremacy. Kincaid is fully aware, however, that her 'prejudices have no weight to [the English] ... no force behind them' and, in contrast to the powerful narratives of Englishness, they 'remain opinions' (Kincaid, 1991: 40). Phillips' outlook, on the other hand, is more positive. Reflecting on the growing number of young British people who have embraced cultural diversity, he declares himself hopeful of a truly multicultural Britain, in which there is no longer a dominant cultural group. He argues that it was these early West Indian immigrants 'who helped to introduce Britain to the notion of postcoloniality' and that it will be their descendants 'who will help Britain cross the Rubicon of the English Channel and enter the European age of the twenty-first century' (Phillips, 2002: 282). And yet, Kincaid's angry and despairing tone and Phillips's hopeful and insistent tone are themselves signs of the immense struggle for a new narrative. As several critics have pointed out, the anti-European stance and the promise to restore Britain's global importance that fed into the Brexit debate have been fuelled by an idealisation of a British imperial past, which has evaded a critical engagement with its racist dimension (Virdee and McGeever, 2017; El-Enany, 2017). The more strictly insular UKIP rhetoric, on the other hand, successfully tapped into the cliffs' long-standing significance as a racialised border (Virdee and McGeever, 2017).[13] The cliffs conveyed the message of anti-immigration so well not simply because they offered a blank canvas, but rather because the whiteness itself was the message.

While the representations of the cliffs as given by Isherwood, Raban, Phillips and Kincaid demand a more dynamic understanding of borders and the identities they shape, they also testify to the dominance and continuity of exclusionary narratives of identity, which can be challenged and deconstructed, but hardly ignored. Perhaps the cliffs served so well as 'guards of Brexit' because, as with Theresa May's 'Brexit means Brexit', questions of what they actually stand for have not been asked often and insistently enough. Going beyond the surface meaning of both the white cliffs and Brexit reveals a multiplicity of meanings, unresolved conflicts and oppressed voices that still need to be heard. Baggini reminds us that 'symbols are not static. They are malleable and their meanings can change, subtly and importantly' (Baggini, 2012b: 4). Uncovering the multifaceted meanings surrounding the Dover area and making them more visible in society is thus a means to create a more inclusive view of a necessarily shared cultural space.

Notes

1   See UK Department for Transport (2017). With 9.1 million passengers in 2016, the Dover–Calais route was the busiest among all the ferry routes between Britain and mainland Europe. In the same year, 20.6 million passengers made use of the subterranean rail connection, the Eurostar.

2   With its focus on transnational socio-economic operations and activities, Renaud Morieux's excellent study *The Channel: England, France and the Construction of a Maritime Border in the Eighteenth Century* (2016) acts as a corrective to historical analyses which have focused on the Channel as a

geographical feature that necessarily creates division and opposition, a view that still dominates public discourse.

3   The living conditions for migrants in the area worsened after the closing of the Sangatte refugee centre in 2002. As an increasing number of people arrived in Calais in the wake of the 2015 so-called 'European refugee crisis', the term 'Jungle' became widely used in the media. The French government had the camp cleared in October 2016.

4   *The Poke* (2015).

5   See for example Howkins (2014).

6   As Franco Moretti has shown by mapping the invaders' routes in works such as *The Battle of Dorking* (1871), *How John Bull lost London* (1882) and *The Invasion of 1910* (1906), England's south-eastern corner was considered to be particularly vulnerable to foreign intrusion, no doubt because of its proximity to continental Europe (Moretti, 1998: 139).

7   For a more detailed discussion of Britannia's significance for the nation see Dresser (1989).

8   These images still abounded around the time of the tunnel's completion in the early 1990s. In her study *Bridging Divides: The Channel Tunnel and English Legal Identity*, Darian-Smith reports how resistance to the tunnel was expressed in terms of the 'penetration' and 'rape' of a feminised Kent, 'the Garden of England' (1999: 62–7).

9   It is important to note that British imperial expansion itself has been crucial to the growth and establishment of British travel writing (Korte, 2000; Siegel, 2002; Youngs, 2013).

10 Isherwood here brings to mind the line 'Or lesser breeds without the Law' in Rudyard Kipling's poem 'Recessional' from 1897. George Orwell, in his 1942 essay 'Rudyard Kipling', argues against the common view that this refers to natives encountered in British colonies, and instead posits that Kipling had in mind Germans and the proponents of pan-Germanism.

11 For a discussion of the *Empire Windrush* as a narrative trope of arrival in the British cultural memory, see Lowe (2018).

12 The need to treat the 'pioneers' as full British citizens has gained a new sense of urgency in light of the 2018 Windrush scandal, when it was revealed that numerous members of the Windrush generation, who had come to live in Britain before 1973 and been granted the right to remain, had been threatened with or experienced detention, deportation or the denial of their legal rights.

13 See Virdee and McGeever (2017).

References

Ash, Timothy Garton (2016), 'As a lifelong English European, this is the biggest defeat of my political life', *Guardian* (suppl. 'A Farewell to Europe'), 25 June, pp. 1–3.

Baggini, Julian (2012a), 'Why the white cliffs of Dover are so special', *Guardian*, 19 August. www.theguardian.com/commentisfree/2012/aug/19/white-cliffs-of-dover (last accessed 28 November 2017).

—— (2012b), *A Home on the Rock* (Swindon: National Trust).

Bartholomew, Michael (2006), *In Search of H.V. Morton* (London: Methuen).

Baucom, Ian (1999), *Out of Place: Englishness, Empire, and the Locations of Identity* (Princeton: Princeton University Press).

Bhabha, Homi K. (1990), 'Introduction: Narrating the Nation' in Homi K. Bhabha (ed.), *Nation and Narration* (London and New York: Routledge), pp. 1–7.

Darian-Smith, Eve (1999), *Bridging Divides: The Channel Tunnel and English Legal Identity* (Berkeley: University of California Press).

Dover Museum Website (n.d.), 'White cliffs of Dover'. www.dovermuseum.co.uk/Information-Resources/Articles-Factsheets/White-Cliffs-of-Dover.aspx (accessed 28 November 2017).

Dresser, Madge (1989), 'Britannia' in Raphael Samuel (ed.), *Patriotism: The Making and Unmaking of British National Identity*, 3 vols (London: Routledge, 1989), vol. 3, pp. 26–50.

El-Enany, Nadine (2017), 'Things Fall Apart: From Empire to Brexit Britain', *IPR Blog*, University of Bath Institute for Policy Research (IPR), 2 May. http://blogs.bath.ac.uk/iprblog/2017/05/02/things-fall-apart-from-empire-to-brexit-britain/ (last accessed 12 October 2017).

Fussell, Paul (1980), *Abroad: British Literary Traveling Between the Wars* (Oxford and New York: Oxford University Press).

Habermann, Ina (2010), *Myth, Memory and the Middlebrow: Priestley, du Maurier and the Symbolic Form of Englishness* (Basingstoke: Palgrave Macmillan).

Howkins, Alun (2014), 'The Discovery of Rural England' in Robert Colls and Philip Dodd (eds), *Englishness: Politics and Culture 1880–1920* (London and New York: Bloomsbury, 2nd edition), pp. 85–111.

Isherwood, Christopher (2012), *Down There on a Visit* (London: Vintage).

Kincaid, Jamaica (1991), 'On seeing England for the first time', *Transition Magazine*, 51, pp. 32–40.

Korte, Barbara (2000), *English Travel Writing* (Houndmills: Macmillan Press).

Lowe, Hannah (2018), ' "Remember the ship": narrating the Empire Windrush', *Journal of Postcolonial Writing*, pp. 1–14. https://doi.org/10.1080/17449855.2017.1411416.

Moretti, Franco (1998), *Atlas of the European Novel 1800–1900* (London: Verso).

Morieux, Renaud (2016), *The Channel: England, France and the Construction of a Maritime Border in the Eighteenth Century* (Cambridge: Cambridge University Press).

Morton, H.V. (1984), *In Search of England* (London: Methuen).

Newman, David (2007), 'The Lines that Continue to Separate Us: Borders in Our "Borderless" World' in Johan Schimanski and Stephen Wolfe (eds), *Border Poetics De-limited* (Hannover: Wehrhahn Verlag), pp. 27–57.

Orwell, George (1968), 'Rudyard Kipling' in Sonia Orwell and Ian Angus (eds), *The Collected Essays, Journalism and Letters of George Orwell*, 4 vols (London: Secker and Warburg), vol. 2, pp. 184–97.

Phillips, Caryl (2002), 'The Pioneers: Fifty Years of Caribbean Migration to Britain' in Caryl Phillips (ed.), *A New World Order* (London: Vintage), pp. 264–82.

Pick, Daniel (1993), *War Machine: The Rationalisation of Slaughter in the Modern Age* (New Haven and London: Yale University Press).

The Poke (2015), 'White cliffs of Dover to take out restraining order against Nigel Farage', *The Poke*. www.thepoke.co.uk/2015/07/30/white-cliffs-dover-take-restraining-order-nigel-farage/ (last accessed 28 November 2017).

Raban, Jonathan (2003), *Coasting: A Private Voyage* (London: Vintage).

Readman, Paul (2014), '"The cliffs are not cliffs": the cliffs of Dover and national identities in Britain, c.1750–c.1950', *History* 99:335, pp. 241–69, https://doi.org/10.1111/1468–229X.12054.

Shakespeare, William (1998a), *The Tragedy of King Lear. The Oxford Shakespeare: The Complete Works*, edited by Stanley Wells and Gary Taylor (Oxford: Clarendon Press), pp. 943–74.

(1998b), *The Tragedy of King Richard II. The Oxford Shakespeare: The Complete Works*, edited by Stanley Wells and Gary Taylor (Oxford: Clarendon Press), pp. 367–95.

Siegel, Kristi (ed.) (2002), *Issues in Travel Writing: Empire, Spectacle, and Displacement* (New York: Peter Lang).

Spiering, Menno (2015), *A Cultural History of British Euroscepticism* (Basingstoke: Palgrave Macmillan).

Trower, Shelley (2015), *Rocks of Nation: The Imagination of Celtic Cornwall* (Manchester: Manchester University Press).

UK Department for Transport (2017), 'Final sea passenger statistics: 2016', Gov.uk, Department for Transport. www.gov.uk/government/uploads/system/uploads/attachment_data/file/661355/final-sea-passenger-statistics-2016.pdf (last accessed 10 December 2017).

Virdee, Satnam and Brendan McGeever (2017), 'Racism, crisis, Brexit', *Ethnic and Racial Studies*, pp. 1–18. https://doi.org/10.1080/01419870.2017.1361544.

Wallace, David (2004), *Premodern Places: Calais to Surinam, Chaucer to Aphra Behn* (Malden, MA: Blackwell).

Youngs, Tim (2013), *The Cambridge Introduction to Travel Writing* (Cambridge: Cambridge University Press).

11

From Iron Curtains to Iron Cliffs: British travel writing between East and West

Blanka Blagojevic

'The British do love their boundaries', claims one educational website devoted to English vocabulary (Grant, 2013). As border studies scholarship highlights, drawing boundaries and 'border making' is 'an old human practice' (Popescu, 2012: 7), and in recent years, there has been growing concern with borders again. However, although 'the creation of places', and, as a consequence borders, appears to be a natural process and geography seems to impose its own logic, borders are not natural phenomena, and their relevance is dependent on the meaning that humans assign them (Diener and Hagen, 2012: 1). Also, geographical studies suggest that '[b]orders are never finished'; they have a 'transitory' quality to them and 'are always in the making, always being imagined and reimagined' (Popescu, 2012: 21).

In this chapter I intend to test this last claim about border durability. My analysis focuses on how the term 'border' has been used in the discursive mapping of British popular geopolitics,[1] in both media and literary texts, where the term 'Iron Curtain' has been used, both to denote a soft and a hard border,[2] since the early twentieth century. I will give an account of the flexible nature of the British border with Europe, the East, or sometimes simply with the Other, and then proceed to discuss three British travel narratives concerned with the Iron Curtain: David Shears' *The Ugly Frontier* (1970), Anthony Bailey's *Along the Edge of the Forest: An Iron Curtain Journey* (1983) and Tim Moore's *The Cyclist Who Went Out in the Cold: Adventures along the Iron Curtain Trail* (2016). I argue that by looking at the usage of the term 'border' in general, as well as the term 'Iron Curtain' in particular, we can trace the trajectory of the British relationship with the Continent and especially Eastern Europe.

In his 1944 travel narrative about the Balkans, Bernard Newman, a historian and author, observes that the British geographical imagination of the Continent has been marked by a rather 'limited outlook' and 'lack of interest',[3] despite some politicians' claims 'that our frontiers were on the Rhine' (Newman, 1944: 8–9). The interwar period produced different geographical imaginaries of the British borders. Patrick Wright, who wrote a cultural history of the term *Iron Curtain*, mentions Lord D'Abernon, the British ambassador to Germany's proposition that the English Channel should 'be considered an "iron curtain"' in his 1925 diary; thus, pushing the British discursive border further west (D'Abernon, *Ambassador of Peace*, 177; qtd. in Wright, 2007: 225). Historian Brendan Simms notes in his study of the 'Euro-British encounter' that in the post-war period, the borders of British geographical imaginations shifted once again, as far east as the Elbe, according to former Prime Minister Harold Macmillan's 1950 speech to the Assembly in Strasbourg (Simms, 2016: 178). Jan Morris confirms the notion that borders retain their soft, or imaginary quality, stating how '[t]he English, in their jingo days ... said that wogs began at Calais' (Morris, 2006: 65). Conversely, Morris recalls British Labour Foreign Secretary Ernest Bevin's policies, where Bevin envisioned future post-war Europe as a place where Britain would not have hard borders with the Continent and where 'a Briton [could] take a train to Paris without needing a passport' (Morris, 2006: 80). In contrast to this 1945 sentiment, the British border of post-1989 Europe, with its newly softened border regime, remained 'the surliest frontier in western Europe', creating 'a disagreeable experience' with 'merciless faces of her Majesty's customs officers interrogating' travellers 'beneath the unforgiving lights of the green channel' (Morris, 2006: 80).

These examples suggest that British geographical imaginations of the British borders with Europe, whether soft or hard, have had a shifting quality, confirming border studies' claims about the transitory and partly imaginary nature of borders. Writing about hard borders, including the Iron Curtain and Berlin Wall, Marc Silberman, Karen E. Till and Janet Ward observe that such barriers are immune to permanence. Walls, borders and boundaries often 'fall' or 'shift'; and when 'demarcated' they are 'transgressed' (Silberman *et al.*, 2012: 1). In order to understand this seemingly paradoxical conjunction between the hard and the transient, it is useful, as Silberman also proposes, to draw on Henri Lefebvre's writings on modern spaces and his concepts of *representations of space, spaces of representation* and *spatial practice* in order to rethink the conceptualisation of hard borders (Silberman *et al.*, 2012: 5–8). Lefebvre approaches space as a threefold of physical, mental and social elements (Lefebvre, 1991: 21) – a conceptualisation of space that chimes with the dual conception of borders as both physical and discursive spaces. Lefebvre further posits that space has 'a reality of its own' and that it is also 'a means of control ... of domination [and] of power', where the 'social and political (state) forces seek, but fail, to master it completely' (Lefebvre, 1991: 26). Lefebvre's 'conceptual triad' comprises *spatial practice, representations of space* and *representational spaces* (Lefebvre, 1991: 33). The first, *spatial practice*, varies according to the type of society, time and dominant means of production, essentially containing spaces of 'daily reality', of 'the routes and networks which link up' both private and public places (Lefebvre, 1991: 38). Spatial practice tests the 'specific spatial competence and performance of every society member' (Lefebvre, 1991: 38) and is related to the 'perceived' (Lefebvre, 1991: 40). By contrast, *representations of space* are understood as 'conceptualized space, the space of scientists, planners, urbanists, technocratic subdividers and social engineers, as of a certain type of artist with a scientific bent' (Lefebvre, 1991: 38). This spatial aspect is related to the 'dominant space' of a society (Lefebvre, 1991: 39) and to the so-called 'conceived' (Lefebvre, 1991: 40). And finally, *representational spaces* are 'directly *lived*' and can be conceived as 'the space of "inhabitants" and "users"' (Lefebvre, 1991: 39; emphasis in original). This is 'the dominated' and 'passively experienced' space which 'the imagination seeks to change and appropriate' (Lefebvre, 1991: 39). Lefebvre also frames this third spatial category as 'linked to the clandestine or underground side of social life, as also to art' (Lefebvre, 1991: 33).

All three categories representing physical, mental and social space are interrelated (Lefebvre, 1991: 27) and 'contribute in different ways to the production of space' in general (Lefebvre, 1991: 46). Furthermore, Lefebvre situates culture between 'representations of space and representational spaces' (Lefebvre, 1991: 43). In other words, cultural artefacts produced within a particular space will at times combine ideology and knowledge to speak to, and for, the dominant space. At other times, however, such products of culture emerging from the dominated space may be seen as symbolic and discursive attempts to subvert forces of state power and its dominant discourses. As Lefebvre points out, the state 'provokes opposition' and '[t]he violence of power is answered by the violence of subversion' (Lefebvre, 1991: 23).

Therefore, if we follow Lefebvre's conception of cultural products as positioned between oppositional views of space, the three narratives analysed here can be viewed accordingly as positioned between the dominant and the dominated spaces, at times speaking on behalf of one or the other. David Shears' *The Ugly Frontier*, Anthony Bailey's *Along the Edge of the Forest: An Iron Curtain Journey* and Tim Moore's *The Cyclist Who Went Out in the Cold: Adventures along the Iron Curtain Trail* all present voices of outsiders, people who are neither permanently bound by the hard border of the Iron Curtain nor required to be completely savvy in terms of the spatial practices that constitute the life around this border.[4] The three narrators are neither part of the panoptical force of the state embodied in the border patrol personnel or the soldiers manning the watch-towers, nor of the inhabitants who have grown accustomed to the border regime's intricacies. Theirs is the role of privileged users, of semi-engaged visitors, who gain access to representational spaces which they help to co-create in turn by narrating them. On the other hand, they are inevitably faced with the daily reality of spatial practices through their contact with the inhabitants, learning from them what it is like to negotiate such a controlled space. As they gain some insight into the dominated space, their narratives speak from that perspective to a degree. Their narratives, as cultural artefacts, can thus be said to inhabit the Lefebvrian indeterminate space between dominant and subaltern discourses.

The Iron Curtain is now one of the 'relict' borders of the world,[5] having in British geographical imagination served to describe British distancing from the Continent, notably the military menace of Germany and the USSR (Kaye, 2009: 7–8; Wright, 2007: 43, 82, 222). For many, the Iron Curtain metaphor was introduced by Winston Churchill in *The Sinews of Peace* (delivered in Fulton, Missouri in March 1946), where he traced the metaphorical division of Europe, proclaiming that 'From Stettin in the Baltic to Trieste in the Adriatic, an iron curtain has descended across the Continent' (Applebaum, 2013: xxi). However, as social historian Patrick Wright reminds us, '[t]here had been many "iron curtains" before Churchill went to Fulton in 1946'. The actual 'theatrical origins of the Iron Curtain would largely be forgotten in the Cold War decades', not least because its original intended use as a safety apparatus to guard the auditorium from stage fires would later be replaced by other materials (Wright, 2007: 375).

American literary critic J. Hillis Miller emphasises that the '[t]opographical setting connects literary works to a specific historical and geographical time' (Miller, 1995: 6). The three travel narratives situated along the physical Iron Curtain thus inevitably evoke the *zeitgeist* of the Cold War era. To begin with, all three refer to Churchill's speech, citing him carefully: Shears paraphrases the speech on the very first page of the first chapter (Shears, 1970: 9); Bailey does it in the opening pages of his narrative when describing his motivation 'to travel [its] length' (1983: 7–8); and Moore in the middle of the travelogue after having entered the former German section of the border (Moore, 2016: 189). By merely looking at the paratextual elements of the three narratives, such as book titles, cover design and table of contents pages, the three books grow progressively more obvious in their references to the Cold War. If

we compare their titles, it can be noted that as time progresses, the evoca-
tion of the Cold War symbolism and the very term 'Iron Curtain' become
more conspicuous: David Shears' *The Ugly Frontier* (1970) does not directly name the border he is travelling along as the 'Iron Curtain', nor does
he particularly iterate Churchill's term. Instead, he coins a number of
substitute terms such as 'a dueling scar', 'a monstrous anomaly' (Shears,
1970: 9), 'unnatural barrier' (Shears, 1970: 14) and 'the Wire and the Wall'
(Shears, 1970: 34). The book's cover design displays an illustration of a
brick wall that could be found anywhere or even be mistaken for a win-
dowless front of a typical British terraced house. Shears also admits in the
first chapter that '[t]he name Iron Curtain has fallen into disuse in recent
years', by which he means the late 1960s (Shears, 1970: 9). Despite these
obfuscating discursive tactics, the table of contents of *The Ugly Frontier*
is heavily laden with technical and material border references – such as
'Drawing the Border', 'Building the Barricades', 'The Border-watchers' and
'The Border Regions' – in addition to two references to Berlin, not least
because his entire journey only covers the German inner border (Shears,
1970: 1).

The paratexts of Anthony Bailey's *Along the Edge of the Forest*, published
thirteen years after Shears' account, already point to the obvious link
with the Iron Curtain. The book cover sports a stylised colourful map of
Central Europe with several photographs depicting the obvious symbols
of the Curtain – Brandenburg Gate, portions of the Berlin Wall, and a
tiny image of a watchtower at the back of the book. Although the main
title remains neutral, its subtitle, 'An Iron Curtain Journey', denotes
both the travel genre and the narrative's main topography. The opening
pages contain a 'Chronology' of the main events of the Cold War and the
table of contents page, which bear obvious references to the hard 'iron'
border. Unlike Shears' *The Ugly Frontier*, Bailey's approach is not narrowly focused on the inner German border and the Berlin Wall alone.
Rather, his journey begins in Lübeck Bay and ends in Trieste, meandering
along the way between the former Czechoslovakia and Austria, as well
as between the former Yugoslavia and Italy. *Along the Edge of the Forest*
also includes descriptions of the author's entries through the Iron Curtain
at the most closely watched German section of the border: Checkpoint
Charlie in Berlin. By contrast, David Shears' narrative contains no
descriptions of the narrator's visits to the East, although it gives detailed
technical descriptions of the border's infrastructure, travel and communication routes, including technical drawings, accounts of both successful
and fatal escape attempts, its history, and several case studies of divided
communities along the intra-German border. All the data that Shears
gathers and presents come from West German and Allied sources as well

as from mostly military personnel involved in the border observation on the western side of the divide. Thus, Shears writes:

> It would be impossible to list all the people who helped in the preparation of this book: local officials and ordinary citizens in communities up and down the border and in Berlin. All the Western border-guarding agencies proved most co-operative, arranging among other things trips by helicopter, jeep and boat along the land and water frontier. Numerous Bonn government officials gave generously of their time and knowledge. (Shears, 1970: 5–6)

Shears' approach and his acknowledgement throw into relief the hardness and impenetrability of the interstate border between the two Germanys, suggesting that Shears' discourse consists of predominantly Lefebvrian 'representations of space', in that his version of the Iron Curtain is already mediated and prefabricated by the representatives of the state, with the border-zone space as a product of 'technocratic subdividers' (Lefebvre, 1991: 39). Both Shears' and Bailey's own spatial practice within the Iron Curtain is, to a significant degree, limited to the routes and networks of the American and British military or the German border patrols. Bailey begins his journey at the Baltic coast where he joins 'the West German patrol boat' (Bailey, 1983: 9). Later on, in Berlin, he meets with 'a U.S. military patrol for a trip along the wall' in an army jeep (109). Similarly, David Shears describes 'fly[ing] in an American army helicopter along the border, [driving] with British military patrols or sail[ing] along the Elbe in a West German Customs launch' (Shears, 1970: 14).

Despite these similarities, however, Bailey's and Shears' texts display certain differences in their motivation and narrative goals. Shears admits that *The Ugly Frontier* 'is the result of … a desire to know more about the hard physical facts of German division' and further still that the book 'is an attempt to describe as factually as possible just how the frontier operates' (Shears, 1970: 5). While Bailey uses the prerogatives of a Western observer with connections and access to the technocratic spaces and their privileged users, he registers more personal motivations, showing significantly more interest in the actual competences and living experiences of ordinary people on both sides of the Curtain. He further claims that he is interested in observing people's spatial practices, 'look[ing] at the ground and at the people living along the border' and 'the effects of living close' to the border (Bailey, 1983: 8). Furthermore, Bailey is willing to experience the spatial practices of the border regions as directly lived spaces, and do 'reconnaissance along the frontier' not only in military vehicles but also in his private car (Bailey, 1983: 8). As Bailey's narrative progresses, we encounter more and more examples of his direct observation of these representational spaces of the Iron Curtain with their elements of opposition to the state power, or what Lefebvre would call 'violence of subversion' (1991: 23), from the cheeky graffiti messages on the western side of the Berlin Wall, which read, for example, 'The Wall Must Go', or 'East German High Jump Training Area' (Bailey, 1983: 99), to East German bitter-sweet subversive jokes and the fact that 'many watch a lot of West German TV', while West Berliners are said to attend 'a good deal of excellent music and opera in East Berlin' (Bailey, 1983: 123). That this was possible in the historical moment where Bailey was writing in the early 1980s might be seen as evidence of a certain thaw, and easing of tensions. Significantly, both books dedicate space to escape attempts. Shears devotes a chapter to stories of attempts both tragic and successful (Shears, 1970: 52–69). He ends on a rather pessimistic note, opining that such attempts are bound to become rare because '[f]light from the East has become so hazardous' and that some rare successful examples are 'due to exceptional circumstances or exceptional luck' (Shears, 1970: 69). Bailey recounts escape stories which by now have become part of collective memory, preserved in a museum near Checkpoint Charlie in Berlin, dedicated to escapes and containing vehicles and paraphernalia which the escapees used. The museum commemorates failure and the tragic deaths of escapees inducing 'sadness' and evoking the air 'of an uncivil, murderous peace' that speaks eloquently to the violence of the Cold War hard borders (Bailey, 1983: 102–3).

As both Shears and Bailey dwell on spatial practices rigidly regulated by the hard border regime on both sides of the Iron Curtain, they attempt to understand, or perhaps even find a rational justification for, its existence. They both go into some depth of German history and arrive at the conclusion that the present border merely reflects earlier historical divisions. Shears appears to feel a need to naturalise the border: 'Was it reasonable to suppose that the line dividing the Soviet zone from those of the Western Allies, purposefully following old provincial borders, would in fact enhance genuine political, religious or ethnic distinctions within Germany? Seen in historical perspective, it might be argued that it was. Even in the Middle Ages, roughly the same line divided Germans' (Shears, 1970: 24–5). Like Shears, Bailey attempts to put the current division into perspective by linking it to long-term historical events, repeating the notion of the 'atavistic' roots of the Iron Curtain extending back to the age of Charlemagne and being reinforced again in Napoleon's campaigns. Even though he admits that the present state of the divide is largely due to the border drawing games of the Allied forces (Bailey, 1983: 17–19, 20), he feels the urge to find a historical justification for the border. Predictably, perhaps, both authors are pessimistic about the future regarding the durability of the Iron Curtain. Shears opines that the 'outlook is bleak' (Shears, 1970: 213) and that 'the Ugly Frontier ... will last indefinitely' (Shears, 1970: 217). Bailey also speculates about 'the chances of German reunification – and what did West Germans think of it?' (Bailey, 1983: 82). His answers are ambivalent, in that some of his sources suggest that the reunification 'was unlikely to come about', whereas others posit that 'West Germans should work for reunion in perhaps thirty or forty years' time' (Bailey, 1983: 82). As his journey along the border progresses, a conversation with an informed American political adviser once again reveals the instability of the apparent hard border. As their conversation traces the issue of divisions from the Roman *limes* to the Iron Curtain, they conclude that '[t]hings that look very stable can change overnight' (Bailey, 1983: 113). In that regard, the nuanced discursive differences in Shears' and Bailey's texts are significant because they reflect elements of both top-down and bottom-up geopolitical imaginaries which appear to confirm the transitory nature of all borders. And yet, both Anne Applebaum in her historical study of the Iron Curtain and Larry Wolff in his intellectual history of Eastern Europe agree that the fall of the Iron Curtain and the events of 1989 came as a surprise. Applebaum notes that in the 1960s, after the Berlin Wall was erected and the Curtain began to materialise, 'it seemed as if these barriers could last forever' (Applebaum, 2013: xxviii). Larry Wolff, on a more personal note, remembers a conference held in 1988 where the gathering of high-quality academic expertise provided no sign of such developments as occurred in 1989, although they took place only a year later. Wolff notes that '[n]either [he] nor anyone else had the faintest notion of what the opaque future was hiding just out of sight' (Wolff, 1994: 3). The geographers Diener and Hagen endorse this, noting that: 'During the Cold War ... international borders remained divisive issues but appeared static and fixed against the backdrop of superpower confrontation' (Diener and Hagen, 2012: 16).

Despite their differences, which are sometimes only subtle, the two travel narratives compared so far – *The Ugly Frontier* and *Along the Edge of the Forest* – can be said to form a compatible thematic pair since they were both written and published in the Cold War era. The third travel narrative, however, came out around a quarter of a century after the fall of the Iron Curtain. This fact alone makes Tim Moore's *The Cyclist Who Went Out in the Cold* a very different read. Not only is Moore's book endowed with the advantage of historical hindsight, but it is also written in a completely different tone, perhaps possible only now. The book is by far the most light-hearted of the three, containing numerous instances of that travel genre staple: humour. This is more or less equally distributed between authorial self-deprecation and humour deployed as a mechanism for othering the former communist Eastern Europe, thus rhetorically defending the author against possible charges of condescension.

Another stark difference, and *The Cyclist*'s main advantage, is the freedom of choosing the course as well as the means of transportation. In post-Wall Europe, one does not need to depend on the elaborate police and military transportation network. To make the crossing still as challenging and memorable as possible, so he has a tale to tell, Moore takes the longest version of the Iron Curtain's route from northern Finland to the Black Sea. The means of transportation is a second-hand East German shopping bicycle – MIFA 904 – which he describes as an 'East/West, cross-Curtain vintage hybrid' (Moore, 2016: 20). The flexible itinerary and vehicle of choice ensure that *The Cyclist*'s track can zigzag freely from the east to the west of the former hard border. Despite this flexibility, however, the choice of itinerary suggests the narrative's orientation towards the Cold War era, which was filled with binary oppositions separating the two parts of the Continent. The differences that the travelogue seeks to explore are therefore not only the product of the residual memory of the Cold War's ideological and material divisions featured in the text's rhetoric but are also sought in physical landscapes still bearing visible traces of those differences. Thus, the very title of the book may be said to display rhetorical residues of 'the nostalgic Cold War repertoire', referencing le Carré's classic *The Spy Who Came in from the Cold* (Boym, 2002).

Despite its humour and light-hearted tone, the Cold War repertoire is conspicuous in Moore's narrative. For example, in Vyborg, early on in his journey, Moore experiences his 'first encounter with urban Russia', which, in his words, 'showcased everything that lay in wait – fear, filth, incompetence and colourful family fun – all in one ramshackle package' (2016: 88). As is typical in the genre of travel writing, seemingly authentic descriptions are heavily filtered through the 'act of writing' (Thompson, 2011: 62). As Thompson states in *Travel Writing*, instances of 'radical difference' can trigger either 'horror' or 'delight' in both the author and his (implied) readers (Thompson, 2011: 66), negotiated through rhetorical devices (Thompson, 2011: 68), as is the case with Moore's examples of shabbiness of the former Eastern bloc. As Moore himself admits, this rhetorical 'horror' and 'delight' were present in the Cold War, as he was 'brought up to regard East Europeans with fear, or pity' whose living standard provided 'goofy' examples of technology which one could not help but 'warm to' (Moore, 2016: 7). Moore's signature humour appears in the narrative when the author needs to negotiate the previously stated 'radical difference'. The employment of similes to illustrate the ludicrousness of his transportation choice and the vehicle's inappropriateness is an occasion to provide what Thompson calls a 'point of comparison' with the readers' own Western culture (Thompson, 2011: 68). Thus, the MIFA bike is described as 'a vinyl breezeblock' or 'the sort of thing Mad Max's auntie might have ridden to the bingo' (Moore, 2016: 22).

Apart from the differences rooted in both spatial and temporal advantages over its predecessors, Moore's *The Cyclist* displays one more discursive trait which is absent from Shears's and Bailey's books: nostalgia. Svetlana Boym defines nostalgia as 'a sentiment of loss and displacement, but ... also [as] a romance with one's own fantasy' (Boym, 2007: 7). Moore's narrative abounds in nostalgic elements interspersed with sobering reminders of the darker side of the Cold War. He frames the nostalgic motivation behind his quest as being 'about history, about the days of my old MIFA 900' (Moore, 2016: 222) while the conscious decision to begin the journey at the height of the cold season sets the apocalyptical Cold War atmosphere of 'a monochrome nuclear winter' (Moore, 2016: 15). The nostalgia of *The Cyclist Who Went Out in the Cold* could be said to display the characteristics of a 'reflective nostalgia' which 'explores ways of inhabiting many places at once and imagining different time zones' (Boym, 2001: xix). This can be seen in the organisation of Moore's text: the paperback edition contains no table of contents, requiring the reader to leaf through the book in order to locate each chapter, demarcated by a fragment of the route alongside an illustrated map, usually titled after a country or a region. This practice fragments and spatialises the otherwise linear reading experience of *The Cyclist*'s journey and symbolically both revives and displaces the Iron Curtain experience. This in turn has the effect of evoking the condition of 'reflective nostalgia', which, in Boym's definition, contains both 'a longing for continuity' and a realisation that revisiting the Cold War in the post-1989 conditions means experiencing 'a fragmented world' (Boym, 2001: xiv). This somewhat chaotic nostalgic experience of the fragmented border confirms Popescu's notion of the 'renewed border instability' due to '[t]he collapse of [the] bipolar international system along with its figurative and literal border landmarks – the Iron Curtain and the Berlin Wall' (Popescu, 2012: 18).

Reflective nostalgia 'can be ironic and humorous'; it 'savours details and memorial signs' and uses these elements to create a narrative that is 'ironic, inconclusive, and fragmentary' (Boym, 2007: 15). These 'ironic and humorous' elements are staples of Moore's text, which have already been shown to be epitomised by the vehicle's post-apocalyptic incompatibility. This is supplemented by close attention to nostalgic detail in the travelogue, from the peculiar choice of the vintage bicycle to fond reminiscences of an earlier car trip across Eastern Europe, which is steeped, as the author himself admits, in 'nostalgic memories of a three-month journey' which he and his wife made in the early months after the fall of the Curtain (Moore, 2016: 3). Details range from insisting on sporting a GDR jersey to visiting the actual MIFA factory in a small town of Sangerhausen 'which lay deep in the old East' and which makes the narrator feel 'most at home since setting off', despite having never previously visited the place (Moore, 2016: 214). What makes the place so homelike is that here the cyclist is exposed 'for the first time to the hard-core, full-strength GDR, away from those borderlands diluted by proximity to the old West' and where everything 'was grubby and decrepit' and everyone 'more impoverished' (Moore, 2016: 214).

The latter two occasions prove to be sobering, if awkward, reminders that memory and nostalgia may be difficult to translate into another memory culture. Thus, on the occasion of wearing the GDR jersey in the streets of former East Germany, the narrator is confronted with many 'a stare of incredulous hatred' (Moore, 2016: 184), so that he feels compelled to hide the communist emblem under gaffer tape. The visit to the MIFA factory turns out to be a miscalculated and disappointing occasion as well. While the author 'imagined that [his] 900's back-to-the-roots pilgrimage would have meant as much to its creators as it did to [him]' (Moore, 2016: 222), he admits with sadness that the vintage bike 'was evidently an uncomfortable reminder of an unhappy past' (Moore, 2016: 223). Such cultural missteps when 'we try to repair longing with belonging', as these two examples illustrate, may lead to misunderstanding, as Svetlana Boym notes (Boym, 2001: xvi).

Tim Moore's text is radically different from the first two Cold War travelogues; not only in style, with its nostalgic and humorous rhetoric, but also in the spatial practices that it both exhibits and detects along the Iron Curtain route. David Shears' 'ugly frontier' contains almost exclusively top-down representations of space. Keeping most of his sources anonymous, Shears depends heavily on data and information provided by government officials, the police and the military forces, citing statistics pertaining to communications, infrastructure and travel links between the two Germanys.[6] Spatial practices are heavily regimented through a state force whose power is felt as 'sinister peace' (Shears, 1970: 34), while the lived spaces themselves are filled with the matching props: 'concrete barriers' of checkpoints (Shears, 1970: 17), 'with barbed wire and ploughed "death strips"' (Shears, 1970: 39); roads that are 'barricaded or guarded' (Shears, 1970: 39); 'bunkers', 'watchtowers', road blocks, 'no-man's-land', 'minefields and fences' (Shears, 1970: 171). This setting evokes a panoptic quality, the border creating in the landscape what Foucault describes as 'a strict spatial partitioning' (Foucault, 1995: 195). The space, as a product of the Cold War binaries, becomes 'a segmented, immobile, frozen space' with its sectors divided between Allied forces who incessantly patrol the border zone and thus represent the typical spatial practice in the area that aligns with Foucauldian partitioning. Anthony Bailey's Iron Curtain of the early 1980s still retains the panoptic qualities of Shears' 'ugly frontier' of the late 1960s, which Bailey describes in detail: 'Between the actual border and the DDR fence there was generally a cleared strip of ground, of varying width. There were also usually two fences, with an area of ground, of varying width that was often sown with mines. The fences were roughly three meters tall, and made of metal cut and then stretched into a grid pattern' (Bailey, 1983: 15). Bailey's description abounds with elaborate technical details, conjuring the look of the fence on both sides, and painting a vivid picture of the border's space with its 'plowed strip[s]', 'deep ditch[es]', 'vehicle barrier[s]', 'lights and electric- and sound-alarm systems', and types of 'observation towers', where newer ones have 'windows made of ... reflecting glass that made it difficult to see what those inside the observation post were doing' (Bailey, 1983: 15). These descriptive details, which paint the Curtain as 'a machinery that assures dissymmetry' (Foucault, 1995: 202), confirm over and over again that the landscape of the Iron Curtain is constructed as a panoptic space where the invisible power is all-seeing, rarely allowing the inhabitants to see but almost exclusively to be seen, turning them into 'the object of information, [and] never a subject in communication' (Foucault, 1995: 200). When reading these descriptive passages, it is important to remember that the author is only able to obtain such specialist knowledge of technical details because he has a privileged status and easy access to those who are directly involved in exercising political power through technology,[7] which is part of the representations of space.

In terms of spatial practices that are present in the hard border zone of the Iron Curtain, as far as the older two travelogues are concerned, they are mostly focused on the infrastructure built for and available to the representatives of state power. As previously stated, in both books, descriptions of the movement of border officials and other state personnel proliferate. The lives of ordinary people are foregrounded mostly through accounts of escape attempts of East German citizens. The dominant argument in Shears is that '[e]ven many Germans know remarkably little about the workings of the few links that still remain between East and West ... and the way the border is watched and guarded', in part because of the paucity of written testimonies about this division (Shears, 1970: 5). Bailey confirms this, noting that the representatives of the state have the best knowledge of this border, and with reference to escape attempts, stating that '[b]order guards still have a greater chance of getting across than civilians' (Bailey, 1983: 105). Moore's text once again departs from these lines of thought, as the actual traces of the Curtain are fewer and often less visible. The book regales the reader with humorous strings of cycling anecdotes whose focus shifts just as much to the weather conditions, physical exertion, and to locating food and accommodation as it does to political history. What is more, the Iron Curtain has now become a bicycle-friendly trail, a tourist attraction and, in places, a natural park, echoing concerns of other critics that 'it may be dangerously easy to let the importance of this barrier and the impacts it wrought fade away' (Havlick, 2014: 127). Nevertheless, Moore's seemingly light-hearted discourse notwithstanding, *The Cyclist* also makes frequent reference to the histories of European countries and the Cold War. Moore's memory still moves between 'how deeply ingrained the fear of annihilation was in those days' (Moore, 2016: 132) and how being born in the mid-1960s was 'a traumatic time to come of age' (Moore, 2016: 133). Almost predictably, the author evokes the English tradition of invasion scare narratives, imagining what it would be like if the USSR invaded Great Britain. He is quick to deflect this threat again, concluding humorously that 'we'd all be much less fat and Coventry would look a lot better' due to the 'Communist authorities' sensitive respect for cultural heritage' (Moore, 2016: 146); still, the spectre has been raised for his implied British readership. 'What kind of Communist would I have been?', he wonders, admitting to having been 'a state socialist' (Moore, 2016: 207), but concluding that he would probably be a fellow traveller like most other people in the Eastern bloc (Moore, 2016: 207–8).

Comparing the paratextual elements of Moore's book to the earlier two travelogues, it can be said that Moore's narrative exhibits more similarities to Bailey's than to Shears's, while still displaying a significantly different approach. Bailey's cover design shows actual photographs from field trips superimposed over a political map, whose subversive potential lies in distinguishing each country of the Eastern bloc as well as showing Germany united. This visual mapping strategy stands in contrast to the monolithic mental maps of the Cold War era, which were often imagined to be dividing the world and Europe with 'super-borders of the blocks' (Balibar, 2002: 80). By contrast, Moore's paperback cover depicts an anonymous winter landscape with coniferous trees, watchtowers, barbed wire walls in the background and the fast-moving cyclist in the foreground. The illustration style is reminiscent of cartoons or even children's book illustrations. The colour scheme recalls the Union Jack, consisting of white, blue and a rather intense red. The sinister effect of the Cold War imagery – that of the watchtowers, searchlights and barbed wire fences – is largely muted through a cheerful, slightly retro drawing style. The inside covers reveal the itinerary starting in Kirkenes, Norway and ending in

Tsarevo, Bulgaria, also depicting the political map of Europe with distinct state borders. This route, however, does not clearly demarcate the Iron Curtain, so that the only concrete paratextual proof that the book is about the Iron Curtain journey is the secondary title, 'Adventures along the Iron Curtain Trail'. Examined chronologically, the three novels demonstrate a progression in the British popular imagination of Eastern Europe, beginning with the static, binary division of the 1960s when Shears wrote *The Ugly Frontier*; to the first glimpses of 1980s optimism that the hard border might not last indefinitely in Bailey's *Along the Edge of Forest*; to Moore's 2016 *The Cyclist*, which reflects the post-1989 world of fragmentation, irony and humorous nostalgia.

Crucially, the narratives reflect the degree of British engagement with the Continent. As Brendan Simms has suggested, the Cold War ensured Britain's rhetorical and geopolitical proximity to the Continent, expressed in Macmillan's pronouncement that the British frontier was not only on the Rhine but also on the Elbe (Simms, 2016: 178).[8] This political interest in European affairs results in part from the physical presence of the British troops in Germany including the area around both the Rhine and the Elbe during the Cold War. Both Shears and Bailey acknowledge that fact directly. Thus, in *The Ugly Frontier* we learn of the BAOR, the British Army on the Rhine (Shears, 1970: 100) and 'Britain's "presence"' on the Elbe (Shears, 1970: 102), while Bailey's narrative presents details about the blurriness of this seemingly natural borderline (Bailey, 1983: 48), such as the fact that the Elbe border issue had remained unsolved mainly due to the indecision of Great Britain and that 'the British solution' was – to paraphrase one of the narrator's interlocutors – not to solve the problem but to live with it (Bailey, 1983: 48).[9] Even Moore, when crossing the Elbe, is aware of the former frontier, citing data about the number of people who tried to escape into the West at this portion of the border during the Cold War (Moore, 2016: 200–1). However, the memory of the British presence is at best oblique, acknowledged briefly when the author, after having crossed the Elbe into small former East German towns, comes across a remaining 'death strip', thus giving voice to a British, or even English, geo-cultural imaginary shaping of Britain's relationship with Europe.

Discussing the archaeology of the Iron Curtain, Anna McWilliams notes that '[t]he Iron Curtain was first "created" in words by Churchill, then physically created ... and then again changed and recreated through words' (McWilliams, 2013: 43). As these travelogues show, the physicality of the Iron Curtain has diminished since the height of the Cold War era. At the same time, the phrase itself – as well as the memory of it – continues its discursive existence and remains present in British cultural and medial discourses, often being an eye-catcher in news reports. This is reflected in headlines from the years leading up to Brexit: 'We're gonna have to build the Wall!'[10] (Wogan, 2007); 'An Iron Curtain Cycle Trail' (Pyzik, 2014), 'Refugees Cross as Hungary Builds "New Iron Curtain" to Stop Them' (Thorpe, 2015), 'Russia: Nato Building "New Iron Curtain"' (BBC, 2016); 'Don't Give Us an Iron Cliff of Dover to Replace the Iron Curtain' (Roberts, 2016). All these headlines suggest that there is a deeply ingrained symbolism of the Iron Curtain as a political and cultural divider, a trope which the addressees of these news items will easily recognise. What is interesting to observe is the spatial flexibility of the Curtain, which seems to be able to move discursively across the Continent, from the Russian border all the way to the English Channel. In other words, the Iron Curtain, whether it is understood as a piece of reflective nostalgia or not, has become displaced and is now used in popular geopolitics and broader culture as a powerful symbol of exclusion and isolation. As Larry Wolff remarks, 'the maps in the mind' drawn with the Iron Curtain 'are deeply rooted and powerfully compelling' (Wolff, 1994: 3). Gabriel Popescu agrees that the borders 'leave lasting memories' since they influence '[p]atterns of social interaction in space', or – as Lefebvre would put it – social practices (Popescu, 2012: 2). Étienne Balibar makes a similar observation, claiming that 'the "blocs" of the recent past have left deep marks on institutions, law and mentalities' (Balibar, 2002: 81).

Sustaining a 'wall in the head' mentality[11] and still fresh collective memories of the Cold War, the Iron Curtain remains a central trope of British views of and the relationship with the Continent. Reasons for this may be found in the interrelation of political and cultural discourses. Klaus Dodds lists 'Britain's four geopolitical traditions':[12] Little England, Cosmopolitan, European and American Britain (Dodds, 2007: 47), suggesting that the British relationship with Europe has been of varying intensity throughout history. Historian Stephen J. Lee observes that since Britain has been in decline as a world power since at least the First World War, it has sought 'a more distinctively regional role' which meant 'closer involvement with Europe' (Lee, 1996: 9). The British travel narratives discussed here reflect this geopolitical orientation and British interest in continental affairs.

This is contrasted, however, with an endorsement of 'splendid isolation',[13] or – as Dodds would frame it – of the geopolitical orientation towards 'Little England'. I have already noted Anthony Bailey's conclusion in the case of the Cold War border on the Elbe, where the British were viewed as responsible for the failure of the resolution of the border issue. Tim Moore's assessment of the British understanding of Europe is even sharper, since his book was published after the Brexit referendum results.

Thus, he notes that '[e]nsconced on our little island under the banner INVASION-FREE SINCE 1066, it's hard for us to envisage the ethno-political ebbs and flows that have swept through continental Europe' (Moore, 2016: 150). It was not always so, as can be glimpsed from Shears' description of the intense British involvement in the drawing of the post-war continental border in the final years of the war as well as the early period of the Cold War, but Britain's active role and interest seem to have come to a halt (Shears, 1970: 19).

In the years leading up to Brexit, the isolationist pattern and Euroscepticism in the media gathered momentum. In 2011 an article in the *Guardian* discussed the issue of Euroscepticism, raising a rhetorical question: '[s]o is today's isolation splendid or miserable? Is it better or for worse?' (White, 2011). Some years later, writing for the BBC, journalist Sam Wilson discussed the same issue, ascribing the isolationist tendencies to 'Britain's island mentality' and 'that imperial hangover' reflecting mostly the geopolitical orientation of the 'Little England' type which demonstrated its vitality in the Brexit referendum (Wilson, 2014). As the Brexit negotiations continue in 2019, it is hard to prognosticate what kind of changed spatial practices and representations of space will emerge as a result of these polit-ical changes and how they will be reflected in the cultural discourses of the future. Surely, however, the Lefebvrian triadic concept of space will remain relevant as an analytical tool as we investigate the spaces Brexit will create for the British relationship with the Continent in the near future. This analysis highlights the interconnectedness and mutual influences of literary, cultural and geopolitical discourses as well as the relevance of interdisciplinarity in understanding a phenomenon like Brexit. The approach can thus illu-minate broader discursive tendencies that shape popular geo-cultural and political imaginaries in the British–European relationship. A Lefebvrian analysis attentive to various interrelated dimensions of material and social space can help explain a seeming paradox: hard borders may look forbid-ding and permanent, but they always collapse at some point, while the soft borders in the mind prove much more durable.

Notes

1   Scholarship on geopolitics differentiates between 'formal' (academic), 'prac-tical' (foreign policy and political institutions) and 'popular' geopolitics, where the term 'popular' refers to the discourses of mass media, films, litera-ture and cartoons as the 'popular' aspects of 'geopolitical imagination', which in turn is understood here as 'geopolitical representations of self and other' (Dodds, 2007: 45–6).

2   German sociologist Klaus Eder proposes that borders can be classified as *hard* and *soft*. The border infrastructure – fences, cross-border personnel and customs office represent the *hard* border. The 'soft borders', he argues, 'are boundaries that we draw between people' and that '[t]hey are in the images people have of their world' (Eder, 2006: 256).

3   My usage of the term 'geographical imaginations' follows the definition given by cultural geographers where these space-focused templates are said to provide ways of seeing the world, describing 'how individuals and communities understand themselves and their relations with each other across space' (Atkinson *et al.*, 2005: 3).

4   The Iron Curtain has featured not only as a topographic staple of the spy genre but also in many Anglophone travel narratives and photojournalism books, especially those focusing on Eastern Europe, either as the dominant backdrop or at least as a prominent motif. See, for example, Rory MacLean's *Stalin's Nose* (1992), Giles Whittell's *Lambada Country* (1992), Jan Morris's *Fifty Years of Europe* (1997), Brian Rose's *The Lost Border* (2005), Tom Arnold's *Checkpoint Charlie* (2006), Michael Palin's *New Europe* (2007), Paul Kaye's *Fragments* (2009) and Jason Smart's *The Red Quest* (2013).

5   Gabriel Popescu defines 'relict borders' as 'boundary lines that no longer mar[k] political divisions but that were still visible in the landscape' (Popescu, 2012: 18).

6   See especially chapters 9 and 10: 'Transport and Travel' and 'Communications' (Shears, 1970: 131–168).

7   The term 'political technology' was discussed by Elden (2013: 16–17, 322–3). Space in this context is a product of political, cultural and technical influences which exert control and power over it through territorial division. The term can be closely related to the process of 'political territoriality' which is understood similarly as a 'form of power over space' (Popescu, 2012: 12). See also Sack (2009).

8   See also 'The British zone of occupation in Germany, 1945' (Simms, 2016: xxxii–xxxiii).

9   British preference towards this status quo strategy was noticeable during the Brexit negotiations particularly during the winter of 2018/19.

10   The BBC's commentator's response to the voting results during the song contest when several Eastern European countries were in the lead while the UK contestants were at the bottom of the list (Wogan, 2007).

11   The term 'Mauer in den Köpfen' [a wall in people's heads] first appeared in the novel *The Wall Jumper* by West German author Peter Schneider published in 1982. For a discussion of the novel and German 'Wall literature' [*Mauerliteratur*] in the broader context of border literature, see: Rüdiger Görner, 'Border in Mind or How to Re-invent Identities' in Barta (2013: 48–57).

12   For a more detailed exploration of the four geopolitical orientations of Great Britain, see Ash (2004).

13 Splendid isolation is a term describing a British foreign policy in the second
    half of the nineteenth century when Britain chose to remain uninvolved in
    European affairs. For a historical analysis of the policy, see Charmley (1999).

References

Applebaum, A. (2013), *Iron Curtain: The Crushing of Eastern Europe* (London:
    Penguin Books).
Ash, Timothy Garton (2004), *Free World. America, Europe, and the Surprising
    Future of the West* (London: Vintage).
Atkinson, D., P. Jackson, D. Sibley and N. Washbourne (eds) (2005), *Cultural
    Geography: A Critical Dictionary of Key Concepts* (London: I.B. Tauris).
Bailey, A. (1983), *Along the Edge of the Forest: An Iron Curtain Journey*
    (London: Faber & Faber).
Balibar, E. (2002), *Politics and the Other Scene* (London: Verso).
Barta, P.I. (ed.) (2013), *The Fall of the Iron Curtain and the Culture of Europe*
    (London: Routledge).
BBC (2016), 'Russia: Nato building "new Iron Curtain"', 14 August.
Boym, S. (2001), *The Future of Nostalgia* (New York: Basic Books).
    (2002), 'Dubravka Ugresic', *Bomb*, Summer, p. 80. https://bombmagazine.org/
    (last accessed 30 April 2018).
    (2007), 'Nostalgia and its discontents', *Hedgehog Review* 9:2, pp. 7–18. https://
    iasc-culture.org (last accessed 17 March 2018).
Charmley, John (1999), *Splendid Isolation? Britain and the Balance of Power 1874–
    1914* (London: Hodder & Stoughton).
Diener, A.C. and J. Hagen (2012), *Borders: A Very Short Introduction* (Oxford:
    Oxford University Press).
Dodds, K. (2007), *Geopolitics: A Very Short Introduction* (Oxford: Oxford
    University Press).
Eder, K. (2006), 'Europe's borders: the narrative construction of the boundaries of
    Europe', *European Journal of Social Theory* 9:3, pp. 255–71.
Elden, Stuart (2013), *The Birth of Territory* (Chicago: University of Chicago Press).
Foucault, M. (1995), *Discipline and Punish: The Birth of the Prison*, trans. A.
    Sheridan (New York: Vintage Books).
Grant, D. (2013), '15 idioms and metaphors about boundaries, walls and fences'.
    https://owlcation.com/ (last accessed 25 May 2018).
Havlick, D.G. (2014), 'The Iron Curtain trail's landscapes of memory, meaning,
    and recovery', *Focus on Geography* 57:3, 126–133.
Kaye, P. (2009), *Fragments* (San Francisco: Blurb).
Lee, S.J. (1996), *Aspects of British Political History 1914–1995* (London: Routledge).
Lefebvre, H. (1991), *The Production of Space*, trans. D. Nicholson-Smith
    (Oxford: Blackwell).
McWilliams, A. (2013), *An Archaeology of the Iron Curtain: Material and Metaphor*
    (Stockholm: Södertörn University). www.diva-portal.org/ (last accessed 17
    July 2016).

Miller, J.H. (1995), *Topographies* (Stanford: Stanford University Press).

Moore, T. (2016), *The Cyclist Who Went Out in the Cold: Adventures along the Iron Curtain Trail* (London: Yellow Jersey Press).

Morris, J. (2006), *Europe: An Intimate Journey* (London: Faber & Faber).

Newman, B. (1944), *Balkan Background* (London: Robert Hale Limited).

Popescu, G. (2012), *Bordering and Ordering the Twenty-First Century: Understanding Borders* (Lanham: Rowman & Littlefield).

Pyzik, Agata (2014), 'An Iron Curtain cycle trail may peddle the delusion that borders don't exist', *Guardian*. www.theguardian.com (last accessed 27 August 2016).

Roberts, Miles (2016), 'Don't give us an Iron Cliff of Dover to replace the Iron Curtain', *Daily Telegraph*. www.telegraph.co.uk (last accessed 2 August 2016).

Sack, Robert David (2009), *Human Territoriality: Its Theory and History* (Cambridge: Cambridge University Press).

Shears, D. (1970), *The Ugly Frontier* (New York: Alfred A. Knopf).

Simms, B. (2016), *Britain's Europe: A Thousand Years of Conflict and Cooperation* (London: Allen Lane).

Silberman, M., K.E. Till and Janet Ward (eds) (2012), *Walls, Borders, Boundaries: Spatial and Cultural Practices in Europe* (New York: Berghahn Books).

Thompson, C. (2011), *Travel Writing* (London: Routledge).

Thorpe, Nick (2015), 'Refugees cross as Hungary builds "new Iron Curtain" to stop them', BBC News. www.pri.org (last accessed 2 June 2016).

White, M. (2011), 'The European question: will it be splendid isolation or miserable?', *Guardian*. www.guardian.com (last accessed 15 August 2016).

Wilson, Sam (2014), 'Britain and the EU: a long and rocky relationship', BBC News. www.bbc.com (last accessed 15 August 2016).

Wogan, Terry (2007), 'BBC-Eurovision 2007 final – full voting & winning', YouTube. www.youtube.com/watch?v=Wvglef7casl (last accessed 27 August 2016).

Wolff, L. (1994), *Inventing Eastern Europe: The Map of Civilization on the Mind of the Enlightenment* (Stanford: Stanford University Press).

Wright, P. (2007), *Iron Curtain: From Stage to Cold War* (Oxford: Oxford University Press).

12

Fifty years of Unbelonging: a Gibraltarian writer's personal testimonial on the road to Brexit

M.G. Sanchez

1

It was bound to happen sooner or later. I knew it from the moment I picked up the paper that July afternoon and saw the headline on the front cover. *Revealed*, it said. *The shocking scale of racist hate since the Brexit vote.* Henceforth I could sense it in the air, a hint of atmospheric turbulence, the sound of slow-beating wings approaching closer and closer. When the dark angel finally alighted before me, I was on the way to the local supermarket. Out of nowhere, a guy came up to me and quietly asked me if I could spare a cigarette. He was about six foot two. Skeletally thin. Crumpled jacket. Bags of wrinkles bulging like seedless testicles under his eyes. When I shook my head and replied that I didn't smoke, his bead-like eyes contracted even further and his face morphed into an upthrust snout. "Ere, you're not from round 'ere, are you?' he asked challengingly, all meekness having evaporated from his tone, his voice reeking of flinty, hard-edged *Northernness.*

Stupidly, caught off guard as I was, I shook my head.

'Then why don't you fuck off back to where you come from?' the man shouted, his lips pulled back as if he were about to hack up a gob of spit.

I should have told him that I'm a British citizen. That my partner is English and that I have lived in this country for fifteen out of the last twenty-one years. That I have a PhD in English Literature. That my father was born in London, and I worked for several years as a civil servant for the Employment Service. That even people who don't like migrants, on hearing that I come from the Rock, usually turn around and, with the sweetest, most generous expression on their faces, looking mightily pleased with their benevolence, say, *but you're all right, aren't you, you're from Gibraltar.*

But no, none of this came to my lips. Instead I thrust my hands into my pockets and, looking down, head tilted forward, conscious that I was being stared at now from both sides of the street, scampered away from the homeless man and his vituperative words.

'Go on, *fuck off!*' my antagonist repeated in an even angrier voice, working up some saliva in his mouth and then spitting it out, emboldened, no doubt, by the fact that not a single passer-by had intervened. 'Get the fuck out of *my country!*'

I nodded subconsciously and continued walking in a daze. Behind me the man kept hurling saliva-drenched obscenities, but they now sounded lukewarm and half-hearted, distinctly unenthusiastic, and after a while he quietened down and went back to the far more pressing business of trying to cadge a cigarette off somebody else. Relieved, I sighed and gradually slowed. Then I whipped out my mobile phone and called my partner:

'Was it just a pint of milk you wanted from Morrison's? Or did you also want me to buy a loaf of bread? I've completely forgotten.'

2

Before I continue, let me tell you something about myself. I'm a male Caucasian, aged forty-seven, five foot eight and around 170 pounds, with thinning grey hair and grey-green eyes. I don't look like a photophobic ginger-haired Scandinavian albino, true, but neither do I look like a gnarled and tousle-haired Mediterranean fisherman. The relative paleness of my complexion can be explained by the fact that, even though my sur-name is Sanchez and I come from Gibraltar, I have English ancestry on both the maternal (the Whitelocks) and the paternal side (the Browns). People in the UK occasionally think that I'm Polish – possibly because of my jawline (which is broader and more angular than most Englishmen's) and my nose (which is bulbous at the apex, but unusually flat along the bridge, a direct consequence of having been beaten up in a Scandinavian island some twenty-five years ago) – but the truth is that most of the time nobody would even notice that I am not a born and bred Englishman. Actually, the only time when it becomes apparent is when I open my mouth and the slightly hesitant, syncopated tones of my Gibraltarian accent can be heard floating in the air.

3

I shouldn't have been so shocked by what happened that morning on the way to Morrison's, considering that I had grown up in the Gibraltar of the 1970s and 1980s. In those days, our dockyard was run by the Royal

Navy and countless frigates, destroyers and aircraft carriers would sail into port. With the ships came thousands of British sailors, many of whom would get shit-faced in our bars and wouldn't think twice about insulting you. Spics, dagos, Gibbos, wops: these are some of the colourful terms they routinely employed against us Gibraltarians. Once, I remember, I was having a drink with two friends at a local wine bar. We had just taken part in the Gibraltar International Half Marathon – and were celebrating the achievement with a few shandies. While we were discussing the day's events, a group of about fifteen British squaddies staggered through the door. Loud voices, sunburned faces, shirts dripping in alcohol-saturated sweat. I suggested that we get up and go somewhere else, but M. and F., being slightly older, and therefore, in the language of Gibraltarian street slang, *más pasota*, said that they had no intention of going anywhere because of '*algunos guiris borrachos*'. Ten, perhaps fifteen minutes passed. Then, from the other side of the bar: "Ere. Anif yer lot want ter buy us ah lager n' lime?' Looking up, we saw a stocky man wearing a Leeds United shirt, about six foot two and with a flushed face, his tattooed knuckles protruding around a pint glass containing some fluorescent green liquid. 'Excuse me?' one of my eighteen-year-old friends whispered. 'Do you mind repeating that?' But the man wasn't prepared to elaborate any further; instead he turned back to his mates and, rolling his eyes, with an expression of pure racist contempt, said three words which still resound in my head all these years later; '*Bloody fucking spicks*.'

Looking back, what most astonishes me is that I never mentioned this episode to anyone. I simply accepted the situation, assimilated it without complaints. That's what it was like on the Rock in those days. We clung to Britain because she defended us in a hostile world and were regularly forced to turn a blind eye to the faults of our protectors. In any case, who could we have complained to? The military police cruising around in their white provost vans? The Naval authorities down at HMS Rooke? The stern, white-helmeted guard by the dockyard gates? I can almost imagine the kind of brush-off that would have been waiting for us had we dared:

> *Come on, son. Them lads don't mean nobody no harm. It's just a bit of banter, innit? Got to realise some of these boys have been cooped up aboard ship for many months. Messes with your head, all that does, gets you proper hyper and wired, real desperate, like, to neck a few bevvies and have a laugh. Best just to forget about the episode, matey, and carry on doing what you're doing. No harm done, if you know what I'm saying, eh?*

4

The episode mentioned above took place in 1984. To uncover my first brush with racism, however, we must go back to the end of the 1970s. My mother used to work as a supply teacher in those days, and at some point she was offered the opportunity to do a ten-month training course in the UK. We duly packed our bags and soon after moved to High Melton near Doncaster, where her college was based. My school was in the village of Sprotbrough, a short bus ride away. The area had little experience of immigration, and, as the only foreigner in the entire school, I was an easy target for bullies. There was one boy in particular who never left me alone. He sat next to me in class and was always trying to provoke me – punching me in the arm, kicking me under the table, pulling my ears as I was bent over my desk, spitting into my hair as I walked past him in the cloakroom corridor. Once he was waving a pencil in my face and I tried to push his hand away. The pencil snapped in two and its tip got stuck in the webbed flap of skin between my right forefinger and middle finger. Mr B–, our swarthy, long-haired teacher who used to remind me of an Indian swami whenever he sat cross-legged with his recorder in the activities room, rushed to my side and carefully pulled out the fragment wedged in my hand. I still bear a small scar where the graphite penetrated through the different dermal layers, a discoloured welt of unusually pale skin, itself surmounted by the faintest of grey dots, which for a long time made me think that part of the pencil had remained stuck inside.

For sheer trauma, though, nothing beat the Wednesday morning singing assembly. Unlike regular morning assemblies, this one lasted half an hour and was organised by Mrs P–. She was the school's music teacher, a big-boned, physically imposing woman with fringed black hair and shiny red nails. We'd trail into the school gym from our respective classrooms and then sit there in rows on the cold parquet floor, cross-legged and knocking knees with each other, facing Mrs P– and the piano on which she played her songs, continually being urged to sing louder and louder:

We sailed on the sloop John B, My Grandfather and me
Around Nassau town we did roam
Drinking all night, got into a fight
Well I feel so broke up I want to go home.

But I couldn't sing. I just couldn't do it. I don't know whether it was because I was shy or because I was self-conscious about my foreign accent or because I was so fed up with being bullied that I couldn't dislodge the words from my mouth. All I know is that I tried and tried – but only a muffled croak came to my lips, a husky whisper that contrasted with the animated, high-pitched cries of my English schoolmates and – alas! – was always noticed by our music teacher:

> 'Come on, Master Sanchez from the Rock of Gibraltar! Sing! Or I will have to ask you to come and keep me company right here by the piano!'

And, of course, that's where I soon find myself, *there*, in front of the whole school, trying to sing but still unable to dredge up the damn words, hating that woman with the black hair and the shiny fingernails, hating the kids who are staring at me and struggling not to laugh, hating the other teachers who sit there without lifting a finger, but, above all, more than anything else, hating myself for not being able to open my bloody mouth and sing …

5

And yet the worst example of racism I ever suffered did not happen in Gibraltar or even in mainland Britain, but about 4,000 kilometres away from the Rock, on the Baltic island of Åland. I had gone there to take part in the 1991 Island Games, a sort of mini-Olympics for islands and small territories. I was twenty-two years old, a quiet, dreamy, wavy-haired youth who had abandoned a History degree course at the University of Manchester a year earlier due to homesickness. One evening, as my running friends and I were relaxing inside the large marquee that had been set up near the beach for the game's competitors, we were approached by a party of drunken thirty-somethings from the Isle of Wight. None of us knew it at the time, but the new arrivals were members of the Isle of Wight judo team and that same morning they had been involved in a spat with the Gibraltar judo delegation over competition rules. Spotting the word 'Gibraltar' embroidered on our red and white tracksuits, they moved to an adjacent table and began to call us 'filthy dagos' and 'fucking spicks' and other choice terms of abuse. There were three of them: two short, muscular, thick-necked baldheads, and a tall, lanky individual with a bristly, grey-flecked moustache who reminded me of the character Boycie from *Only Fools and Horses*. At twenty-two, I was the oldest in our group, so it fell upon me to ask them to please leave us alone. *Come on, fellas*, I nervously pleaded with one of the men, *these are supposed to be the friendly games, like it says on the official games T-shirt, know what I mean?* Next thing I knew the bloke headbutted me and flung me to the ground with a judo throw. Women's screams, crunching glass, overturned stools and tables, the patternless echo of scurrying feet. Trapped in a choke hold, I lay on the floor with my assailant standing over me and repeatedly punching me on the side of the head. I could feel the blood pouring into my eyes, accumulating in my mouth, clogging my nostrils. And then, quite abruptly, the punches stop and I am left alone in the centre of the marquee, collapsed in a marionette-like heap, breathing through a mouth full of warm blood, pinpricks of light exploding in front of my eyes.

And then, an instant or two later, everything fractures again and I find myself in hospital. Bright fluorescents. Medicinal smells. A masked doctor standing half-crouched over me. Though I cannot study his face, I sense that the medic treating me is young and a touch hippyish. From the corner of my eye, I see a suture needle being pushed into the flap of skin under my eyebrow and then coming out after a couple of seconds, a sliver of metal quivering under the glare of the ceiling lights, slowly enclosing my eyebrow in an ever-tightening cocoon of black thread.

Later still, in an interview room down at Mariehamn police station, I learn that two of my other companions have also been attacked. My interviewer is a brunette woman with a pistol holster strapped to her waist. Pink enamelled nails. A face mottled by rosacea. Halfway through the interview, she brings out a Polaroid camera and takes a close-up of my head. She then places the film face-up on the table, waiting for the image to develop. In ten or fifteen seconds a representation of my face starts rupturing through the chemically treated paper, slowly acquiring form and colour. When it is ready, I see that my eyes are reduced to a pair of barely open slits and that the upper half of my face is enfolded in a band of fig-coloured bruising, almost as if I were wearing a Zorro mask.

'Do I look as bad as that?' I ask the policewoman.

Instead of answering me, she picks up the photo, places it in a document folder and then asks me if I am willing to identify those who had attacked me. I nod my head and say 'yes'.

And then I am in a police van heading down to the same beachside park where I was assaulted earlier. I am convinced that coming to the park has got to be a waste of time, as I'm pretty sure that our attackers must have fled by this stage. But when we get there, we find them with their beer glasses less than fifty yards from the marquee. This time they are in a group with seven or eight other Isle of Wight athletes. I spot the guy who attacked me, cradling a pint glass to his chest. When he sees me, he turns to his mates and says something under his breath that makes them all laugh. It only lasts a fraction of a second, this collective outburst of laughter, but its brazenness fills me with so much anger that I suddenly start trembling all over. Flanked by two local policemen, I take a couple of steps forward and stop in front of my aggressor. 'It's him', I say, almost jabbing him in the eye with an accusatory finger. 'And these are the other two who were with him.'

The three British judokas were arrested shortly afterwards and taken into custody. During the next three or four days, I traipsed around the island in a sunken state, no longer able to focus on my running events, a baseball cap pulled low over my brow. Despite the fact that we had been warned not to mention the incident to anybody back home, news of the assault somehow leaked to the Gibraltarian press, and an article duly appeared in the *Gibraltar Chronicle* a day or two later, describing how myself and another local athlete were 'recovering from facial injuries caused by an unprovoked attack'. The article was seen by my mother, who nearly fainted with worry on reading the news. When I finally heard that our assailants had been put on a plane and deported from the island, I did not feel either relief or vengeful satisfaction; just a curious sense of emptiness, the way you sometimes feel when you wake up midway through a bad dream and find yourself staring at the reassuringly familiar objects around you. Thinking about it now, I should have insisted to the police that my attacker be taken to court and prosecuted for his actions, but I was only twenty-two years old and painfully naïve, and all I wanted to do was go home and forget about the whole episode. At some point over the next few days a short piece about the attack appeared in one of the English tabloids under the title 'Yobs thrown out of island in disgrace' – or words to that effect. Also, as I passed through Gatwick airport with the rest of the Gibraltar contingent on the way back to the Rock, a British Customs officer turned to one of his colleagues by the entrance to the green channel and, nodding in my direction, without removing his hands from his pockets, casually said, 'Look, there's that guy who got roughed up in that tournament in that Scandinavian island. Must have done something bad to deserve a beating like that, don't you think?'

6

For a few years after my 'Åland experience' I flitted between different jobs, finding it hard to settle into a routine. Sometimes I'd walk to the top of the Rock and sit on a craggy ledge somewhere, chain-smoking Marlboro cigarettes; other times I'd stay in my room, too dispirited to rouse myself from my state of lethargy. When I at last emerged from that semi-depression, I decided to return to the UK and resume my studies. I knew that this wouldn't be easy, but I was desperate to turn things around and overcome my personal demons. To add to my difficulties, there were one or two individuals who tried to convince me not to press ahead with my plan. At the construction site where I worked, for instance, there was an electrician who was hell-bent on making me change my mind. 'Don't go', he once said, looking down at me from the top of his foldable aluminium ladder, power drill held like an oversized Luger in a hirsute hand. 'It's very cold in the UK and the English *son toh unoh malaje* and none of the women will have anything to do with you, 'cos they don't like foreigners there. You didn't last last time you went, and you won't last now. *Mejoh quedarseh aquí en Gibraltah.*'

7

But I still went. And almost to my surprise, things weren't as bad as the guy with the power drill had intimated. The University of Leeds, where I got a place to study English Literature and Language, was a neutral and aseptic place and, though I have to admit that I sometimes felt a little lost wandering through its endless fluorescent-lit corridors, I never experienced any of the prejudice or xenophobia which by now I associated with the English mindset. On the contrary, I met many wonderful people and made all sorts of friends. In the gap between my MA and my PhD, I was a bit low on cash, so I applied for a part-time job working for the Employment Service. My interviewer was a chap from Huddersfield. At the end of my interview, he told me that ten other people – all English – had already applied for the job, but only two of us – myself and a local girl from Horsforth – had interviewed well. 'Anyhow', he said, picking up the folder on his desk and rapidly closing it. 'My gut instinct tells me you are the right person for the job, so if you want it, it's yours.'

I spent four and a half years at that government office block in Leeds. On the ground floor, where my section was based, everybody knew that I was from Gibraltar, but on the other three floors I somehow came to be known as 'Maltese Mark'. I think this was because Gibraltar wasn't much in the news in those days and also, I suppose, because it is easier to remember 'Maltese Mark' than 'Mark from Gibraltar'. Anyway, I didn't really mind. 'Maltese Mark' suited me fine.

My time at 33 Park Place served to change my thinking on a number of levels. During the years of my colonial youth, most of the English people I had come in contact with were soldiers and sailors – nearly all of whom were aloof and high-handed when sober, and aggressively, shockingly insulting when drunk. Rightly or wrongly, this had implanted the belief in my head that the English were an arrogant and mean-spirited lot, a belligerent, inward-looking people who took pleasure in distancing themselves from the rest of the world. But in those offices in Leeds I came to realise that the cross-section of Englishmen I had met in Gibraltar was by no means representative of the other Brits back home. Yes, there was a lot of 'gradism' within our offices and I once overheard someone on the third floor sneeringly describe me as 'that asylum seeker sitting on reception' – but none of this took away from the fact that, on a day-to-day basis, I was treated kindly and respectfully, with scrupulous fairness. What I learned – or rather intuited – from those Leeds years is that there have always been, and always will be, *two Englands*. There is the 'Little England' of Charles Trevelyan and the British Union of Fascists, of Reginald Dyer and the transatlantic slavers, of Enoch Powell and the Northern mill owners, of Tommy Robinson and the English Defence League, a retrogressive, insular, profit-driven, fiercely self-righteous England, always looking at foreigners with suspicion, firmly convinced of its own superiority. And then there is the 'Greater England' of William Wilberforce and Dr Barnardo, of Josephine Butler and the Earl of Shaftesbury, of Jo Cox and Jeremy Bentham, of George Orwell and the Fifteenth International Brigade, a progressive, reformist, noble, compassionate, open-minded England, an England which spends more on foreign aid than any other country with the exception of the United States, which repeatedly extends a hand to those in need.

8

Of course, there were still racist incidents during those years. There was the guy I've already mentioned who described me as an 'asylum seeker'. There was the postman who refused to accept my Gibraltar driving licence as proof of identity when I went to the local depot to collect a registered parcel. There was the crew-cut yob in a curry-house in Keswick who, leaving his friends to come to my table, asked me if I considered myself a white person. There was the time I had a row with my English girlfriend on a bus, and some fellow in front of us all of a sudden turned around and, quite brazenly, winking at her in the manner of someone uncorking a witticism, said, 'Don't worry, luv. I can't understand him either with that fucked-up accent of his'.

9

It is 2 September 2016, and I'm back in Gibraltar on holiday. I have come to see my mother and to attend to some personal business. A few days ago, while I was sitting at one of the Main Street cafés, I saw an Englishman walk past with a T-shirt (presumably homemade) bearing the slogan 'THE EU CAN FUCK OFF'. He was brawny and shaven-headed, with an array of interlocking tattoos wrapped around the length of his right arm and a clunky metal watch resting on his left wrist. Why are so many people in the UK scared of outsiders, I wondered, gazing at the bloke. How can all that institutionalised respect for cultural diversity co-exist with such systemic prejudice and xenophobia? Part of the problem, I think, stems from the fact that Great Britain is an island nation and many of its citizens are not as used to dealing with foreigners as they are in mainland Europe. Barricaded in their imaginary fortress, their self-worth massaged by moribund imperial ideas of British pre-eminence, Little Englanders have always found it difficult to engage with their European cousins, preferring instead to sit back and view foreigners with that peculiarly 'English' mixture of aloofness, fear and condescension. The situation hasn't been helped either by the populist British media, who for years have been tapping into the population's latent xenophobia and plying their readers with targeted editorials. Consider, if you will, the front-page headlines spewed by the *Mail* in the run-up to the Brexit referendum:

13 April 2016: MIGRANTS SMUGGLED TO UK FOR JUST £100
19 April 2016: OSBORNE's 3M MIGRANT BOMBSHELL
19 May 2016: MIGRANTS SPARK HOUSING CRISIS
20 May 2016: EU BOSS: WE DO MEDDLE TOO MUCH
27 May 2016: RECORD NUMBER OF JOBLESS EU MIGRANTS IN BRITAIN
12 June 2016: FURY OVER PLOT TO LET 1.5m TURKS INTO BRITAIN
15 June 2016: WE'RE FROM EUROPE – LET US IN!
21 June 2016: CAMERON'S MIGRANT DECEPTION

Two days after that last headline in the *Daily Mail*, the population of the UK voted by a narrow margin to leave the European Union. Many of my English friends were in a state of shock, oscillating between feelings of outrage and despair, trying to understand where it had all gone wrong, unable to comprehend how their fellow countrymen could have willingly and without coercion opted for an isolationist future. As a passionate supporter of the Remain campaign, I shared their frustration and their pain, but not their sense of disbelief. On the contrary, I had been *more or less expecting something like this to happen.* For close to twenty years, after all, I have been experiencing the intolerance and the divisiveness which gave birth to the Brexit movement. I encountered it in the form of standoffish postures and judgmental expressions, in the resentful looks that followed me whenever I visited a hospital or a library or a post office, in the barely civil treatment that has been meted out to me by a myriad of bartenders, waiters and supermarket check-out operators. If you ask me, the phenomenon we now call Brexit was there all along, hidden but gathering momentum, rapidly percolating through into the mainstream, its separatist agenda rendered palatable by the drolleries of Mr Farage, its anti-European paranoia buttressed – and ultimately legitimised – by the rantings of the right-wing press. Add to all this the rampant social inequality, the long-brewing political resentments, the intense suspicion of foreigners, as well as the cloying, irrational nostalgia for the good old days of empire – and the startling thing about all this Brexit business is not that the UK voted to leave on 23 June 2016, but that almost half of the electorate – 16,141,242 people – still wanted to remain part of the European Union. To misquote the Duke of Wellington, I never expected it to be such 'a damn close-run thing'.

Index

Aachen Memorandum, The (Roberts) 138–9, 143–55
Abroad: British Literary Travelling between the Wars (Fussell) 205
Abulafia, David 18
Achebe, Chinua 170
Acheson, Dean 37
Act in Restraint of Appeals of 1532 129
Act of Settlement 133
Act of Supremacy of 1534 129
Adenauer, Konrad 24
Aftermath, The (Brook) 10
Aftermath, The (Kent) 11–12
Agriculture and Horticulture Development Board 29
Åland 238
Aldiss, Brian 143
Alfred the Great 152
Aliens Act of 1905 105
Aliens Restriction Act of 1914 108
Along the Edge of the Forest (Bailey) 215–22, 228
Alteration, The (Amis) 136
Amis, Kingsley 136
Anderson, Benedict 70, 179, 182, 186–7
anti-Catholicism 132–7, 193
see also anti-Catholic novels; Catholicism

anti-Catholic novels 132–3, 135–7
see also anti-Catholicism
anti-European novels 54–6, 60, 132, 137–9
Antigua 209
anti-immigration discourse 84
apocalyptic novel 163, 167–71
Applebaum, Anne 222
Armitage, David 130
Army of Salonica 21
Ash, Timothy Garton 199
atom bomb 58
Attlee, Clement 50
Auden, W.H. 127, 205
authenticity 170
automation 58

Baggini, Julian 200, 211
Bailey, Anthony 215–22, 226
Baker, Roy Ward 115–24
Balfour, Arthur 39
Balibar, Étienne 229
Balkans, the 79, 83, 215–16
Ball, George 25, 27
Barnes, Julian 6
Bartholomew, Michael 204
Batten, Gerard 61
Battle of Britain 200
Battle of Dorking, The (Chesney) 138
Baucom, Ian 204

BBC Reith Lectures *see* Reith
    Lectures (BBC)
Beddowes, Daniel 61
Bentham, Jeremy 242
Berger, John 171–5, 177n.16
Berlin Wall 164, 216, 221–2
Bevin, Ernest 30, 50, 216
Bhabha, Homi 199
Black, Jeremy 128
Blair, Tony 33, 93, 182, 184
Blake, Robert 127–8
Blue Water Empire (Holland) 5
Bogdanor, Vernon 19
Böhm, Karlheinz 119
Bonaparte, Napoleon 20, 31, 131, 221
Bookseller, The 180
borders 126, 199–201, 203, 207, 211,
    215–32, 231n.2
Bosworth, Battle of 181, 187, 193
Boym, Svetlana 187, 224–5
Bradbury, Ray 145, 156n.8
Brave New World (Huxley) 145,
    148, 154
Brexit
    binarism of 1, 31, 126
    and 'BrexLit' projects 7, 12n.2
    campaigns for 97, 189
    class and 1–2, 9, 27–35, 87, 108,
        128, 181–93
    fundamentalism of 34
    historical underpinnings of 18–19,
        27, 61–2, 187, 244
    implications of 29, 165–6, 179,
        229–30, 234
    inevitability of 243–4
    ironies of 37
    lead-up to 155, 229, 243
    negotiations of 18, 29, 32,
        36, 38, 99
    referendum for 1, 17, 33, 38, 71,
        87, 95, 97–100, 139, 143, 151,
        181–2, 200
    rhetoric of 22, 30, 163, 168, 229
    see also Leave campaign; Remain
        campaign

BrexLit 7, 12n.2, 22, 61–3, 162–4,
    167–71, 179–94
Bridging Divides
    (Darian-Smith) 212n.8
Britain, Battle of 200
British Army on the Rhine 228
British constitutional order 93
British Council 12
British countryside 27–9
    see also English countryside
British culture 150
    see also English culture
British Empire 3, 11, 22, 37, 203
British exceptionalism *see*
    exceptionalism
British Expeditionary Force 20
British farmers 27–9
British identity 3, 7, 37, 56, 107,
    110–15, 134, 140–50, 155, 156n.7,
    202, 242
    see also English identity
British Nationality Act of 1948 208
Britons: Forging the Nation (Colley)
    88–9, 130
Brockington, Grace 48
Brontë, Charlotte 132–3
Brook, Rhidian 10
Brooke, Rupert 47–8
Brown, Alice 93
Brown, Ford Madox 203
Brown, Gordon 139
Bryant, Arthur 151
Buchan, John 111
Bulgaria 69, 77
Burk, Cathleen 108
Burkett, Jodi 3–4
Burt, Kendal 115–24
Byron, George Gordon (Lord) 130–1

Calais 199
Calhoun, Craig 175n.7
Cameron, David 33, 71, 78–82, 96,
    128, 151, 155n.1
Campaign for Nuclear Disarmament 4
CAP *see* Common Agricultural Policy

capitalism 2, 165, 172–4
Cardinal Newman 133
Cash, Bill 155n.2
Catholicism 130, 132–3, 140, 184
    see also anti-Catholicism
Cautions to Continental Travellers
    (Cunningham) 131–3
Chamberlain, Joseph 29
Channel, The (Morieux) 211n.2
Charlemagne 145–6, 221
Charlemagne Prize 156n.5
Checkpoint Charlie 219, 221
Chesney, George 138
Chilton, Paul 70
Churchill (Teplitzsky) 5
Churchill, Randolph 203
Churchill, Winston 18–19, 21, 24,
    50–3, 64n.11, 107–8, 145,
    218, 228
Cipollini, Flavio 61
Civilization and its Discontents
    (Freud) 126
class 1–2, 9, 27–35, 87, 108,
    128, 181–93
Coasting: A Private Voyage
    (Raban) 206–7
Cold War 3–4, 91, 218–19, 221,
    223–7, 229
collective memory 221, 229
Colley, Linda 88–9, 130
colonialism 164, 208–10, 234–44
Commissioner, The (Johnson) 138
Common (Moore) 4
Common Agricultural Policy (CAP)
    28, 74, 83
Common Market 25–7, 32, 98
communism 45, 76
Concert of Europe 48
Confederation of British
    Industry 24, 34
Confessions of a Recovering
    Environmentalist
    (Kingsnorth) 175n.6
Congress for Cultural Freedom 63n.3
Conservative Party 7, 39, 51, 69–85, 92

Conservative Unionism 29
Constructing Post-Imperial Britain
    (Burkett) 4
Continental Drift (Grob-Fitzgibbon) 4
Continental Society for the Diffusion
    of Religious Knowledge see
    European Missionary Society
Convergence or Divergence?
    (Black) 128
Cornwell, Bernard 180
cosmopolitanism 183, 193
Coudenhove-Kalergi, Richard
    von 49–51
Crimean War 20
Croatia 69, 81
Cromwell, Oliver 130, 183
Cromwell, Thomas 187
Cross Channel (Barnes) 6
cultural genocide 168
cultural heterogeneity 166
cultural imagination 183
cultural memory 203–4, 212n.11
Culture and Society (Williams) 132
Cunningham, John William 131–3
Curtius, E.R. 54
Cyclist Who Went Out in the Cold, The
    (Moore) 222–30

Daddow, Oliver 144
Daily Express 109, 115, 119, 204
Daily Mail 243
D'Ancona, Matthew 189
Darian-Smith, Eve 212n.8
Darkest Hour (Wright) 5
Dark Mountain Manifesto
    (Kingsnorth) 165
Dark Mountain Project, The (Hine and
    Kingsnorth) 162, 167, 170
Dawson, Christopher 49
de Gaulle, Charles 26–7,
    64n.11, 137
Deighton, Anne 153
Deighton, Len 163
De l'esprit des Lois (Montesquieu) 128
Delors, Jacques 31–2

Democratic Unionist Party (DUP)
    35, 37, 98
Denmark 94
devolution 4, 92–5, 99
Diana, Princess 181–2, 189
Diener, A.C 222
Dodds, Klaus 229
Dover 9, 199–211
'Dover' (Auden) 205
Dover from Shakespeare Cliff
    (Turner) 202
Down There on a Visit
    (Isherwood) 205
Downton Abbey 5
Doyle, Arthur Conan 138
Duffy, Gillian 139
Dummett, Ann 108–9
Duncan Smith, Iain 74–6
Dunkirk 21
Dunkirk (Nolan) 5
DUP *see* Democratic
    Unionist Party
Dyer, Reginald 242
dystopia 138–9, 143–55, 162–4,
    167–71, 182

Eaglestone, Robert 2
Ecologist, The 162
economic integration 46
ECU *see* European Currency Unit
Eden, Anthony 44, 50–1
Eder, Klaus 231n.2
EEC *see* European Economic
    Community
EFTA *see* European Free Trade
    Association
Eisenhower, Dwight David 21
El Alamein (Second World War
    battle) 51
Electoral Reform Society 17
Eliot, T.S. 54, 59–60
Elizabethan settlement 18
Empire's New Clothes, The
    (Murphy) 22
English, The (Paxman) 128

English Channel 6, 9, 127, 150, 174,
    200, 202, 205, 211, 216
English countryside 190–2, 204–5
    see also British countryside
English culture 170
    see also British culture
English Defence League 242
English identity 3, 171, 173–4,
    180, 203–4
    see also British identity
English language 60, 162–3, 185
English nationalism 37, 90, 155,
    171–3, 179, 190
Englishness 4, 175n.5, 179–81, 184,
    191, 201–2, 209
English PEN 55
English Reformation 18, 129, 187, 202
English and Their History, The
    (Tombs) 18
enlargement 69–85
Entente Cordiale of 1904 47
environmental crisis 37, 172–3
ERC *see* European Research Council
EU *see* European Union
EU, The (Beddowes and Cipollini) 61
Euro-British literary studies 11
Europa (Parks) 137
Europe
    common culture of 46, 49, 59–60,
        80, 129, 146
    as a cultural entity 60, 127
    Great Britain's attitudes toward 1–2,
        22, 27–8, 84–5, 89, 92, 129,
        132–3, 149, 228
    as 'the Other' 4, 11, 17, 88–90,
        126–40, 153, 170
    as a world power 12, 63n.2, 73
    see also Euroscepticism
European Coal and Steel Community
    44, 50, 136, 156n.6
European Commission 29, 31, 96
European Community
    and Great Britain 24–5, 50, 78, 143
    image of 92
    opposition to 137–9

and potential federation 44–7,
55–6, 59
and Scotland 95
see also Concert of Europe;
European Economic Community
(EEC); European Union (EU);
League of Nations
European Council 74–5
European Currency Unit (ECU) 41n.8
European Economic Community
(EEC) 4, 88, 90–1, 94, 127,
136–7, 172
European Free Trade Association
(EFTA) 23, 25
European identity 27, 56
European integration 93–4
European Literature and the Latin
Middle Ages (Curtius) 54
European loyalty 47–8
European Missionary Society 131
European Regional Policy 93
European Research Council
(ERC) 63n.1
European Single Market 98
European Union (EU)
and Boris Johnson 20
enlargement of 69–85
formation of 62, 146, 164
institutions of 74, 76, 83,
172, 176n.8
migration within 78–9
opposition to 30, 61, 74, 150,
153, 203
and Scotland 95–6
and Theresa May 19
see also freedom of movement;
Treaty on European Union
European unity 37, 44–63, 145–6
Europe of the Regions 94
Europhobia 11, 131, 137–9, 143–55
Eurosceptic fiction 127–8,
138–9, 143–55
Euroscepticism 2, 4, 82, 126–32, 138–9,
143, 147–51, 154, 155n.1, 203, 230
see also Great Britain

Euroslavia (Palmer) 139, 143
exceptionalism 5, 8–9, 17, 127, 132,
136, 151, 193, 208
Express 115

Fahrenheit 451 (Bradbury) 145, 156n.8
Fairbairn, Carolyn 34
Falcon, Richard 118
Falklands War 32, 207, 209
family tradition 168–9
Farage, Nigel 91, 154, 157n.10, 201, 244
fascism 136, 242
Fatherland (Harris) 163
Featherstone, Simon 180, 182
Federation of British Industries see
Confederation of British Industry
feudalism 181, 187
fictionalisation 132, 143–54
Films and Filming 119
financial crisis 78
Fine Gael government 36
First World War 20–1, 47–9, 63n.7,
108, 151
Fisher, Herbert 151
Flies, The (Sartre) 59
Ford, Ford Madox 48
Forster, E.M. 11
Foster, Arlene 36
Foucault, Michel 225–6
Fourth Conquest, The (Upward) 133–7
France 40n.2, 57, 89
Franco-Prussian War 202
Frankau, Gilbert 136
Frankopan, Peter 18
Franks, Oliver 45
Freedland, Jonathan 181–2
freedom of movement 69–85
see also European Union (EU)
French, John 20
Freud, Sigmund 126
'Fuck business' (Johnson) 189
Fussell, Paul 205

Gaitskell, Hugh 152
Ganesh, Janan 22

geographic determinism 128–9
George, Lloyd 48
Geraghty, Christine 111
German identity 110–15
German uniformity 109
Germany
  after the Second World War 12n.6,
    26, 50, 57, 107–24, 163
  Nazism in 48, 55, 109, 152
  and relationship to Europe 46,
    55, 218
  as threat to Great Britain 45,
    107–24, 135, 154
  unification of 20, 47, 222
Gibraltar 4, 9, 23, 203, 234–44
Gibraltar Chronicle 240
Gilbert, Lewis 110–15
Gilroy, Paul 180, 190
Glissant, Edouard 174
globalisation 58, 165–6, 170, 172
Goethe, Johann Wolfgang von 46, 54
Gollancz, Victor 115
Good Friday Agreement 36, 97
Goodhart, David 176n.9, 187
'Gordon Riots' of 1780 130
Gove, Michael 155n.2, 189
Graham, Winston 180
Grand Tour 129
Great Britain
  and attitudes toward Europe 1–2,
    22, 27–8, 84–5, 89, 92, 129,
    132–3, 149, 228
  class relations in 1–2, 9, 27–35, 87,
    108, 128, 181–93
  as a composite nation 89,
    140n.3, 180
  economy of 75, 90
  expansion of 206
  foundational myths of 151
  and France 202
  and geographic relation to
    continental Europe 199
  and Germany 107–24
  imagined community of 81
  as an island nation 3, 5, 7–8, 30, 53,
    128, 151–2, 199, 209, 230, 243

and the Mediterranean 5, 23
  military of 20–21, 110–15, 145,
    152, 235–6
  national emblems of 148, 150,
    199–211, 227
  perceptions of 242
  and relationship to Europe 5–6, 11,
    19, 24–5, 52–3, 100, 135, 144,
    179, 199, 215
  as the 'society of individuals' 112
  and the United States 37
  as a world power 4, 18, 23–4, 26, 37,
    40, 45, 52–3, 79, 151, 207–8, 229
  see also Englishness
Great British Dream Factory, The
  (Sandbrook) 4
Great Depression, the 29
Great Famine of the 1840s 132–3
Great Reform Act of 1832 93
Gregory, Philippa 179–94
Grizedale Hall 121
Grob-Fitzgibbon, Benjamin 4
Guardian 163, 165, 180, 199–200, 230

Hadrian the Seventh (Rolfe) 136
Hagen, J. 222
Hague, William 72–4
Hansard 70–1
Harris, Robert 163–4
Havrie, Christopher 93
Heath, Edward 28
Hellenic heritage 63n.6
Henrician Reformation 181, 187, 193
Henry VII 181, 183, 185, 192
Henry VIII 18, 129–30, 180–1, 187–8
Heroic Failure (O'Toole) 163
Herriot, Édouard 49
Higgins, Charlotte 180
Hine, Dougald 167
Historians for Britain 17–18
historical novels 162–4,
  167–71, 179–94
Hitler, Adolf 24, 31, 55, 61, 109, 111,
  118, 145
Hölderlin, Friedrich 54
Holland, Robert 5–6

homosexuality 205–6
Horizon 54
Horne, Alistair 26
Horne, Stephanie 123
House of York 187
Howard, Michael 73, 77–8
Howe, Geoffrey 32
Hugo, Victor 46
human rights 80
Hundred Years War 202
Huxley, Aldous 145, 148, 154

imagined communities 69–85, 89, 169, 179, 183, 186
Imagined Communities (Anderson) 186
immigration
    in Brexit campaigns 30, 34, 126
    discourses of 9, 69–85, 193, 203, 236–7
    growth of 139, 174
    histories of 132–3, 140, 200–1, 208
    see also class; race
Imperial Economic Conference 29
imperial nostalgia 2, 4, 34, 180–1, 209, 244
individualism 110–15
In Search of England (Morton) 204–5
insularity 9, 26–7, 51, 152, 200–6, 211
International Red Cross 47
Internet 127
Into Their Labours (Berger) 172
invasion novels 138, 163, 202, 227
invasion scare narratives 5, 7–8, 61, 107–8, 118, 138–9, 153, 164, 183, 187, 201–3, 212n.6, 227
Ireland 4, 9, 12n.3, 35–6, 41n.11, 87, 98, 132
    see also Northern Ireland
Irish reunification 87, 98
Iron Curtain 215–32
Isherwood, Christopher 205–6
island fortress *see* island story
island myth *see* island story
island nation *see* island story

island story 3, 5, 7–8, 30, 53, 128, 151–2, 199, 209, 230, 243
Isle of Wight 238
isolationism 8, 22, 61, 88, 206, 230, 232n.13

James, Harold 24
James, Rowland 136
Jameson, Storm 55
John, Elton 183
John Bull 19–20, 40, 115, 175–6n.7
Johns, W.E. 110
Johnson, Boris 1, 19–20, 37–9, 61, 138, 154, 157n.10, 179, 189
Johnson, Stanley 138
Jones, Barry 92, 94
Judt, Tony 107
Juncker, Jean-Claude 31

Kant, Emmanuel 46
Keating, Michael 92, 94
Kennedy, Joe 167, 171, 175n.5, 176n.9
Kennedy, John F. 26
Kenny, Michael 180
Kincaid, Jamaica 209–11
King, Cecil 41n.14
King Lear (Shakespeare) 202
King's Curse, The (Gregory) 179–94
Kingsnorth, Paul 162–5, 167–71, 175n.6, 179–80, 186–7
Kipling, Rudyard 212n.10
Krüger, Hardy 115–24
Kunzru, Hari 175n.2

Labour party 28, 38, 51, 81, 92, 152
Lanchester, John 35, 175n.4
language-identity nexus 70
Larkin, Philip 47
Last Kingdom (Cornwell) 180
Last of England, The (Brown) 203
Lawrence of Arabia 21
League of Nations 48, 63n.6
Leasor, James 115–24
Leave campaign 2, 35, 127, 138, 201
le Carré, John 223
Leconte, Cécile 150

Lee, Stephen J. 229
Lefebvre, Henri 216–17, 220, 230
LGBTQ rights 166
Liberal Democrats 73
liberalism 165
liminality 23, 199, 205, 207, 209–10
Lindsay, Isobel 94
linguistic imperialism 169
literature 2, 6–9, 46, 54–5, 132–3, 150, 240
Lloyds of London 45
London Blitz 21
Lord Byron see Byron, George Gordon (Lord)
Luxemburg European Council 69, 74
Lynn, Vera 207–8

Maastricht Treaty, the 92, 137, 152
McCrone, David 93, 95
Macfarlane, Alan 128
McGuinness, Martin 87
Macmillan, Harold 25–6, 108, 216, 228
McWilliams, Anna 228
Mail 243
Major, John 20, 33, 72–3, 152
Manchester Guardian 49
Mann, Heinrich 48–9
Mann, Klaus 49
Mann, Thomas 49
Mantel, Hilary 180, 182
Marr, Andrew 32, 34
Marshall Plan 24
Marx, Karl 175–6n.7
Mary, Queen 20
Masterman, Charles 48
Maudling, Reginald 25
May, Theresa 1, 17–19, 23, 29–39, 98–9, 174, 179, 188, 201, 211
Mayle, Peter 6
Mayne, Richard 37
'MCMXIV' (Larkin) 47
Mediterranean, the 5, 18, 23, 235
melancholia 2, 4, 34, 180–1, 183, 209, 244

memory 156n.5, 200, 225, 228
Miller, J. Hillis 218
Milton, John 130
Möhner, Carl 110–15
Mohr, Jean 177n.16
Monboit, George 176n.8
Monnet, Jean 37, 51
Montesquieu, Charles 128
Moore, Alan 136
Moore, D.C. 4
Moore, Tim 222–30
More, Kenneth 110–15
Moretti, Franco 212n.6
Morgenthau, Hans 56
Morieux, Renaud 211n.2
Morris, Jan 2, 216
Morton, H.V. 204–5
multiculturalism 200, 208, 210
Murphy, Philip 22
Murray, Gilbert 63n.6

Nairn, Tom 181–2
Napoleon see Bonaparte, Napoleon
Napoleonic Code 205
Napoleonic wars 18, 47, 54, 131
Nasser, Gamal Abdel 31
National Farmers Union 29
national homogeneity 111
national identity 7, 76, 110, 134, 140, 144, 156n.7, 164–5, 202–4, 207, 242
nationalism 48, 90, 144, 171, 173, 181–2, 190, 201
nationhood 51, 170, 179, 190
   see also imagined communities
nativism 22
   see also English identity; Leave campaign
NATO see North Atlantic Treaty Organisation
Nazism 55, 57, 109, 118, 137, 145, 153, 164
neoliberalism 2, 166, 172, 188
New Labour 4, 93, 180

Newman, Bernard 215
Newsnight 36
New Socialist 175n.5
Nicol, Andrew 107
Nineteen Eighty-Four (Orwell) 145,
    149, 154
Norman Conquest 152, 162–3, 199
'Norman Yoke' 4, 8
North Atlantic Treaty Organisation
    (NATO), 73, 107
Northern Ireland 87, 97–8
    see also Ireland
Norway 94
nostalgia 2, 4–5, 34, 179–81, 187, 192,
    209, 224–5, 244
Notes from the Cévennes (Thorpe) 6
Nuremberg rallies 137

Observer 56
OEEC *see* Organisation for European
    Economic Cooperation
Old Men at the Zoo, The (Wilson) 137
One That Got Away, The
    (Baker) 115–24
Only Fools and Horses (Sullivan) 238
organicism 165–7, 172–4, 188–93
Organisation for European Economic
    Cooperation (OEEC) 53
Origins of English Individualism, The
    (Macfarlane) 128
Orion Magazine 177n.17
Orwell, George 54–6, 109, 114, 126–7,
    129, 145, 149, 154, 212n.10, 242
Other Boleyn Girl, The (Gregory) 181
O'Toole, Fintan 61–2, 163–4, 168, 174
outsiders 217
Oxford Movement 133

Palmer, Alan 186
Palmer, Terry 139, 143
Palmer, William 133–7
Pan-Europa 49
panopticism 218, 225–6
'Papal Aggression' of 1850 132–3
Parks, Tim 6, 137

Parr, Catherine 181–5
Parrinder, Patrick 179
Parris, Matthew 37
Partisan Review 56
Passage to India, A (Forster) 11
paternalism 52, 184
Paterson, Lindsay 92–3
patriotism 190, 202
Pavane (Roberts) 136
Paxman, Jeremy 112, 128
PEN Congress 56
peripheralism 23
Phillips, Caryl 208–9
Pick, Daniel 203
Picturegoer 118
Pig Earth (Berger) 172
Pilgrimage of Grace 187
'Pioneers, The' (Phillips) 208
plague epidemic 186
Plaid Cymru 90–1
Plain, Gill 110
Plantagenets 183, 186, 190
Poke, The 201
Poldark (Graham) 180
Pole, Margaret 181–5, 192
political correctness 134
Politique Etrangère 59
Pompidou, Georges 27
Pope Leo 146
Pope Pius IX 132
Popery Acts 130
Popescu, Gabriel
    224, 229, 231n.5
populism 139, 188
postcolonialism 11, 181
postcolonial melancholia 2, 4, 34,
    180–1, 209, 244
Potsdam Conference 30
Powell, Enoch 84, 242
Priestley, J.B. 108–9, 114
progressiveness 188
propaganda 148
Protestant Association 130
Protestant unionism 98
Protestantism 89, 132–3

Quarterly Review 54
Quigly, Isabel 116, 120

Raab, Dominic 9
Raban, Jonathan 206–8
race 35, 47, 61, 180, 193,
    208–9, 234–44
    see also immigration
Rau, Petra 108, 120
Readman, Paul 202
Real England (Kingsnorth) 165,
    167, 179
Reckwitz, Andreas 166
Rees-Mogg, Jacob 39, 179, 189
refugees 126, 212n.3
Reith Lectures (BBC) 45
religion 89, 128–32
Remain campaign 176n.8, 243
Renaissance, the 129
Restraint of Appeals, Act of 1532 129
Review of Reviews (Stead) 46
Reynolds, David 30
Richard II (Shakespeare) 202
Richard III 183
Risorgimento 47
Road to Somewhere, The
    (Goodhart) 187
Road to Somewhere, The
    (Kennedy) 167
Roberts, Andrew 19, 138–9, 143–55
Roberts, Frank 51
Roberts, Keith 136
Robinson, Nick 126
Robinson, Tommy 242
Rolfe, Frederick 136
Roman conquest 200
Romania 69, 77
Roosevelt, Franklin Delano 21, 24, 145
Rose, Sonya 107
Russia 48, 73, 83, 223
    see also Soviet Union (USSR)

Sandbrook Dominic 4
sandwich hypothesis 93
Sartre, Jean-Paul 59

scapegoating 2, 32
Schengen agreement 82
Schleswig-Holstein Question 20
Schmidt, Helmut 119
Schuman Plan 45, 52–3
Scotland 38–9, 87–8, 91, 95–7, 99
Scottish National Party (SNP) 38, 87,
    90–1, 94–7
Second World War
    and the cliffs of Dover 206
    German 'othering' during 108
    and Great Britain 21–2
    legacy of 57, 138, 140, 145, 147, 152
    post-war period of 6, 8, 10, 24,
        44–63, 90, 107–24, 136, 163, 216
    and the United States 21
    writers during 54–56
Seeley, John Robert 3
self-determination 185
sense of place 167–71, 173
Settlement, Act of 133
Seventh Man, A (Berger and Mohr)
    177n.16
Shakespeare, William 190, 202, 206
Shears, David 215–22, 228
Sheehan, James 62
Shelley, Percy Bysshe 131
Silberman, Marc 216
Simms, Brendan 216, 228
simultaneity 182
Sinews of Peace, The (Churchill) 218
Single European Market 32–3
Sink the Bismarck! (Gilbert)
    110–15, 123
Sinn Fein 90–1
SNP *see* Scottish National Party
socialism 173
Society of Singularities (Reckwitz) 166
'Soldier, The' (Brooke) 47
sovereignty 30–1, 90–1, 126, 139,
    148, 203
Soviet Union (USSR) 107, 218,
    223, 227
    see also Russia
Spanish Civil War 206

spatiality 216–17, 220, 225–6, 229–30
Spectator 116
Spender, Stephen 54, 57–8, 62
spheres of influence 75, 83
Spitfire Parade (Johns) 110
splendid isolation *see* isolationism
Spy Who Came in from the Cold
    (le Carré) 223
SS-GB (Deighton) 163
Stalin, Josef 145
status quo 6
Stead, William 46
Štěpánek Karel 110–15
Stern, James 124
Stewart, Rory 36
Sturgeon, Nicola 38, 87, 97
Suez crisis 23, 31
    as historical event 37
Sun 31–2, 139
Sunday Telegraph 137
Super-State (Aldiss) 143
Supremacy, Act of 1534 129
surveillance 144, 149
Swoop, The (Wodehouse) 138

Taming of the Queen, The
    (Gregory) 179–94
Test Acts 130
Thatcher, Margaret 20, 27, 32, 92,
    129, 209
Thatcherism 4, 27, 34, 181
Thier, Katrin 168
Things Fall Apart (Achebe) 170
Third Reich 152
Thorpe, Adam 6, 163
Tice, Richard 127
Till, Karen E. 216
Times 37, 117
Timothy, Nick 40n.7
Tombs, Robert 18
Tomlinson, Jim 108
Toryism 27, 32, 38, 145
'Toward European Unity' (Orwell) 56
Tractarian Movement 133
Tradescant (Gregory) 181

Trafalgar, Battle of 156n.7
Trafalgar Square 111, 147
transference of empire 145–6
translatio imperii 145–6
travel writing 9, 12n.5, 205–11,
    212n.9, 215–30
Travel Writing (Thompson) 223
Treaty of Maastricht *see* Maastricht
    Treaty, the
Treaty of Rome 17, 25, 28, 164
Treaty on European Union
    Article 48 96
    Article 49 96
    Article 50 4, 9, 37, 201
Trevelyan, Charles 242
Trevelyan, George Macaulay 151
Tribune (socialist magazine) 54
Trower, Shelley 201
Trump, Donald 38, 165
Tudors 179–94
Turkey 78
Turner, J.M.W. 202, 206

Ugly Frontier, The (Shears) 215–22, 228
UK Independence Party (UKIP)
    3, 61, 69, 91, 127, 150, 201,
    203, 211
Unborn Tomorrow (Frankau) 136
*Uncivilization: The Dark Mountain
    Manifesto* (Hine and
    Kingsnorth) 167
Under Home Rule (Palmer) 133–7
Union of 1707 38–9
United Kingdom *see* Great Britain
United States 20–1, 37, 44, 49, 53, 63n.7
'Unity of European Culture, The'
    (Eliot) 60
Upward, George Allen 133–7
'Us and Them' discourses 82
USSR *see* Soviet Union

Vansittart, Robert 108
Verhaeren, Émile 48
V for Vendetta (Moore) 136
Victoria, Queen 146

Villette (Brontë) 132–3
vraisemblance 136, 138

Wake, The (Kingsnorth)
    162–4, 167–71
Wall, The (Lanchester) 175n.4
Wallace, David 199
Ward, Janet 216
Warm South, The (Holland) 5–6
War of Spanish Succession 19
Wars of the Roses 181, 183
Waterloo 20, 89, 147,
    151, 156n.7
Wellesley, Eileen 48
Wellington House 48
Wells, H.G. 132
Western sphere of influence 73
What Buchenwald Really Means
    (Gollancz) 115
While England Slept (James) 136
white cliffs of Dover 9, 199–211
Whitebrook, Maureen 155

Wideacre (Gregory) 181
Wilberforce, William 242
William III 19
Williams, Melanie 116
Williams, Raymond 132, 163
Williamson, Gavin 23
Wilson, Angus 137
Wilson, Sam 230
Wilson, Woodrow 48–9, 63n.7
Windrush 208–11
Wodehouse, P.G. 138
Wolfe, Billy 91
Wolff, Larry 222, 229
Wolsey, Thomas 189
Woolf, Leonard 109
Wright, Patrick 216, 218

xenophobia 30, 49
    see also immigration

Year in Provence, A (Mayle) 6
Young, Hugo 137

Lightning Source UK Ltd.
Milton Keynes UK
UKHW021543180522
403185UK00017B/563